The American Land

Smithsonian Exposition Books

Distributed to the trade by
W. W. Norton & Company
New York, N.Y.

First Edition

Contents

Photographs in order to page 12: modern King Canute at work restoring winter-eroded eastern beach; dawn at Hopewell Village National Historic Site in Pennsylvania; Cathedral Spires, near Talkeetna, Alaska; Iowa's capitol reflected by a modern office building; farms sprinkled along the Colorado River Valley; Texas wildflowers speak of the land's fruitfulness; and a California oil refinery rises above a variety of human habitats.

The Smithsonian Institution
Secretary, S. Dillon Ripley

Smithsonian Exposition Books

Director: James K. Page, Jr.
Senior Editor: Russell Bourne
Business Manager: Thomas A. Hoffman
Administrative Assistant: Christine Nonnenmacher

Staff, The American Land
Editors: Alexis Doster III, Joe Goodwin, Robert C. Post
Picture editor: Nancy Strader
Production editor: Ann Beasley
Graphics Coordinator: Patricia Upchurch
Copy editor: Bettie Loux Donley
Indexer: Florence H. Blau
Assistants: June Armstrong, Francine Atwell

Marketing consultant: William H. Kelty

Editorial consultants: Edward S. Ayensu,
    Wilcomb E. Washburn, Charles E. Little

Design direction: John R. Beveridge, Beveridge & Associates, Inc.

Section-opening illustrations: Celia Strain

Separations: Lanman Lithoplate, Inc.

Typography: Custom Composition Company

Printing: Rand McNally and Company

Library of Congress Number 79-67295
ISBN 0-89599-004-0

Introduction

A case could be made that America's unique contribution to literature is the western novel, a properly democratic creation. And in every western, no matter how much a potboiler it may be, a major if unlisted character in the plot is the land. Indeed, throughout our history and that of the people who arrived before us, the land—so vast, so promising, so dangerous—has been a preoccupation, a major force in the shaping of our national character.

In this regard, there has always been a mutual feedback loop. The land is an objective, real thing with its own origins and forces, all of which are subject to the disinterested probings of the scientific method. But even the most scientifically objective viewer has his own perspective, his own vision of that land. And—here is the feedback loop—the individual and the collective visions of the land at any time in history have affected what we do to the land. We are now living on a piece of real estate which is the result not only of plate tectonics but of an almost equally titanic force: the cumulative visions of generations of inhabitants and the actions they have taken in accordance with those visions.

"Where did you grow up?" is a question we are all often asked these days, just as it must have been asked of trappers in Ohio (then called the North West) and miners in California. Where you grew up has much to do with who you are. To be afforded a daily view of the Big Sky in one's formative years, and all of the concomitant insights that go along with such an experience, obviously affects the personality in different ways than growing up in the shadowed, starless canyonlands of an eastern metropolis.

In a sense, then, this is a book of visions of the land—focused through the prism of the Smithsonian Institution which lies athwart a peculiar piece of real estate—the Mall—itself here because of a vision hatched in the minds of a foresighted American, Thomas Jefferson, and a creative Frenchman, Pierre L'Enfant. The Institution also lies athwart a great deal of our history as the restless collector of artifacts and perceptions, the encourager of perspicacious explorers, whether of geographic or scientific realms.

Over many decades the Smithsonian has published the works of those scientists and wanderers—headwaters traced, canyons color-coded, Indian languages chronicled—contributions to Americans' understanding of their land and its "mysteries." Whereas the land in such discrete volumes has continued to appear as a vague, unspoken hero, more recent times have prompted a series of urgent, explicit questions: What should we decide about water resources in western deserts? How shall we use the land between city and wilderness? What are we to make of Alaska?

Hence this rather disparate book of personal visions and specific findings. In the free tradition of American letters about the land, the editors have elicited the thoughts of truly independent writers, organizing their contributions not by linear argument but by areas of debate.

It is not, the editors freely confess, a book that provides all the answers—for they are yet to be found. Nor is it a book that covers the entire subject. There are but 33 chapters—fewer than the states of our union, far fewer than all available visions of the land. But these selected areas represent points of particular concern (or curiosity) at the Smithsonian, and for all the aid and counsel supplied to us by curators and staff of the several museums and galleries, we would like to offer this expression of gratitude. Our hope is that we have served their cause accurately, however enthusiastically.

This book is, finally, a kind of a song, each verse of which suggests yet another whole song. Its essential music, we trust, will come through clearly. As certain Indian tribes say about themselves, we are the land and the land is us.

—The Editors

13

Visions

She was a dusky, voluptuous goddess, at her thigh a cornucopia overflowing with the fruit of the land: America as perceived by the first artists epitomized abundance and fulfillment. Explorers caught sight of that enticing vision and followed it into the heartland, cresting Allegheny ridges like those at left.

A mapmaker of George Washington's time lettered into the empty spaces beyond the mountains these words: "A Fine Level and Fertile Country of great Extent, by Accounts of the Indians and our People." Thus did cartography combine with legend and art and poetry to spur men on.

In this section of the book, Dr. Joshua Taylor points out a curious national harmony in the ways artists of different times portray the rich beauty of the land, even as styles change and society shifts geographically. His examples are found among the great landscape paintings in the Smithsonian collections.

In other pages of this section, authors suggest that the vision of America may resemble a palimpsest, a document overwritten many times. The vision is a changing artifact of the mind in which new images and visions created in one era cover but do not hide older images.

The original Americans, Indians, knew that the land seemed to change in the eyes of successive beholders, to reveal, perhaps, new meaning. Vine Deloria, Jr. notes that wandering tribal groups seeking new land ". . . found ruins and wondered where the

former inhabitants had gone, why they had not found peace in their place."

Alfred Meyer, whose raft pilgrimage down the Mississippi opens the book, reports on the river's shrines, some historic—still haunting the American consciousness—and some new. Roderick Nash, who has analyzed major writings about the American land, explains the continuing pertinence of our treasured literary visions, which parallel those in the graphic arts.

Spanish conquistadors, lusting after gold, and most of the English and French explorers who followed them, failed to see the land itself as the real treasure. That vision has been vouchsafed for later generations, and for none perhaps so much as for our own. Yet even today few men can see the country true and whole.

The vision, never fully revealed, has inspired the people of the land to face—as pioneers—the unknown, to accomplish impossible things, to create what Thomas Wolfe called the "fabulous country."

Sight of sails by Indians; view of New World by mariners: first great vision of an era of discovery and confrontation. French settlers of northern borders ally themselves with Indians. Spaniards invade the Southwest, where Indians shape a civilization around that miracle from Europe—the horse. Englishmen settle the East, pushing on across the Appalachians, while explorers Lewis and Clark reconnoiter the Pacific route, encountering voracious bears and whale-hunting Indians. Last great primitive vision: covered wagons by the thousands, settlers filling the all but limitless frontier.

Bronze Tom Sawyer, left, and Huck survey their hometown, Hannibal, Mo.

Mississippi Pilgrimage

By Alfred Meyer

When the raft stopped along a bank, the people became curious. They gathered around and invariably asked: "Where'd you put in?"

"La Crosse, Wisconsin," we would say.

"Where you headed?"

"New Orleans."

"All the way?"

"With luck."

"I always wanted to do that," they said.

Older men brooding in flannel shirts and dungarees said it. Women perched on little cushioned chairs in the sun on the docks said it. Boys and girls in swimsuits or shorts and T-shirts said it—and asked to come aboard, and along.

It was only a raft trip down the middle of America that my son and friends and I were taking, straight through the American land, north to south. Yet it seemed to sound the same chord on so many guitars—they all wanted to play

float with one corner serving as bow, its catty-corner as stern.

Yet the raft seemed ungainly as a square. So we sawed off three corners—the stern and the two sides. Now at least we knew which was forward and possessed, besides, a legitimate bow on which to paint *Huckleberry Belle.* Trimming the corners also provided an historical distinction. "The only seven-sided raft ever to go down the Mississippi!" we boasted as other vessels came within hailing range.

Strange shapes are nothing new on the Mississippi, of course, for the river traditionally has demanded innovation in the design and construction of the craft that would ply its fast-running, shallow waters. After initial exploration of the river by Père Jacques Marquette and Louis Jolliet in 1673, the redoubtable Sieur de La Salle canoed all the way to the river's mouth, named the territory Louisiana in honor of the French king, and (before his tragic death at the hands of his own mutinous men) forecast the next century of fur enterprise on the river. It was an era of specially built bateaux, capacious yet river-swift, an era followed by the development of flatboats, keelboats, and shoal-draft sidewheelers and sternwheelers. It was these last, grand steamers that carried the river's commercial traffic so successfully until the advent of diesel-powered, tunnel-sterned towboats in the 1900s.

La Crosse, Wisconsin reporters give sendoff to erstwhile crew of Huckleberry Belle. *Once on the river, author found that barges, above, "looked like alligators when they bore down on us, silent and deadly."*

along with us. At times during the trip, I imagined I was in company with legions of explorers and voyageurs, of keelboaters and steamboat men. And that I could see both coasts through the foliage of willows and cottonwoods on either bank, and even through the Appalachians to the east and the Rockies to the west. The vision we were given was extraordinary: a whole continent and an entire civilization. An extraordinarily large vision for such a small raft.

By small, I mean a little less than 20 feet by 20 feet. Stevan Johnson, a Seattle architect, had designed the raft, but rather unorthodoxly (though, admittedly, few standard manuals are available on raft design). Johnson called for oil drums for flotation, with the drums arranged in three double-barrel rows, the center row the longest. Thus he claimed the raft was fundamentally a trimaran. The drums were strapped to a grid of pipe and framed with 2 x 12s. Atop the frame sat a 20-foot square fir deck. The idea was that the raft would

of the river's current. Then a shout, "We're moving, Dad!"

At that moment the shadow of La Crosse's Mississippi bridge passed over our raft, then slid quickly off the stern like a dark ruler. The wind had freshened and, joining forces with the current, bullied us downriver. The anchor bounced along the bottom of the river, seemingly toothless, needing a slow-down to bite.

"Well," I announced, as though in control, "we wanted to drift down the river, didn't we? Let's do it. Haul up the anchor. How far do you suppose the next town is?"

It was 12 miles and we couldn't make it, not with so revolving and buffeted a *Belle.* The wind kept coaxing her toward the east bank where the mouths of sloughs sucked at her like giant sink drains. Into one of these beckoning sloughs the raft swirled irrevocably.

We had hoped that the slough opened to the river again a little to the south. It did not. The raft ended up in a small pond. Yet salvation lay close at hand, in the person of a bass fisherman who eventually towed us to Brownsville, Minnesota, where we could buy another motor.

Two fogs set in before departure, one insectile, the other atmospheric: clouds of mayflies mingling with clouds of mist. Transparent wings, thousands of pairs, covered *Huckleberry Belle.* Covered the roof, the walls, and the deck. Crackled like cellophane when walked on. Stuck to the fingers when plucked off a wall.

Numberless, ephemeral, the mayflies had graduated from their last nymphal stage in the river bottom mud and emerged from the water into the air to spend their day-long lives searching for mates, beginning the next frantic generation. They drove fish and birds into a feeding frenzy that morning. The fish hit at masses of floating larvae, while the birds snatched flyers out of mid-air. Despite the dampening mist, excitement reigned.

"The flies tell you the river's still healthy," said a Brownsville riverman, long since retired and now fishing to earn some money. He got up early to say goodbye and to give us a five-pound walleye, which he had carefully wrapped in newspaper. (River etiquette involves gifts: cake, sausage, and beer in Germanic La Crosse; mostly fish everywhere south.) He also told us what to watch for downriver.

My son Paul and his friend had been a little unnerved when the motor fell off, but then a form of self-reliance took over, stimulated by the initial surge of adrenalin and the following realization that a more primitive existence could promise adventure. Which is why a raft trip had appealed to them in the first place.

At 4 p.m. on the 27th of June we set out for New Orleans on our distinctive little raft. A houseboat carrying reporters and cameramen escorted us down the Black River, the tributary along which the raft was built. When we hit the Mississippi, at 4:30, the houseboat blasted a salute on its horn and turned back. We were on our way, 1,800 miles to go. But at 4:35, no more than an eighth of a mile en route, a sickening whir filled the air. I beheld the strangest sight: Our Mercury outboard motor had parted company with the raft and danced alone on the water. Screaming, it hovered for a moment on the surface in a veil of blue smoke, then plunged down, stifled. The rubber fuel line stretched, then snapped. Oh, boy! Motorless and rudderless on the Mississippi.

"Throw out the anchor!" I hollered, at the same time trying to fix the spot where the motor sank with reference points on the shore. It seemed a long time before the anchor took hold. Taut, the anchor line hummed, indicating the strength

But while crisis heightened their excited awareness of themselves and the river, its absence tended to dull it. Once truly underway, Brownsville behind and systems of propulsion and steering intact once again, rafting became somewhat routine. For the days grew long and hot. As we increased our daily mileage, the eighth day out chalking up 57 miles, the boys concentrated less on the riverbanks and more on the intricacies of their own raft-bound society.

Yet the river refused to let us conclude that this was a private voyage or an inward journey. We kept bumping into history, myriad reminders that this was at least a common stream of American life . . . perhaps more than that, perhaps an intimation of some universal current.

A storm caught us below Nauvoo, Illinois, where the Mormons had built their second temple and near where Joseph Smith, their first prophet, was assassinated by an anti-Mormon mob. It was from Nauvoo that the Mormons fled across the Mississippi with their new leader, Brigham Young, to seek in the barren deserts of the Rockies the God-appointed dwelling place for his wandering tribes. Against a freezing north wind on February 4, 1846, they went, ferryboats carrying the first contingents through ice floes, solid ice supporting those who came later. So the river proved for them both a route to and a barrier for safety, epochal as the Red Sea for the ancient Israelites.

For us the wind was from the south, searing upriver like the hot breath of a hair dryer. No floating against such a headwind, so we motored along as the day grew hotter and hotter. The old fisherman in Brownsville had warned us of a particular widening or pond that we now approached.

"It's long," he said, "and it's wide, maybe a mile and a half, two. It's just south of Nauvoo. And you won't find much anchorage on the banks, either. Scoot through it as fast as you can."

We scooted as fast as we could. But not fast enough. Halfway across, the hair dryer turned from medium to high.

We made for shore. But scarcely had we turned toward the west bank when the wind escalated once more, to perhaps 25 knots. It kicked up three-foot seas which pounded the raft hard and firehosed the deck. We no longer ran a river but—a mote on a gray enormity—found ourselves tossed on an ocean. No Marquettes or Jolliets to be found here; this was the trackless stuff of Columbus and Magellan, abstract instruments required.

Of course, we all *knew* better. Yet the sensation settled in, undeniable, unfathomable. Then the wind shifted. We

Far north, far north are the courses of the great river, the headwaters, the cold lakes . . . . Till at last it is Mississippi, The Father of Waters; the matchless; the great flood . . . the god.

—Steven Vincent Benét

Some 400 thousand sunsets have colored the river since Indians of the Mississippi culture began to reap corn from the fertile floodplains, caught catfish, sturgeon, garfish (skin and bones, below), and enjoyed a vigorous river commerce similar to today's. As those early inhabitants did centuries before them, youngsters come to the river, opposite, "just to have a look." Below left, Huckleberry Belle *pulls into shore near delta destination.*

Helmsman Meyer keeps out of way of tow-boats, barges carrying 230 million tons of nation's bounty annually. Sprague, *below, which burned in 1974, set world record for tow of 60 coal barges covering six acres.*

Coal-laden barge glides through Twin Cities locks, bound for power plant upstream. For past 100 years man has altered river, constructing system of locks and dams to open upper Mississippi to commercial navigation.

changed course and headed into it, looking for the lee of a bank. Foam hissed, spat, and dribbled across the troughs of waves. A plastic dishpan flew off the raft like a Frisbee, gayly Sunday blue. At length, astonishingly, dim shapes—vegetation—took form out of the haze.

In the lee the wind flagged only slightly. But at least it didn't drive the raft into tangles. I headed downriver, hugging the insubstantial shore, a marshy transition between pure river and solid ground. No landmarks appeared to make *A Navigator's Guide to the Upper Mississippi* intelligible, nor any device, natural or unnatural, to which to tie a raft. It cleared later and we stopped at a sandbar to dry out and romp in the sun. Before getting underway again, one of the crew removed a tick from the back of my neck.

Two days later the transistor radio was talking about how the storm we'd encountered had continued north and triggered floods. "So far, floodwaters have accounted for nine drownings," reported the announcer grimly. Still, it was remote news, a distant catastrophe possibly connected to us by that storm and perhaps by the river itself. How long would it take for the floodwaters up north to catch up with the *Belle*?

An impersonal though immensely powerful force, flowing blindly through time, through Earth, and through lives is the Mississippi. Why, then, do the people come to the river? Why in towns without docks, or boats, or beaches and those with giant levees hunched like shoulders between them and the river—do they, at night and on Sundays, drive or walk to the river "just to have a look"?

Still in search of the answer, we left La Grange and headed for Quincy and Tom Sawyer country.

At Hannibal we briefly left the *Belle* unattended and visited the caves south of town where Tom and Becky Thatcher rendezvoused. There we almost froze to death. That night a full moon bathed the river—one of those nights, magical and pastoral, that makes every fiber of self ineffably restless and the soul aware that a large goodness lies diffused over the Earth, particularly over this ever-moving current in the land. The perfume of a Midwestern summer hung thick in the air. Fish leaped and splashed, and a band in town played long into the night. At 4 o'clock in the morning I gave up trying to sleep even though all sounds of revelry by then had stilled, as in an emptied stadium.

I groped my way out on deck to look at the river and find some peace. Instantly, a charge of apprehension seized me. Was it a dream? I reeled and my heart thumped as I saw a silver fleet of ghost craft making its way down the river. Doz-

... civilization in America has followed arteries made by geology .... It is like the steady growth of a complex nervous system for the originally simple, inert continent.

—Frederick Jackson Turner

ens of vessels slid noiselessly past. One came close by, its prow and stern arching ornately high into the night. Vikings? Or, more ancient yet, was this a procession of Valkyries escorting dead heroes to Valhalla?

Then I knew. The one close by turned into a 75-foot willow tree, its roots and branches resembling flourishes of naval architecture. The river teemed with woody flotsam of all sizes, uprooted and uplifted by high water. I noticed that the raft rode higher in relation to the dock than when I first went to bed; the floodwaters of Minnesota had finally caught up with us. Crawling back into my berth, it pleased me that what Mark Twain extolled as the "June Rise" in *Life on the Mississippi* overtook us in Hannibal, of all places.

Vision after vision. The Blessed Virgin appeared on the riverbanks at Portage des Sioux, Missouri, in broad daylight. However, it was no vision but a statue, 50 feet high, illuminated at night, and, according to Quimbey's *Harbor Guide,* unique among madonnas in that it is fiber-glass reinforced. Our Lady of the River was erected in 1951 in gratitude that the floods of that year receded.

The Missouri River spilled in a few miles south and before much longer a gleaming landmark became visible in the distance: the St. Louis arch, gateway to the West. Below St. Louis, the current picked up to a heady 11 miles per hour. With Cairo in sight and the mouth of the Ohio directly ahead, Paul put Olivia Newton-John's version of "On the Banks of the Ohio" on the tape recorder and turned it up loud. That was when the johnboat approached.

The boat came off the Ohio and pulled up straight to the raft. A johnboat is a blunt-bowed aluminum craft, outboard-powered, 15 feet long, usually painted a military olive drab. It is by far the most common and utilitarian fishing boat on the river. Two dour-looking men sat on thwarts. Both wore industrial baseball caps. One cap said "Caterpillar," the other, "Reject Right to Work."

"Where you all going?" asked Caterpillar. A huge, corpulent man with crooked teeth, he wore bib overalls. Right to Work, by contrast, seemed dangerously thin. His cheeks had caved in, a day's growth of white stubble lined them like hard cotton. His cold, deep-set eyes inventoried the raft.

"New Orleans," I answered evenly. I didn't like this. The thought crossed my mind that we had been stopped by pirates, or worse. I then flashed on the terror of James Dickey's novel, *Deliverance,* in which a canoe party is accosted by brutish backwoodsmen. Linked by Caterpillar's enormous arm, the johnboat and the raft drifted down fast in the current. Right to Work sat at the outboard, looking hungry.

In the shadow of St. Louis' Gateway Arch, Paul celebrates his birthday. Families pushing west in 1800s saw the crossing of the river as a symbolic embarkation in their quest for new land and independence.

"I'll be damned," said Caterpillar. It occurred to me that it was the first time on the river I had heard a truly indigenous southern drawl. An old North-South antagonism appeared ready to erupt.

All of a sudden, Right to Work reached down with both hands into a large container near his feet. He took hold of something and with one motion hurled it onto the deck of the raft. An eight-pound catfish flopped where it landed.

"Y'all have a good trip now, heah?" said Right to Work. With that, he started the motor and the johnboat spurted away. Grinning, Caterpillar waved and waved, and shook his head.

"I think we're in the South," I told Paul. "The real South. I imagine that catfish means a pretty penny to those old boys."

Gift of the river, fresh catfish sautéed in butter is worth taking a long raft trip for. That evening, the sky turned into a watermelon again, cool and sweet.

Who owns the Mississippi River, or any of our giant rivers? The Water runs out of a mountain down to the sea.

—Walter J. Hickel

The stretches between towns and stops grew longer as July blazed down. The blue of the Ohio quickly mingled with Mississippi tea, the current slowed back to a leisurely five or six, and the pace of barge traffic increased dramatically below St. Louis. Though it was obvious from maps that the river wound through rich agricultural country—soybeans, some cotton, and, farther south, rice—it was far less obvious from the river itself, for willows and cottonwoods screened everything beyond the banks. Two elements, however, belied the impression that we coursed through uncultivated land: Crop dusters buzzed back and forth and, here and there along the shore, vast grain elevators soared upward, like windowless cathedrals consecrated to fertility.

I also knew from maps that hundreds of prehistoric American Indian burial mounds lay beyond the banks throughout the rich alluvium of the Mississippi Valley. Some of these mounds, described by Smithsonian archeologist Bruce Smith (see pages 148–155), were built for ceremonial purposes; others contained the remains of chiefs and other members of the tribal elite. So the river's riches had beckoned the red man as it later beckoned the invading white.

"But what about the black man?" asked Paul.

"We'll get to that in Memphis," I said. "That's where the Cotton Exchange is."

Memphis came as an intense relief from the long, riverbound miles because of culture—sophisticated, stimulating, urbane. Jazz at Blues Alley, good restaurants everywhere, even Shakespeare on the bank.

However, it was another, less entertaining aspect of culture in Memphis that placed the entire trip and even the river itself into a new perspective. First came Graceland, Elvis Presley's home, just outside Memphis. The road in front was jammed with Presley's fans. Though the gate to the mansion stood tightly locked, throngs congregated before it. They peered through the gate, touched its iron grillwork as though it were an icon, and in some cases scratched graffiti—"Long Live the King"—into the brick wall that surrounded the fabled property.

Another king was dead, too: Martin Luther King. At the Lorraine Motel, where King was shot, business proceeded as usual—except for his room on the second floor. The room, left as it was, is now a shrine. King's portrait hangs on the outside wall on the balcony. A candle burns nearby. "I have been to the mountain-top," runs a quote below.

Shrine. The word seems to take on a new significance when related to the Mississippi. In Memphis, the thought bit me; in Vicksburg, it really grabbed hold. At Memphis's Cotton Ex-change Paul learned that cotton no longer dominates southern agriculture, though the men in shirt-sleeves shouting prices at the Exchange seemed unaware of it. One wall was covered with cotton bales. In Vicksburg he learned that Negro slaves had been essential to the cheap production of cotton and tobacco in the mid-19th-century South, and that the rapidly industrializing North opposed slavery.

"So that's why blacks came?" he asked.

"Mostly."

"And why there was a war?"

"Yes."

"And Martin Luther King was an abolitionist?"

"Not quite. He was called a civil rights leader. Though, come to think of it, that's not far off from being an abolitionist."

We toured the Vicksburg battlefield one sweltering day, crammed into a Volkswagen and listened to a tape-recorded guide. Like Hannibal and Memphis, Vicksburg was full of tourists, most of them bent on visiting the battlefield and pausing before the ornate monuments commemorating army regiments and fallen men, Union and Confederate.

That night, back on the water and embarked on the last stretch to Baton Rouge and New Orleans, I knew how I would always think of the river: a route for traders and pilgrims dotted with historic ports and shrines of differing cults. Our own road to Canterbury.

And then we made it! Past Baton Rouge, which, from the river, looked like an erector set, and into New Orleans, where music—the best of it Cajun—wafted through the soft night like an earthy reward for completed voyages, or pilgrimages.

It had been harrowing at times: Toward the end, river traffic became so intense that we avoided the main channel and picked our way meekly along the shore, the raft shuddering in the slamming wakes of imperious ocean-going freighters, lords of the river.

The last day, with the *Belle* safely off river, I walked down to the banks and took stock. Paul and I had survived, had learned to live within the forced intimacy of our cabin, and within the vast universe of the river. We had seen enough to know why the people come down to the river.

They come to wonder at the blindness and neutrality of the force. Some may consider what lies upriver or down, but mainly, I think, they stand in awe, realizing, however dimly, that this moving water with a name—Mississippi—is their example of the energy of the universe. Against that energy, life is small. The people know the river flowed before they were born and will flow when they are gone.

It rolls through the tropic magic, the almost-jungle, the warm darkness breeding the warm, enormous stars . . . .

–Steven Vincent Benét

Beyond the Horizons

By Wilcomb E. Washburn

Nowhere is our Euro-centered history more parochial than in the account of the "discovery" and "exploration" of America. The presence of native inhabitants—called "Indians" because of Columbus's belief that he had reached Asia—has been traditionally ignored by American historians just as servants and slaves were formerly ignored. The land was—in this view—"virgin" or vacant until the arrival of Europeans. Yet the ancestors of the Indians who greeted Columbus were discoverers and explorers too. These adventurers had come a few thousand years earlier from Asia, evidently crossing the Bering Straits on foot when the Arctic ice cap created a bridge. First, they probably headed for the plains beyond the Rocky Mountains. From there different groups moved off east and west, some into the narrow valleys and landlocked basins of California and the Southwest, some into the bottomlands of the Mississippi Valley, some into the eastern woodlands. Others moved down the "funnel" of Central America and further into South America, finally reaching the tip of Tierra del Fuego.

Exploration of the American land by Europeans began about A.D. 1000. Pushing west from the Scandinavian peninsula to Iceland and then to Greenland, Norsemen by chance discovered land beyond Greenland. Leif Ericsson and his cohorts sought to promote settlement there by naming it "Vinland"—meaning land of vines or land of sweet grasses. The location of the settlements in North America remains in doubt. But the debate is—as one can say in admiration or contempt—academic because the settlements did not survive.

The discovery of America by Europeans was finally and demonstrably achieved through the enterprise of Christopher Columbus, although Columbus died believing that he had reached Asia. As the coastlines discovered by others stretched farther north and south, however, it became apparent that this was not Asia but an unknown world of continental proportions. For all its attractions it remained, both spiritually and physically, a barrier between Europe and Asia. Successive explorers of America continued to hope that around the corner, up the river, over the next ridge, one would finally get on the road to India. After the epic circumnavigation of the world by the Magellan expedition in 1519–22, it was realized that a passage around or through these new land masses would still leave one confronting another great ocean. But recognition of the actual distance to the goal did not discourage explorers. If a water route existed, man was capable of sailing it even in the relatively small ships of the 16th century. Not until the 19th century would movement on land become easier than movement on the water.

Florida, for centuries regarded as a useless waste of sand and swamp, was nevertheless a focal point of early European interest because it sat astride the Gulf Stream that carried the Spanish bullion fleets from Cartagena and Havana on their way back to Spain. As the English spokesman for expansion Richard Hakluyt put it, Florida was a potential "bridle" placed on the Spanish in America. The French, English, and Dutch all sought to share the wealth revealed by Columbus's voyages, if not by taking it directly from the land or from the Indians, then from the Spanish, who had taken it from both.

In 1562 Jean Ribaut planted a column bearing the arms of

France on a bluff overlooking the St. John's River east of present-day Jacksonville. Two years later he returned to establish a fort on the site; it was named Fort Caroline in honor of the French king, Charles IX. Spain's answer to these interlopers was to fortify Florida, too. In 1565 Spain and France, on a collision course in Florida, collided. Pedro Menéndez de Avilés, sent by the King of Spain to root out the French, massacred most of Ribaut's party at the Matanzas River. Fort Caroline was wiped out and Castillo de San Marcos established at St. Augustine, giving Spain control over this strategic area which it retained into the 19th century.

Meanwhile, Coronado and other Spanish conquistadors were seeking golden cities among the Pueblos of Arizona and New Mexico (whose towns actually are golden only in the setting sun), and putting the stamp of Spanish culture on that enduring land. But wealth eluded them. And, though native inhabitants were conquered by successive Spanish invaders, their independence was never entirely extinguished.

Because oceans were the highways of the Age of Expansion, New England was nearly established in California before it was established on the Atlantic Coast. "Nova Albion"—New England—was the name given to the region of California where Francis Drake stopped for repairs during his voyage around the world between 1577 and 1580. After sailing through the straits that bore the name of their discoverer, Magellan, and working his way perhaps as far north as the present Canadian border, Drake was forced by the cold to turn back to a "convenient and fit harbor"—probably the harbor now called Drake's Bay just north of San Francisco. Fog and mist kept the skies overcast during his stay, June 17 to July 23, 1579. His men were "continually visited with like nipping colds . . . insomuch that if violent exercises of our bodies, and busy employment about our necessary labors, had not sometimes compelled us to the contrary, we could very well have been contented to have kept about us still our winter clothes." Though Drake held conferences with the local Indians who were friendly, and left a plate of brass proclaiming English sovereignty over the area, New England was actually fated to be 3,000 miles away.

In 1585 Sir Walter Raleigh, Queen Elizabeth's brash and gallant favorite, sought to found a colony on the east coast of America, which he named Virginia in honor of the Virgin Queen. The settlement at Roanoke Island, on the Outer Banks of today's North Carolina coast, was located offshore for defense against Spanish and Indians, though one of the captains of the voyage wrote that on the nearby mainland "the soil is the most plentiful, sweet, fruitful, and wholesome

of all the world: there are above fourteen several sweet smelling timber trees, and the most part of their underwoods are Bays and such like: they have those Oaks that we have, but far greater and better." Raleigh's men also found the natives "most gentle, loving and faithful, void of all guile and treason, and such as live after the manner of the golden age."

During the period of national peril from the Spanish Armada, however, the settlement was cut off from supplies. By the time contact was reestablished it had disappeared. The "Lost Colony" remains an enigma. Did the colonists amalgamate with the native inhabitants? Did they survive?

Raleigh's hope was eventually realized by the colonists at Jamestown in 1607. After grim seasons of starvation and war, the settlement began to prosper, and supporters like the Reverend Samuel Purchas, encouraging emigration from England, spoke in glowing terms of Virginia's charms: "But looke upon Virginia; view her lovely lookes (howsoever like a

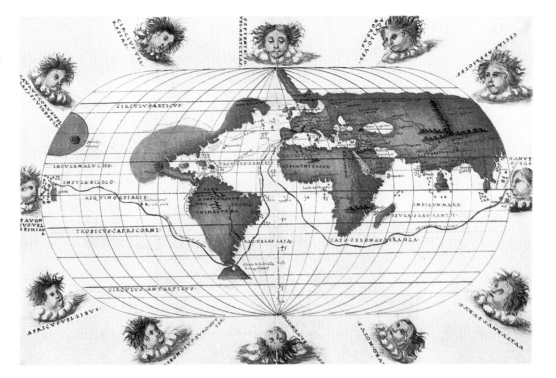

Preferring to overlook North America's coast and to envision the South Sea beyond, early explorers' dreams influenced cartographer Baptista Agnese. He included Magellan's 'round-the-world route on his c. 1540 map.

the gallant Pilgrim settlement of 1620 in Massachusetts, one finds, just to the west of the village, a pond called by the curious name of "Billington Sea." The name derives from the dashed hopes of Francis Billington who, on January 8, 1621, soon after debarking from the *Mayflower,* climbed a tree and spotted what he rashly proclaimed to be a "great sea." In derision the pond retained the character attributed to it by the optimistic Billington.

In Canada, French explorers with the same misconceptions as the English were meeting with the same disappointments. Sieur de La Salle, seeking a passage to the Orient, was unhappy to find that the great "Father of Waters" flowed into a gulf of the same ocean crossed by Europeans in coming to America. Still, his discoveries, and those of other Frenchmen such as Louis Jolliet and Jacques Marquette, fostered optimism that the Missouri River, the main western tributary of the Mississippi, would provide a passage to the South Sea. Explorers dreamed of a short portage from the headwaters of the Missouri to the headwaters of a river running westward.

Louis Hennepin, one of La Salle's company, in his *New Discovery of a Vast Country in North America,* wrote that the Missouri was formed from several other rivers which flowed from a mountain about 12 days' journey from its mouth. Allowing his imagination free rein, Hennepin added that "from this mountain one might see the Sea, and now and then some Great Ships." Europeans sometimes expected to meet Chinese or Tatars in their explorations of the Northwest. The reports of Asians there, derived either from wishful thinking or from the resemblance of the natives to the people from whom they were descended, spurred expectations of eventually finding a "Passage to India."

It was in the towering mind of Thomas Jefferson that a plan was conceived to dispel ignorance about the unexplored regions of the Northwest. From the time of his boyhood Jefferson had absorbed tales of this land, both fanciful and true. His schoolteacher, the Reverend James Maury, reasoning on the basis of symmetrical geography, believed that the sources of rivers flowing east into the Mississippi were just as liable to be near the sources of rivers flowing west into the Pacific as the rivers flowing west into the Mississippi were close to the rivers flowing east into the Atlantic. No one knew for sure, even in 1800, that the remote and rugged ranges variously termed the "Stoney Mountains," the "Shining Mountains," or the "Rocky Mountains" far exceeded the Appalachians in their breadth, height, and extent.

Jefferson carefully considered the conflicting evidence concerning the Northwest. The area was vast and so it is not

modest Virgin she is now vailed with wild Coverts and shadie Woods, expecting rather ravishment then Mariage from her Native Savages) survay her Heavens, Elements, Situation; her divisions by armes of Bayes and Rivers into so goodly and well proportioned limmes and members; her Virgin portion nothing empaired, nay not yet improoved, in Natures best Legacies; the neighbouring Regions and Seas so commodious and obsequious; her opportunities for offence and defence; and in all these you shall see, that she is worth wooing and loves of the best Husband."

During the early years of English settlement in Virginia and in New England, the dream persisted of a South Sea just beyond. The dream was nourished by maps from Giovanni da Verrazzano's cruise up the coast in 1524. Looking westward for a passage to Asia, Verrazzano had thought he saw a sea. Like John Cabot and other explorers before and after him, Verrazzano did not have time or stomach for more detailed explorations (which would have revealed that he was simply looking across the Outer Banks of North Carolina). As a result, North America appeared on some maps as long and gangling with another ocean just beyond.

Englishmen as well as Frenchmen and Italians searched in vain for this South Sea. When one visits Plymouth, the site of

surprising that all reports—whether of deserts or rich agricultural soils—should have embodied some element of truth. On the whole, the reports, particularly those derived from French explorers, emphasized positive aspects to the point that a powerful image of the "Garden of the World" was created. Father Marquette, in speaking of the Mississippi Valley, had asserted that "no better soil can be found either for corn, for vines, or for any other fruit whatever." And one of La Salle's company had reported "vast Meadows, which need not be grubb'd up but are ready for the Plow and Seed." When combined with the image of the Passage to India, which had spurred Europeans from the time of Columbus, the lure was irresistible.

After Jefferson was elected President in 1800, he established a "Corps of Discovery," headed by his private secretary, Meriwether Lewis, who selected William Clark as co-commander. Lewis and Clark left the United States in 1804 with a small party of picked men to "explore the Missouri river, & such principal stream of it, as by it's course and communication with the waters of the Pacific ocean, whether the Columbia, Oregan, Colorado or any other river may offer the most direct & practicable water communication across this continent for the purpose of commerce."

In addition to this objective, the party was trained to make scientific observations of flora and fauna, and to record astronomical data. Jefferson, who anticipated future dealings with the Indian inhabitants of the area, and the possible settlement of whites there, provided for a sensitive and intelligent approach to the powerful nations the expedition would meet. It is only when we compare the success of this expedition with the expeditions of the Spanish conquistadors that we realize the magnitude of Jefferson's achievement. By instructing the men carefully, by providing them with symbols of friendship—the peace medals that became a continuing element in Indian-white interaction—he enabled the small company to traverse half the continent amicably and accomplish its mission safely. The Lewis and Clark expedition was a classic in the annals of exploration. At once heroic and scientific, intellectual and physical, peaceful yet effectual, it was a tribute to the genius of America and to Thomas Jefferson, who did so much to define America's goals.

Even before Lewis and Clark returned, other government expeditions had been sent out. William Dunbar went to explore the lower Red River and the Ouachita. Zebulon M. Pike headed north to look for the source of the Mississippi. He failed in that objective, but in a second expedition, to the southern Rockies, he sighted the summit later named Pikes Peak. Thomas Nuttall explored the Missouri beyond the Mandan villages, then later the Red River and the Arkansas. Nuttall was a scientist, as was Henry Schoolcraft, who explored southern Missouri and Arkansas in 1817–18, and in 1832 finally discovered the source of the Mississippi in Lake Itasca, Minnesota. Many other key discoveries were made by fur trappers: In 1813 Robert Stuart found South Pass, later the route of the Oregon Trail across the Rockies; in the early 1820s Jim Bridger and Peter Skene Ogden explored in the vicinity of Great Salt Lake; and in the latter 1820s Jedediah Smith became the first citizen of the U.S.A. to see the interior of northern California and Oregon.

Meantime, expeditions kept going west under Army auspices. Major Stephen H. Long explored the territory between the Missouri and the Rockies in 1819, for example, and in 1838 Joseph N. Nicollet and John C. Frémont explored the

Florida's strategic position near Caribbean trade routes made France's Fort Caroline, below, a prize for Spain in 1565. Spanish conquistadors march in Navajo petroglyph, opposite, Canyon de Chelly, Arizona.

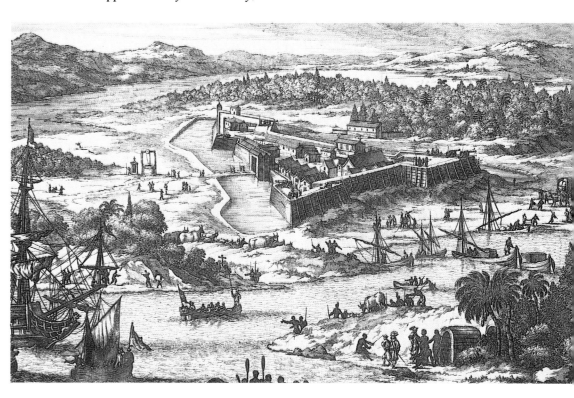

plateau between the upper Missouri and Mississippi rivers. In the 1840s Frémont made three major treks through the Rockies, the Great Basin, and the Sierras, as a result of which he acquired the sobriquet "the Pathfinder."

By the middle 1840s few areas of the American West were totally unknown, yet there still remained—in the words of Joseph Henry, first Secretary of the Smithsonian Institution—"almost a blank" in human knowledge of this vast region. Establishment of the Smithsonian in 1846 coincided with the beginning of rapid expansion into the West. Its initial involvement included cartography, archeology, physical geography, and meteorology. By tabulating astronomical observations it facilitated making accurate determinations of longitude. Its very earliest publication, in 1848, an archeological study of ancient monuments of the Mississippi Valley, laid the basis for perhaps the most impressive series of anthropological explorations ever conducted by a single organization. Its publication between 1849 and 1851 of the results of various surveys of physical geography, particularly of the Mississippi and Ohio valleys by Charles Ellet, helped to facilitate travel and navigation. Close to Joseph Henry's heart was the planning of a comprehensive program of meteorological observations, which he hoped would lead to a general theory of climatic change with resulting practical benefits, especially to farmers. The weather map with which we are now all familiar, "presenting the successive phases of the sky over the whole country, at different points of time," emerged from these studies.

The most prominent Smithsonian field activity in the

Below, even leaders of 1776 America knew little of trans-Appalachian continent. One hundred years later, Smithsonian artist-anthropologist William H. Holmes portrayed Grand Canyon during scientific expedition.

1850s was collecting natural history specimens from all parts of the world but particularly from the Western Hemisphere. The Smithsonian "Castle," completed in 1855, provided a place to house such collections, and the vigorous young Spencer Baird, Henry's assistant in the natural history department, provided the impetus to gather them. Although Henry worried that the emphasis on collections would eventually undermine support for original scientific investigations, he accepted and encouraged the indefatigable collecting spirit of Baird, which he directed into broader channels of research and publication.

1849; similarly, it published a paper on botany by John Torrey of Princeton based on plants discovered by John C. Frémont in California.

The Smithsonian's policy of exerting its influence indirectly derived from the stern insistence of Joseph Henry that it could do more "by stimulating and assisting the researches of original inquiries, wherever found" than by undertaking costly expeditions at its own expense. Henry's method of "piggy-back" research was nicely illustrated in the Smithsonian's association with the expedition organized by Western Union to establish direct telegraph communication between the United States and Russia. When it began its project in 1861, the company called upon Henry and Baird for information concerning the contemplated route. Robert Kennicott, a biologist who had spent three years in "Russian America" under the auspices of the Institution, was assigned to the expedition. Other Smithsonian-trained men went along to make notes and collect specimens. The Smithsonian's ability to staff a scientific expedition was unequaled. In addition to its paid staff, there were dozens of unpaid scholars, some living in the Smithsonian Castle in rooms that were—thankfully—both heated and lighted. Moreover, as Henry proudly put it, "all the prominent cultivators of original science in this country" were available to advance knowledge by collaborating on projects in which the Smithsonian took an interest.

The range of Smithsonian-supported expeditions in the 1860s was extraordinary. Under the supervision of Baird (who was to succeed Henry after the latter's death in 1878), they covered the entire Western Hemisphere. When the question of purchasing Alaska from Russia came to the fore in 1867, Smithsonian scientists provided up-to-date evidence concerning the contents of the "icebox." Quizzed by officials of the State Department and by members of Congress, they helped dispel the popular myth concerning its worthlessness. Subsequent expeditions to the new Territory were guided by Smithsonian expertise.

The role of the Smithsonian in Arctic explorations was significant throughout the 1850s, 1860s, and 1870s. It provided assistance to Dr. Elisha Kent Kane in his 1853 search for the lost explorer Sir John Franklin. In the early 1860s it furnished instruments for the expedition led by Isaac L. Hayes, then analyzed and published his findings. Joseph Henry, in his annual report for 1865, noted that the observations made by earlier explorers in the Arctic regions had "not yet been subjected to the analytical processes by which all the interesting truths relative to the physical geog-

> I climb so high that the men and boats are lost in the black depths below . . . and still there is more canyon above than below.
>
> –John Wesley Powell

During the 1850s practically every expedition that was outfitted—whether by the Army, Navy, Coast Survey, Topographical Bureau, Department of the Interior, or Land Office, or by states, societies, or individuals—was provided with instruments by the Smithsonian, and with staff members it recommended. The notes and specimens these expeditions brought back were subjected to scholarly scrutiny by Smithsonian staff or collaborators, and the results often published by the Institution. For example, it published a memoir by Asa Gray, professor of botany at Harvard, based on a collection of plants made by Charles Curtis in Texas in

raphy of the globe are to be deduced." While Hayes and others did make specific geographical discoveries, such as a new sound opening to the westward near Cape Sabine, of greater import were the fundamental scientific discoveries, such as a more precise value for the Earth's polar depression than had previously been known. Meteorological observations taken in the Arctic helped reinforce the results of experiments Henry had begun.

The Smithsonian played a leading part in arranging the expedition of Captain Charles F. Hall in the *Polaris*, 1871–73, to penetrate as close as possible to the North Pole. Henry and Baird provided instructions on observational techniques in meteorology and natural history, and further instructions were provided by Smithsonian collaborators like J. E. Hilgard and Louis Agassiz. Following the expedition's return, its chief scientist, Emil Bessels, worked at the Smithsonian organizing the data gathered, and this was published in three volumes by the Institution.

The rich collection of archeological and ethnological specimens accumulated from the Northwest Coast and from the Arctic helped stimulate the Smithsonian's researches in these fields. In his reports, Henry expounded on the significance of the material evidence of native groups. These specimens began to arrive just as topographical and geographical surveys started sending back equally rich material from interior regions of the continent. In collecting, Henry was aware of the necessity to act quickly, particularly with regard to ethnological specimens, before the advance of "civilization" destroyed or altered the existing environment.

John Wesley Powell's interest in the ethnology as well as the geology of the western regions had emerged during his first explorations in 1868, aimed at clearing up the mystery surrounding the upper Colorado River. Although earlier explorers had penetrated into different portions of the vast domain stretching from Wyoming to the Gulf of California, no accurate maps existed of the river system that found its outlet in the lower Colorado. Powell devised special boats to carry his party down the Green River in Wyoming, through treacherous waters and dangerous rapids to the Mormon settlements on the Virgin River where the Colorado turns along the present border between Nevada and Arizona. The river was charted, Indian ruins studied, and the basis for Powell's geological theories formed. In the course of the journey, boats were swamped and instruments—many borrowed from the Smithsonian—lost. Starvation threatened. Three of the party refused to push on and were killed by Indians after climbing out of the canyon.

Hostility to Powell increased as provisions ran low. "If he can only study geology," wrote one of the party, "he will be happy without food or shelter, but the rest of us are not afflicted with it to an alarming extent." Yet Powell's scientific achievements were remarkable. His exploration of the Colorado allowed him to "unravel" the "mystery of the rocks," as he put it in his journal. Essentially what Powell recognized, and what he later developed into a more formal theory, was that the topography of the region was the result of uplift, erosion, and sedimentation. More importantly, perhaps, his dramatic exploration led to government support through the Smithsonian Institution for a more comprehensive "Geographical and Topographical Survey of the Colorado River of the West." In the course of this second expedition, made in 1871–72, Powell explored a belt 15 miles wide on both sides of the river and made significant geographical and ethnological discoveries.

When the Bureau of American Ethnology was created within the Smithsonian in 1879, Powell was chosen to lead it. In 1880 he succeeded to the directorship of the U.S. Geological Survey, consolidated from four separate western surveys the year before. Two products of Powell's association with the Smithsonian were an Indian linguistic atlas and the cautionary and pathbreaking *Report on the Lands of the Arid Region of the United States* (1878).

Explorers and scientists, from Columbus to Powell, often acted with pure motives and an inspired vision. Those who followed and profited from their vision have frequently exhibited less elevated purposes. Hence the ambiguity of exploration that—seen from the opposite side of the ethnic divide or from the perspective of a later generation—seems more intent upon exploitation than discovery. "The most utilitarian conquest known to history," Professor Perry Miller pointed out in an essay on "The Romantic Dilemma in American Nationalism and the Concept of Nature," had "somehow to be viewed not as inspired by a calculus of rising land values and investments but (despite the orgies of speculation) as an immense exertion of the spirit." The more rapidly and violently was Nature exploited, the more insistently did American philosophers, poets, and painters seek to identify the true American with the virtues of Nature, pure and undefiled.

America was, in the literature of the 19th century, "Nature's nation." The Christian citizen could resolve the dilemma posed by a brutal, expansive America by assuming that the nation could "progress indefinitely into an expanding future without acquiring sinful delusions of grandeur simply because it is nestled in Nature, is instructed and guided by mountains, [and] is chastened by cataracts." Certainly the scientific face of that expansion helped stimulate the beneficent view of the process that Miller saw in its more exploitative aspects.

Nothing human is perfect, yet humans continue to uphold the ideal: the retention of unspoiled wilderness, the maintenance of friendly relations with weaker peoples, the non-exploitative harvesting of natural resources. However ambivalent, these ideals, too, have been part of the relation between Americans and their land.

Though much of today's exploration is scientific—like the probing of the crystal-hunting spelunker, opposite—Americans remain possessed by a vision of opportunity. Print, below, celebrates telegraph wire going west.

A Land for Landscapes

By Joshua C. Taylor

Asher Brown Durand expressed the serenity of an eastern valley and his own reverence for nature in Dover Plain *(1848). Opposite, Thomas Moran's* Cliffs of the Upper Colorado River *(1882) exalts the untamed West.*

Artists were late in discovering landscape as a meaningful subject for their work. Except as a setting for human activity, landscape at first had little significance for painting beyond recording a specific site. Since art was regarded as the projection of human understanding—helped by a divine spark of genius—there seemed little point in simply representing what one saw. But attitudes toward both art and nature materially changed between the beginning of the 17th century and the time when American artists began noticing the attractions of their own wilderness, some two centuries later.

The first appraisals of American nature were made with an eye toward production: how a patch of landscape would favor agriculture, settlement, shipping, or prosperity in general. Of course, there were remarks about agreeable vistas and natural curiosities, but the wilderness was there to be won, not admired. By the mid-18th century, cultivated Englishmen were beginning to talk about nature as a balm or stimulant to the human mind, how a cataract could provoke sublime emotions, how one could pleasurably lose oneself in the inviting disorder of wild nature, or find calm and assurance in a well-ordered, smoothly contoured landscape. Through the persuasive power of their forms, natural surroundings, it was averred, had an effect on man's character and even on the way he thought.

Such ideas gained currency in America

just as the country was becoming newly aware of itself. So rural estates were planted to afford the proud owner the peace of the smoothly "beautiful" or the spiritually stimulating irregularity of the "picturesque," making the garden a mentor for the emotions and a complement to the mind. Areas were searched for picturesque views and, above all, for overwhelming natural phenomena that could move the reverent observer to an awareness of the sublime. About the only natural event that could be counted on for this latter soul-stirring experience was the thundering Niagara Falls, which was painted at least once by every artist with even a slight interest in landscape from the beginning of the 19th century on.

The drama of American landscape as discovered in other aspects of its wilderness was first revealed by the New York painter Thomas Cole. Prepared to be moved by the jagged forms of storm-struck trees and the contest between light and shade set up by sun and rolling clouds, he found along the Hudson River all of the elements necessary to stir the soul to an awareness of God's rule and the fragility of human destiny. Unspoiled nature, in which America abounded, still spoke God's truth, and through the drama of its ever-changing forms, man could escape his petty concerns to become one with a moral universe. America's raw nature could inspire the human spirit to achieve a level of morality as no man-trammeled European nature could. When Cole went to Europe to study, America's nature poet William Cullen Bryant warned him not to be seduced by the softer aspects of foreign skies.

The generation of American painters inspired by Cole saw little reason to dramatize the spiritual quality of nature in his forceful way, nor were they inclined to interpret a thunderstorm as a hell-and-brimstone sermon. They accepted the fact that nature was a manifestation of God, but saw the face of deity in a more smiling aspect.

By the 1840s nature was not threat but promise. Asher Brown Durand in his great painting of Dover Plain, New York, in 1848 shows nature to be bounteous on two levels. Cows forage in peaceful fields watered by a placid lake, sheep graze beneath the flourishing trees, and in the background grain is being harvested. Meanwhile a group of young people clamber over the undisturbed boulders picking lush berries from the wild vines. But on the topmost rock a young woman shields her eyes to take in the grandeur of the extensive scene. The warm sun, the rolling hills masked in a delicate blue haze, and the open, inviting space provide a spiritual feast no less important or nourishing than the edible products of the land.

Durand and his friends were very conscious of these spiritual values. They spoke of their landscape studies not in terms of composition and technique, but in terms of moral value. Nonetheless, a meticulousness of rendering was important to them. If

nature was to be seen as the manifestation of God's hand, who were they to change it through predilections of their own? Visual truth became a moral principle; to deviate from exact appearance was a kind of blasphemy. The artist's role was not to boast of his own feelings and his creative accomplishments, but to call attention to the verities of nature in such a way that nature, not the artist, moved the spectator. Art, in other words, was only as good as its success in identifying itself wholly with nature. It was the means, as Ralph Waldo Emerson was wont to point out, for a more receptive encounter with nature itself. In *Nature* he had written: "In the woods, we return to reason and faith. There I feel that nothing can befall me in life,—no disgrace, no calamity (leaving me my eyes), which nature cannot repair. Standing on the bare ground,— my head bathed by the blithe air and uplifted into infinite space,—all mean egotism vanishes. I became a transparent eye-

ball; I am nothing; I see all; the currents of the Universal Being circulate through me; I am part and parcel of God."

So artists journeyed through the countryside, sketchbooks in hand, to study art not in European galleries of artistic masterpieces but in the woods, the mountains, and peaceful fields of the United States. One need not be an artist, of course, to commune with nature, and people traveled to mountain retreats and resorts on the rocky seacoast to be won over by the spell of nature. As life became more urban, the importance of such healthful sessions became greater, as did the collecting of landscape paintings. Each painting was a quintessential experience of nature, a moral reminder in an otherwise busy, gainful life.

The mountains and the shore were two attractive poles: the grandeur of high places and tall woods, or the threatening yet consoling vastness of the ever-active sea. Rough waves assaulting rocks, whether on the Isles of Shoals, New Hampshire, or at Marblehead, Massachusetts, seemed to cleanse the mind of other associations, absorbing the entire attention of the seeker after natural truth. The symbol of the seashore as a spiritual restorative was formed early and lasted late, well past the magnificent seas of Winslow Homer and the sun-flecked waves of Childe Hassam. The shore outlasted the mountains in America as an image in art.

By mid-century, although many artists were content with even the most modest aspects of nature—an attitude not unlike Thoreau's—some regularly lamented the fact that for the really overwhelming impact of nature one had to travel through the Alps or take a boat down the Rhine. The early enchantment of Niagara had gradually worn a bit thin. Then the miraculous happened. Artists accompanying surveying expeditions to the West began to bring back exciting images of Yellowstone, the Rocky Mountains, and Yosemite. Here was rugged grandeur second to none. Albert Bierstadt,

who first traveled West in 1859, expressed his awe and admiration of the mountainous scene in huge canvases that drew the imagination into a realm of vast peaks, mirror-like lakes, and mysterious veils of iridescent mist that promised more mountain wonders beyond. While Frederick Edwin Church's paintings of immense spaces and snow-capped mountains in South America were exotic and fascinating in their intricacy, Bierstadt's grandiloquent experiences were a part of America. In fact they quickly became associated with the new American dream of infinite expansion to the West, of new discoveries and potentialities, of a triumphant march of westward progress. There was in Bierstadt's pictorial hymns to western grandeur both a mystic idealism and attention to material fact, two qualities they shared with the spirit of *Westward Ho!*

This was a new kind of landscape painting. It was big, often so in size and always in conception. The eye could not grasp it all at once but had to wander through its spaces, enjoying the passing scene but looking for more. Thomas Moran saw the West as a member of expeditions to the Yellowstone and down the Colorado and painted such epochal works as *The Grand Canyon of the Yellowstone*. As from an eagle's perch, the viewer can focus on an isolated pinnacle and exult in the vast surrounding space. The sun, in these sweeping paintings, is never passive but kindles brilliant fires in the clouds or on the walls of strange eroded

In his panoramic 6- by 10-foot Western Landscape with Lake and Mountains, *Albert Bierstadt, in 1868, opened the eyes of Americans to the grandeur of the West. This epic work may be seen at the Smithsonian Institution's National Collection of Fine Arts.*

Experimenting with light and shadow, impressionists often chose traditional subjects like Niagara, *right, by George Inness (1889). By the turn of the century, such works as Childe Hassam's* Colonial Graveyard at Lexington, *above, John Henry Twachtman's* End of Winter, *below, and Albert Pinkham Ryder's* With Sloping Mast and Dipping Prow, *opposite, were winning acclaim.*

canyons. This was God's country, one liked to say, but the powerful, ragged images seemed, in their challenge, to affirm the importance of man. America began to identify itself with the intractable West, considering its distances and demanding mountains to be both test and symbol of American character. The exultant poetry of Whitman, not the reflective philosophy of Emerson, matched these epic proportions.

A different poetry of landscape, however, developed in these same years in direct contrast to the exclamatory verse of the expanding West. George Inness was no more interested than Bierstadt in losing himself in the moral minutiae of a domesticated woodland, but he shied away from overtowering grandeur. Landscape for him was a way of feeling. He wished his paintings of eastern scenes to mirror his state of mind, not just to imitate the landscape that produced it. More and more his creations in paint became moody evocations with little attention given to the specific place or time. At first such works were rejected as being morally suspect—they did slight justice to the details of God's handiwork or were lacking in American stature. But by the 1870s and '80s there was a growing appreciation for the haunting effect of his sensuous elegies. Alien to the forces of progress, his personal dream in the face of nature confirmed a different aspect of individuality. The deeply rooted strain of feeling reached by sensuous suggestion rather than descriptive statement could be understood either in terms of religion or simply of art. Inness looked upon his reaction to nature as religious—although not in the way of Cole or Durand—because it put him in touch with his own inner spirit which, he assumed, was not unlike the spirit that motivated all men and nature as well. The painting was a creation of the artist who had been inspired by nature; more than a view, it was a landscape of the mind.

Some of the nostalgic mood of Inness's

paintings reflects the quality he found in the works of such French painters as Rousseau and Millet, innovative and initially unpopular artists who had chosen to lead the peasant life in a rustic spot outside Paris called Barbizon. There the forest was wild, the fields rugged, giving evidence of the struggles of the humble peasants who depended on that land. The peasant, ever toiling in the tradition of his ancestors, blended perfectly into this ages-old landscape. But to American painters, attracted by this vision, traditional peasant life seemed more exotic; they tended to accept the scene as a pure Virgilian eclogue with no overtones of social problems. The peasant became only a poetic symbol who, as at times with Inness, might appear in a New Jersey landscape.

Landscape as visual poetry had some notable supporters in the last quarter of 19th-century American art. As with Inness, Ralph Blakelock's nocturnal scenes were based on his own observations, but his paintings were built up of evident paint, form by form, color by color—the way Poe assembled a poem—until the canvas itself evoked the feeling he associated with nature. Nonetheless the paintings relate to the known environment if only because, after looking at a late Inness or a Blakelock, one sees the surrounding landscape differently, as having new potentiality for the reflective mind.

The most powerful visual poet of landscape in America was Albert Pinkham Ryder. Whether he painted a farmyard or a boat tossed at sea, he endowed each object and shape with a mysterious aura. His forms are simple because each one was built up over the years with layer upon layer of paint until there was not a line or shape that failed to carry its haunting message. Ryder also wrote poetry, but whether his medium was words or paint his goal was to open the mind to an expanding radiation of thought and feeling, for which his landscape image was only the starting point. To explore land-

Patterns of the landscape inspired regional artists in the 20th century. Above, Young Corn *by Grant Wood, son of the Midwest; below,* Only One *by Georgia O'Keeffe; below right,* Water Valley *by Karl Knaths.*

scape was to explore the inner life of man.

The association of sentiment with landscape was strong in America—so strong that when American painters were attracted to the new range of prismatic color introduced in Paris by the impressionists, they adapted it to their own expressive purposes rather than following the objective procedures of Monet or Pissarro. John Twachtman ruminated on the somber beauties of autumn or winter or evoked the blissful reminiscence of a protracted summer afternoon. J. Alden Weir found the sunlight falling across the upland pasture of his Connecticut farm an adequate excuse for quiet, reflective contemplation. Even Childe Hassam, who followed more closely than most the new French scheme of divided color, saw landscape not just as vision but as mood. The Americans at this point were unwilling to give up their hard-won right to visual poetry; objective vision was a separate, long-established tradition in America. Landscape belonged not to God or country but to the artist who looked at it.

Even the American artists who embraced those exciting concepts of art from Paris early in the 20th century came back to rethink the new forms in the face of the American landscape. John Marin, fascinated with the intermingling of time and space that made the cubist and futurist paintings so dynamic, discovered the full power of the new vision on the coast of Maine. Georgia O'Keeffe discovered the most eloquent expression of her refined, purist taste of the 1920s in the bleached forms and spare landscape of New Mexico. There also Edward Weston, Paul Strand, and others proved the subtlety of photography, using the dunes and sky to test infinite refinement of photographic line and value. Art in America grew out of the American landscape, and the landscape has never been far from any artist's consciousness—regardless of aesthetic direction.

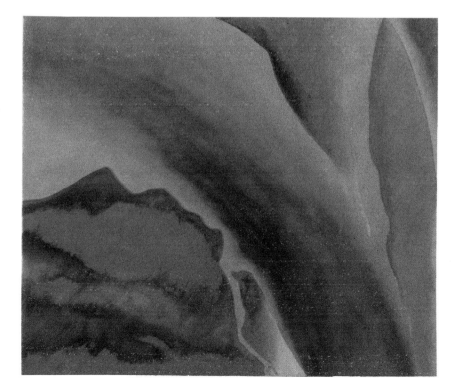

In the 1930s, when Depression America was trying to reestablish direction, eyes were turned once more to the land, and artists rediscovered the country from Maine to California. They might paint the fertile mid-western fields, as did Grant Wood and John Steuart Curry, New England countrysides in the snow, or personal fantasies of small towns and haunted forests. But in the American landscape they found and provided the public with a credible sense of stability through a renewed feeling for place.

The artist in more recent years has, no less than his forerunners, found in the American landscape a means for reaching out to the world around him while remaining in touch with his own inner promptings. The ever-changing complexity of these corners of the environment not yet dominated by man retains a rejuvenating newness to even the most jaded eye. Milton Avery found an everlasting summer of glowing hues and unconstructed forms; Karl Knaths never tired of the shifting puzzles of space and light. The artist has used his sensitivity to the natural prospect as a way of adjusting and refining the response of man to his surrounding world.

In a society devoted to definitions and limits, the immensity of nature has proved a vital challenge to the artist. Earth sculptors have created huge forms that become a part of nature and punctuate its spaces, and—for those who have found that concepts can outstrip the reach of forms—the Earth itself has become a part of the artist's imaginative calculations. On the other hand, some—like Alan Sonfist, in his collage (right) from *The Leaf Met the Paper in Time*—have reacted to a cosmic consciousness by returning to specific nature in its smallest detail.

For art in America, the landscape has meant freedom and expansion, or, when useful, discipline and concentration. But once the artist took possession of his environment, the natural bounty of America was never far from the surface of his art.

American Space

By Roderick Nash

Gertrude Stein said it perfectly: "In the United States there is more space where nobody is than where anybody is. That is what makes America what it is." It was, in fact, geographical space, vast emptiness, that made the New World new. Nothing, Americans gradually discovered, could be something. The discovery powered what is most distinctive and distinguished in American letters. Culture and geography are closely linked; ideas, like trees, are shaped by their surroundings. If there is such a thing as national character, the environment—the basic shared situation—explains it. If ecology is the study of the interrelationships of living things and the environment, then *cultural* ecology should concern the nexus between place and human imagination. A cultural ecologist of the United States could do worse than start with Stein.

The archetypal vision in the American experience was of nothing at all—space, wildness, the open range, the big woods, the big sky. But space, in the context of the nation's history, was full of significance. Emptiness meant the possibility of new creation. Vastness meant elbowroom, intellectual as well as social. Wildness meant release, freedom, and the spine-tingling potential of new beginnings not just for a man, but as Neil Armstrong recognized when he stepped on the moon, for mankind. The initial excitement of the American land lay in the opportunity it afforded to turn a new leaf, to write on a *tabula rasa*. The Puritans understood this in the 17th century as they fled the crowded and restrictive Old World. There still was room to be different two centuries later when Brigham Young led the Mormons to a ridge on the western slope of Utah's Wasatch Range and told them that the basin of Great Salt Lake was the place to pursue perfection. A similar vision impelled counterculture homesteaders of the 1960s to seek empty nooks and corners of the American landscape. Utopianism demands deserted islands. Even the contemporary backpacker who heads for the hills recapitulates the central national experience of escape and rebirth.

The novelist Wallace Stegner set forth these basic American truths in 1960 in a letter to a government commission charged with determining how much wilderness to save for the future. Stegner, it is worth noting, grew up on the Montana-Saskatchewan borderland where, at sunrise and sunset, a man casts a 100-yard shadow. He began his letter by speaking of "the wilderness *idea*" as an American resource just as important as lumber, ore, and grass. The wildness of the New World, Stegner continued, meant "opportunity" which was "the thing that had helped make an American different from and, until we forget it in the roar of our industrial cities, more fortunate than other men." The wild places that remain, he concluded, retard the "headlong drive into our technological termite-life, the Brave New World of a completely man-controlled environment." It followed for Stegner that Americans needed all the wild country left, even if they did no more than think about it as a symbol, because wilderness was "a part of the geography of hope."

A distinctive literary tradition, an *American* tradition, began when European writers started to take cognizance of the vast emptiness of the New World. Two interpretative traditions appeared at the outset. One celebrated the beauty, fecundity, and beneficence of the American land. An example was the Norse account of the fruit-laden vegetation of "Vinland." Another was Columbus's report from the Caribbean that his ships had circled the very nipple of the "cosmic breast"—paradise itself. Subsequent writers entertained visions of bounteous gardens, beauteous maidens, golden cities, and fountains of youth.

The other interpretative tradition was negative, and it too sprang from the unknown vastness of the American land. Wilderness, the first Americans quickly learned, could terrorize as well as enchant. The early accounts are replete with horrors. Some were natural but so far outside the experience of the newcomers as to seem mysterious and sinister. Hurricanes leveled forests, pack ice crushed ships, earthquakes collapsed mountains, and floods raged down enormous rivers. Phenomena like these were not common in the familiar European world. Neither were grizzly bears, alligators, rattlesnakes, and herds of strangely humped buffalo so vast that they blocked trails for entire days. Many of the negative qualities of the American environment were, of course, the products of medieval minds still enmeshed in superstition. Satan, it was believed, dwelt in the "dark and howling"

As America's eyes turned westward, a new, indigenous literature appeared. Going Down the Rapids, *opposite, illustrates writings of James Fenimore Cooper. Above, prairie hunter, from William Cullen Bryant's poems.*

wilderness. Witches frequented the deep woods, and the heathen natives were aligned with the devil against the puny force of the Christian newcomers. Ignorance of the land continued to feed fear for centuries and, in the process, created powerful forces for bringing the American wilderness under the control of American civilization.

Space was one reason for both the wonder and the terror associated with the American land. New World geography was on a scale difficult to comprehend for natives of England, France, and Spain. In 1540, a detachment of Coronado's expedition pushing north from Mexico encountered the Grand Canyon of the Colorado. The Spaniards reported astonishment at finding the oppo-

site "bank" of the river 10 air miles distant. The river, a vertical mile below, at first appeared to them only six feet wide. Totally confused by the geographical scale of things, the leader of the detachment sent three men down the canyon walls to obtain water for the night's camp. They straggled back three days later, observing that "what appeared to be easy from above was not so, but instead very hard and difficult." It was through such trial and error that Europeans came to terms with American geography. "The land was ours," as Robert Frost put it, "before we were the land's."

Contrary to the teachings of historians, victory over the British at Yorktown in 1781 did not really establish American independence. The United States might be a nation on paper, but where was the cultural uniqueness that marked *bona fide* nationhood? The national ego desperately needed something both valuable and distinctive that could transform embarrassed provincials into proud, confident citizens. But the search for a culture ran immediately into difficulties. America's relatively short history, shallow traditions, and minor literary and artistic achievements seemed paltry in comparison to Europe's. "Who," scoffed the English critic Sidney Smith in 1820, "reads an American book?" He was right, of course. What literature existed in the colonies and new nation was highly imitative. But cultural nationalists gradually recognized that in one respect their country *was* different. Specifically, it was wilder. That immense, uninhabited space had no counterpart in the Old World.

But was not this emptiness precisely the problem? The denial came from deism and romanticism and climaxed in the 1830s and 1840s in the philosophy of transcendentalism. It rested on the idea that truth, beauty, and morality shone forth more brilliantly from unmodified, wild landscapes than from environments where centuries of human use had deposited a layer of civilized artificiality over the raw material of nature. America, in other words, was closer to the sources.

William Cullen Bryant wrote in 1811 about "the continuous woods where rolls the Oregon," but the first substantial American literary achievement based upon nature was that of James Fenimore Cooper. After a dismal attempt at copying the English style in fiction, Cooper turned in *The Pioneers* (1823) to a literary exploitation of the backwoods. His protagonist, Leatherstocking, launched a pattern in the American definition of the frontier hero that extended through Owen Wister's *The Virginian* (1902) to the film characterizations by Robert Redford and John Wayne. The "western" was a peculiarly American phenomenon,

demanding wide-open spaces and strong men singing "Don't fence me in."

"America," Ralph Waldo Emerson wrote in 1844, "is a poem in our eyes; its ample geography dazzles the imagination, and it will not wait long for metres." The next year a slight, stoop-shouldered New Englander left his home in Concord, Massachusetts, in order to experiment with his life beside a pond called Walden. Henry David Thoreau's conclusions brought together the main currents in America's effort to come to literary terms with its geography. As a transcendentalist Thoreau believed that nature, rightly seen, yielded truths more profound than those of libraries and laboratories. The poet could *transcend* exteriors and, using his intuition, probe inner meanings. But the process demanded proximity to wildness— "the raw-material of life." Fortunately, as Emerson and Thoreau saw it, America had wildness in abundance.

But while wildness might permit, in Emerson's words, "an original relation to the universe" or be, according to Thoreau, "the preservation of the World," neither man escaped the old association of terror and the unknown. On an 1846 trip to Maine's Mt. Katahdin, Thoreau confessed to being lonely and afraid in the presence of "vast, Titanic, inhuman Nature." The wilderness stripped him of his transcendental confidence in the innate divinity of both man and nature. The link between wildness and culture no longer seemed as simple as it had on the edge of Walden Pond in what was, essentially, suburban Boston. Civilization, he concluded, was not irrelevant to culture. Just as pure fertilizer was not good soil for plants, the intensity of the New World's wildness was too much. The ideal condition was one that blended wilderness and civilization or, as Emerson put it, society and solitude. Thoreau applied the metaphor to the problem of American nationalism. In terms of culture, the Old World was an exhausted field, the New a wild peat

bog. America needed "some of the sand of the Old World to be carted on to her rich but as yet unassimilated meadows." The ideal for men and for nations was to be "half-cultivated."

Another response to Emerson's call for a poet who could do justice to America's "ample geography" came striding forth from "Mannahatta" in the 1850s with a vision of continental proportions. No American writer approaches Walt Whitman in sheer, raw enthusiasm for the physical dimensions of his native land. His best poems are largely geographic; place names roll across his pages like the land itself. Near the end of "Song of Myself" (1855), Whitman transcends human temporal and spatial constraints and absorbs in an intuitive flash the totality of the physical nation: "Space and Time! now I see it is true, what I guess'd at, . . . My ties and ballasts leave me, . . . I skirt sierras, my palms cover continents, I am afoot with my vision." Thus "speeding through space" Whitman learns its meaning. Over time, to be sure, Whitman turned introspective and his early enthusiasm waned. The Civil War, particularly the assassination of Abraham Lincoln, discouraged him with regard to democracy. The materialism of the Gilded Age undermined his faith in ideals. But while increasingly critical of the American *people,* Whitman's confidence in the American *land* remained unshaken. If the American experiment failed, it was because the occupants of the New World had not proved worthy of their geography.

In March 1867 the usually sure hands of a young craftsman slipped and drove the point of a sharp file into his right eye. John Muir stood by a window as the fluid drained into his cupped hand. His left eye, too, went blind from sympathetic shock. Later, in a sick bed, Muir vowed that if his vision returned he would never waste another day working. Instead he would dedicate his life to a celebration of natural objects as "the terrestrial manifestations of God." This, of course, was warmed-over transcendentalism, but Muir, with eyesight restored, carried the philosophy to its practical extremes. His first venture following the file accident was a thousand-mile walk from Indiana to the Gulf of Mexico. March of 1868 found him in San Francisco asking directions to any place that was wild. From the hills behind San Francisco Bay Muir had his first breathtaking view of the Sierra, that "range of light" which was to be his mecca for the next half-century.

In the relationship between Muir and mountains the literary potential of wild America received its fullest expression to that date. Exulting in pine trees, peaks, and waterfalls as "sparks of the Divine Soul," Muir lived the life Emerson and Thoreau merely wrote about. Sensing this, Muir could not suppress a chuckle at writers like Thoreau who could "see forests in orchards and patches of huckleberry brush." Compared to the quality of wilderness he knew in California and later in Alaska, Walden Pond was a joke, a "mere saunter" from the city. By contrast Muir rambled, often alone and with astonishingly little gear, for weeks at a time. He made a first ascent almost every time he climbed a Sierra peak.

When Muir first came to the West most of the region was hardly known, much less coveted for economic development. But by the 1890s Muir saw the need to protect the yet undeveloped land with institutions like national parks and organizations like the Sierra Club. The last years of his life were consumed by a desperate battle to prevent a part of Yosemite National Park from being dammed and flooded. In 1913, however, Congress permitted San Francisco to use the Hetch Hetchy Valley for municipal water storage and hydroelectric power generation. Muir had been one of

the first white men to enter the valley.

Changes were occurring in American life and on the American land. The wildness of the New World was melting away. Consider that the nation's population jumped from 40 to 92 million between 1870 and 1910. Or that coal production climbed in the same period from 20 million to 257 million tons. Industrialization and urbanization were in their primes. In 1890 the United States Census assessed the collective significance of these changes and put a label on the process: the ending of the frontier. Historian Frederick Jackson Turner helped his countrymen understand the significance of this fact. With no more frontier, he explained in 1893, there could be no more frontiersmen. Pioneering, as a way of life, was impossible. The consequences for the national character concerned Turner and many of his contemporaries. What would happen to free people with the end of free land? Democracy, Turner believed, was the product of the frontier experience. He wondered in 1903 if democratic forms of government would persist "under conditions so radically unlike those in the days of their origin."

American writers generally reacted bitterly and pessimistically to the psychological shock of the end of the frontier. Frank Norris worried in 1902 that, in the absence of an untamed West to conquer, Americans would turn to conquering the world. The recent enthusiasm of the nation for an imperialist foreign policy seemed to prove him right. One of Ernest Hemingway's protagonists dreamed of returning from war to fish and camp along Michigan's Big Two-Hearted River only to find much of the country a burned-over wasteland. William Faulkner saw the end of an era in the rapacity of a civilization that in its quest for money and power spared so little of the wildness of the Deep South. The great bears, symbols of the wilderness, had been hounded out of the bottomlands to make

Termed a "bachelor of nature" by his friend Emerson, Thoreau learned by observation. "I am the wiser," he wrote, "in respect to all knowledges . . . for knowing that there is a minnow in the brook."

way for cotton fields. America, once so ripe with promise, ended as a "gilded pustule."

F. Scott Fitzgerald also sensed the contrast between the original wildness and the result of human transformation of the American land. At the end of *The Great Gatsby* (1925) the narrator, Nick, finds Gatsby shot and floating on an air mattress in the swimming pool of his seaside mansion. The novel's long trail of idealism turned to lust and greed had run to its grisly conclusion. Later, in the moonlight, Nick wandered to the edge of Long Island Sound. "And as the moon rose higher the inessential houses began to melt away until gradually I became aware of the old island here that flowered once for Dutch sailors' eyes—a fresh, green breast of the new world." Nick sensed the vanished magic of that virgin land that had given rise to "the last and greatest of all human dreams." It was a vision of perfection, of paradise regained. "For a transitory enchanted moment," Fitzgerald continued, "man must have held his breath in the presence of this continent, compelled into an aesthetic contemplation he neither understood nor desired, face to face for the last time in history with something commensurate to his capacity for wonder." Now Nick was left with only the cold wind blowing through dry lawns.

Some of the nostalgia for the vanishing frontier stemmed from the perception that nature was moral, inspirational, even divine. In the 20th century, however, the rise of the science of ecology created a new framework of understanding. For ecologists of the 1930s and 1940s, like Aldo Leopold, the natural world appeared as an astonishingly complex system of matter and energy upon which all life was totally dependent. Neither benevolent nor malevolent, nature seemed indifferent to man and his desires. Suddenly very small and very vulnerable, *Homo sapiens* found himself stripped of his pretensions to separate creation and lordship over nature. We were, in Leopold's words, "only fellow-voyageurs with other creatures in the odyssey of evolution." Humans might still love nature, and even guide their actions according to what Leopold called a "land ethic," but nature did not love back. Humility marked the maturation of ecological awareness.

When imaginative writers absorbed the significance of ecology, the transcendent confidence of an Emerson, the vaulting egotism of a Whitman, and the religiosity of a Muir quickly disappeared. Thomas Wolfe typified the new perception in 1935. The true history of America, he wrote, runs "back through poverty and hardship, through solitude and loneliness and death and unspeakable courage into the wilderness. For it is the wilderness that is the mother of that nation: it was in the wilderness that the strange and lonely people who have not yet spoken . . . first knew themselves . . . . The real history . . . is a history of solitude, of the wilderness, and of the eternal earth . . . the immense and terrible earth that makes no answer." Wolfe's huge, silent, "terrible earth" could have, as poet-dramatist Robinson Jeffers understood, "intense and terrible beauty," but only for those who abandoned the old illusions. The new approach emphasized frank confrontation with the impersonality of wild nature—a reality neither created

"Home-earth": Thomas Wolfe hymned Americans' roots in Look Homeward, Angel (*1929*).

by nor concerned with human beings.

From this perspective the desert, previously neglected in American nature writing, took on special appeal. Mary Austin, for example, found "room enough and time enough" in the vast arid land of the Southwest. Later Willa Cather and Joseph Wood Krutch joined her in celebrating the timelessness and emptiness of the desert. They understood how the silent, austere, and uncluttered landscape frees the mind. Wallace Stegner thought of the desert as a more "honest" environment than the gentle green hills and placid ponds of the East. "It is," he continued, "a lovely and terrible wilderness . . . harshly and beautifully colored, broken and worn until its bones are exposed, its great sky without a smudge or taint from Technocracy, and in hidden corners and pockets under its cliffs, the sudden poetry of springs."

The most recent literary interpreter of the American desert, Edward Abbey, is, arguably, the most extreme both in his sense of its harshness and in his love of this same quality. Perhaps the intensification of civilization, a process that has reduced the amount of wild land left in the lower 48 states to approximately the amount of paved land, explains Abbey's attitude. In *Desert Solitaire* he begins by "gaping at this monstrous and inhuman spectacle of rock and cloud and sky and space" that he encountered in the Utah canyonlands. His quest is to know this "hard and brutal" land as do the vultures, junipers, and rocks, to know it "devoid of all humanly ascribed qualities." The idea, and here Abbey is one with Thoreau, is "to confront, immediately and directly if it's possible, the bare bones of existence, the elemental and fundamental, the bedrock which sustains us." In time he learns that the rim of a wild canyon is the "brink of nothing and everything." When the spaciousness of the desert is threatened by an expanding civilization, Abbey turns radi-cal, loosing in the novel, *The Monkey Wrench Gang*, a band of environmental guerrillas against land exploiters. Preserving wilderness, it appears, is not merely a matter of saving trees and animals but of safeguarding the highest interests of man.

In Utah in July the temperature hits 110 degrees and Edward Abbey's mind wandered to Alaska. He may never get there, he mused, but he was glad for its wild presence. The *idea* of Alaska sustained him. Geographical refuge, so central to American history as a physical reality, was also important as a concept. Stegner had written of the "geography of hope." Abbey wrote that "we need the possibility of escape as surely as we need hope; with-out it the life of the cities would drive all men into crime or drugs or psychoanalysis."

This troubling idea is worth reflection. Psychologists are beginning to discern links between physical space and mental well-being. "I'm looking for space," sings John Denver, "to find out who I am." In its relation to individual autonomy and identity, solitude has become a precious commodity; meditation promises enlargement of one's "psychic space."

As frontiers on this planet shrink, the search for space turns both inward to the mind and outward to the stars. As a people who have known the exultation of far horizons, Americans understand the importance of these quests.

Inspired by Wolfe, Letterio Calapai created wood engravings, opposite and below.

The Coming of the People

By Vine Deloria, Jr.

There was a time, Black Elk told his biographer, John Neihardt, when the people were many but they were not a nation yet. "All were relatives, but sons did not know their fathers, nor fathers their sons, nor brothers their sisters." If there is a beginning, it is the memory of this primordial chaos when people had no relatives in the Indian way and they were not yet truly people. The Sioux were at that time, according to Black Elk, living on a great body of water, probably the Gulf of Mexico, and in the course of events the Holy Men had visions which led the Sioux through long journeys to the sacred island hill—the Black Hills of South Dakota—and they became a people.

Cultural traditions with a scientific bent view creation as an event distant in time in which the cosmic process began its steady and mechanical progression. The mystical traditions of the East speak of a cosmic dance in which manifestations of individuality, albeit ephemeral, produce the plentitude of life which we see around us. The individual then must achieve the realization that all is really one and return to the cosmic unity. Even the fundamentalist traditions which credit God with instantaneous creation and see in the operations of nature a divine intention to produce goodness are intertwined with the progression and inevitability of things. But it is not so with the American Indians.

These ideas are all too abstract and general. They tell us nothing about the world and less about ourselves. Speculations must not replace experiences. The Crow chief Arapooish, talking with Robert Campbell of the Rocky Mountain Fur Company at one of the last rendezvous, described his land:

"The Crow country is a good country. The Great Spirit put it exactly in the right place; while you are in it you fare well; whenever you are out of it, whichever way you travel, you fare worse . . ." And he went on to tell about its marvels: The Crow country is exactly in the right place. It has snowy mountains and sunny plains, all kinds of climate and good things for every season. When the summer heats scorch the prairies, you can draw up under the mountains, where the air is sweet and cool, the grasses fresh, and the bright streams come tumbling out of the snowbanks. There you can hunt the elk, the deer, and the antelope, when their skins are fit for dressing; there you will find plenty of white bear and mountain sheep.

In the autumn, when your horses are fat and strong from the mountain pastures, you can go into the plains and hunt the buffalo, or trap beaver on the streams. And when winter comes on, you can take shelter in the woody bottoms along the rivers; there you will find buffalo meat for yourselves, and cottonwood bark for your horses; or you may winter in Wind River Valley where there is salt weed in abundance.

Yes, Arapooish concluded, the Crow country is exactly in the right place, and a flood of pleasant memories filled him to confirm his belief.

Our species, for ever so long, has believed that we are strangers in the world and many people have looked to the heavens for a sign that some time, in some place, they would no longer be strangers in the land. And so long as people felt incomplete and sought to find a home they were not really created. The Indians also had this feeling but they had one great virtue which many of the other peoples lacked—they were able to listen to the Earth. And so when they came here they waited for instructions, believing that they would be guided to the right place.

The oldest of the people, the Hopi, came in several migrations and brought with them the knowledge of former worlds, times, and places. Survivors of primordial catastrophes, they had endured the cold of outer space when the Earth's axis refused to turn. Tested in the trauma of a world gone mad with power, they returned to the simple task of finding relatives in order that they might live in harmony with the rhythms of the land. Four migrations around the continent they made, each time seeking to establish their roots and center their universe. The most ancient monuments of the land testify to their travels and, blocked by the massive walls of ice in the north, they finally came to the high mesa of the Southwest where the giant canyon of light informed them of its antiquity. Not far from the center of the Earth, an area

that has existed in geological stability for millions of years, they planted their villages.

Other peoples, then spiritual adolescents in comparison with the Hopi clans, arrived later, also seeking to find the right place and also listening for instructions. The Iroquois and Sioux say they arrived from the direction where the sun rises; the Three Fires, the Chippewa, Ottawa, and Potawatomi, traveled from the mouth of the St. Lawrence to the Great Lakes. The Okanagon moved eastward on a chain of islands and, looking back at the submerging lands they were leaving, steadfast in their determination to find the right place, arrived at the mouth of the Columbia River and moved up its hospitable waters to the mountains where many rivulets had agreed to come together to form the mighty river.

Were some peoples already here? The Klamath, living in comfort in the Cascades, watched the Okanagon arrive, burned red from the ordeal at sea, and were bemused at the

Sioux Holy Man Black Elk, opposite, reflects the agelessness of the land on which he was born some 80 years before. Above, beehive ovens at Taos, New Mexico, display forms as distinctive as the hills beyond.

newcomers living in tents while they busied themselves in their stone houses. Other peoples, coming into their own lands, found ruins and wondered where the former inhabitants had gone, why they had not found peace in their place, and whether this place was indeed special. The Yakimas, discovering relics of a former people, preferred to continue a nomadic life, uncertain at the fate of any group that would dare to effect a permanent settlement. They always hurried through these remnant dwellings on the Columbia for fear that the fate of the ancient ones might become their own.

So over the centuries the people found their places and, like the Crow, they all knew their country was in exactly the right place. No land seemed formidable when it was designed for a particular people. The Hopi, living on the high desert mesa, received special ceremonies to enable them to plant and harvest. The Iroquois, in the eastern forests, learned quickly that they were related to all beings in their country. The Three Sisters, corn, beans, and squash, showed them how to live, and the mutual spirituality of the Sisters kept their lands fertile and hospitable. The peoples of the plains learned from the cottonwood how to make tipis, and the tree became their sacred relative participating in the annual sun dance. It was not simply a task of living in their country as human beings. It was necessary to live as relatives.

How does one find relatives among the peoples of creation? The human being, the old ones relate, is a strange creature. The eagle's eye is stronger. The bear's arm is stronger. The swallow is able to fly. The fish is a better swimmer. The deer is much quicker. The panther can leap farther. The wasp has greater poison. The hawk is a better hunter. The snake is more in tune with the Earth. The dog is friendlier. So the human being must learn from these other peoples. Watch, listen, and learn.

The peoples seem to be the same—but they are not. The Great Spirit teaches the birds to make nests—yet each bird makes a different kind of nest. The Great Spirit teaches animals to hunt—yet each hunts in a different way. The Great Spirit teaches each people to care for its young—yet each people has a different manner of instruction. The Great Spirit provides the outline of how to live; each people contributes the content of life by becoming themselves.

Simple observation was often not sufficient to teach the lessons of life. The peoples were all related and, like relatives, they had to give and share. The humans could contribute very little, but a way was found for them to do so. One day, a long time ago, a great race was held. The race course extended from the Black Hills clear across Wyoming to the Big Horns, far south, and then farther north. It was a serious race, for the two-leggeds—human beings and birds—were racing the four-leggeds to determine which should feed the others. It was the most serious covenant ever established. The winners would feed upon the losers from that day forth. Only when the winners returned to the earth and their bones became the soil and they brought forth food would the losers feed upon them.

The two-leggeds were no match for the four-leggeds. All of the peoples joined in. Sometimes the winds aided the four-leggeds and prevented the wings from flying. Other times the day would be very hot and the four-leggeds would slow down while the two-leggeds caught up. The race was even and it lasted many, many days. But as the days passed and each member of the two groups took their turns running, the magpie devised a scheme: Instead of flying, she sat on the buffalo's horn, catching a ride and preserving her strength. The racers neared the finish line and the four-leggeds, seeing the buffalo chief in the lead and no two-leggeds in sight, began to cheer and shout, shaking the Earth with their noise. As they neared the finish line the magpie flew from the buffalo's horn and crossed the finish line ahead of him, saving the day for the two-leggeds and demonstrating that while physical strength is important, it must be used intelligently.

The cycle of life was established. While the two-leggeds were to feed on the four-leggeds, they were not to fear death for it provided the means of completing the bargain. The bodies of the two-leggeds, after their spirits had departed, provided the soil in which the plants grew to feed the four-leggeds. Neither group ever feared the other for they were relatives and knew that while they might receive, they were also expected to give.

There were, of course, people who could not listen to the instructions of the land. And there were people who forgot the teachings that they had been given. There are many ways that people can be taught. In the Cascades the people began fighting with each other and there was no harmony. The trouble became so bad that the greatest chief of all, known by the whites as ancient Mount Multnomah, exploded, killing the disobedient people and destroying the country which had been so fruitful. When the smoke cleared and the survivors gathered around, all that was left of the great chief was a much smaller mountain and the three wives who sat in mourning over the lost innocence of former days. The white men now call this ruin the Three Sisters and tell us that it is the remnant of a mighty volcano which exploded in a very remote geological era. But the Indians know better. Moun-

The land—mountains, rivers, lakes, and valleys—was sacred to generations before him. True to his heritage, Ernest Tootoosis, a Cree, is a dynamic religious leader and force in the American Indian ecumenical movement.

tains are people too, and when our species brings turmoil and disharmony to the creation, eventually all the other peoples are injured also.

In various parts of Turtle Island this bitter lesson had to be learned. On the Great Plains the people began quarreling. Some said that greed began to dominate human relationships and people no longer cared for their relatives. Others said that selfishness and the determination to exclude other peoples from the bounty that was the High Plains caused the trouble. Either of these faults would have violated the personality of the plains and angered its spirit. On the plains one must be wild and free with no artificial boundaries and no gathering of things to oneself. When the lands became soaked with blood from the quarreling of the humans, the Spirit of the Plains decided to punish the people.

Calling upon his relatives, the Sky and Winds, the Spirit of the Plains let forth a loud bellowing noise, and dark clouds gathered. The land shook, darkness filled the skies, and fires burst forth from the bowels of the Earth. Violent thunderstorms swept the plains clean of people, and heavy smoke and dust filled the air, making it impossible to see. For a long time it was as if Sky and Earth had merged together to prevent people from living on the plains. When the air finally cleared and it was possible to see once again, in the midst of the fertile grasslands were places barren of vegetation, eternally scarred and discolored, and devoid of any ability to produce life. Only small patches of the massive plains were in this desolated condition, and life returned to most of the area very shortly. But generations of people passing near these lands—which came to be called "badlands"—saw and remembered what had happened here.

Southern California is among the most ancient parts of Turtle Island and certainly one of the most fruitful. But inland a short distance lies Death Valley, a tremendous sink much below sea level, and inhospitable to nearly every form of life. It was not always a cursed land. Not so many years ago, at least within the memory of some of the tribes, it was a happy, fruitful land. So fruitful in fact that its riches stirred feelings of greed among the people who lived there, and each wanted the valley exclusively for themselves. The medicine men warned the people to stop fighting with each other but to no avail. The buzzard came as a special messenger of the spirits and warned that the land could not stand senseless killing and might punish the people. No one listened.

Finally, the mountain sheep who used the valley in the summers made a special visit to the warring tribes and demanded they make peace before the land and spirits rebelled.

In the dust where we have buried the silent races and their abominations we have buried so much of the delicate magic of life.

–D.H. Lawrence

Still the people refused to listen. Their pride injured by the intrusion of their relatives into their raiding activities, they defied both spirits and relatives and rejected the overtures of the mountain sheep. So the spirits of the place became very angry. They blew the tops off the mountains and poured hot lava on the warriors who refused to live peaceably. The earth became spongy like jelly and shook continually, causing the warring people to flee hither and yon. Still their pride caused them to refuse to make peace.

Great cracks in the earth appeared, and finally the spirits split open a mountain range and poured ocean water into the valley, creating a vast inland sea. The people scrambled to the heights of the mountains along the lakeshore but the angry spirits pursued them there. The great inland sea dried up, leaving salt flats in its place. As the people sought refuge in the mountains each range was twisted and split into many fragments; with the demise of each range of mountains the valley sank lower and lower. Finally, satisfied that they had punished the people for their transgressions, the spirits caused torrential rains to pour down upon the valley and remove many traces of human habitation which had survived the catastrophe. Only the debris of nature was left to testify to the awful punishments that had been inflicted.

All over the continent, whenever the people lost their humility and began to mistreat their relatives, the land rebelled and rebuked them. The unusual features of the land testify to the events in the experiences of many peoples. So creation, if we insist that it must include the configuration of landscapes, is also history. The water marks on Steptoe Butte in eastern Washington remind us of the great flood that destroyed the transgressors of the natural laws. Grand Coulee, farther up the valley of the Columbia, once poured forth a tidal wave of water that flooded the central plain and created immense sandbars which now appear as small hillocks in the plains of eastern Washington. The lava flows of western New Mexico tell us of the rebellion of the land there also. And the yawning mouth of Crater Lake in southern Oregon is an eloquent voice reminding us to have respect for all creatures.

It is exceedingly strange that we do not today understand that creation is really history—the story of how peoples found their relatives and came to know their sacred places. When we get older we begin to see that creation is history because it is the continual search for cosmic rhythms which remind us of our true selves. Black Elk reflected that "everything the Power of the World does is done in a circle." And he illustrated his insight with the vivid examples that could only come from a person who was in harmony with all of creation

and knew their ways: "The Sky is round and I have heard that the Earth is round like a ball and so are all the stars. The Wind, in its greatest power, whirls. Birds make their nests in circles, for theirs is the same religion as ours. The sun comes forth and goes down again in a circle. The moon does the same, and both are round. Even the seasons form a great circle in their changing, and always come back again to where they were. The life of a man is a circle from childhood to childhood and so it is with everything where power moves."

In the unique and cosmic rhythms, special events stand out and are recognized as those special occasions when Earth, peoples, and the Power of the World shared a unique and sometimes chastising experience.

When a people have finally reached their sacred place and come to understand its ways, they begin to take on its characteristics. "We are a part of the nature around us, and the older we get the more we come to look like it," the Sioux medicine man Lame Deer once remarked. "In the end we become part of the landscape with a face like the Badlands." In the same way, one can move around the continent and discover in the faces of the people almost a mirror of the lands on which they live. Photographers, perhaps unaware of the nature of Indian life and thinking that creation is a distant event, still continue to take pictures of older Indians without realizing that their photographs are capturing the essence of creation itself.

There are, of course, many other stories about the continent, and each tribe preserves its special knowledge and memories about the sacred mountains, rivers, lakes, and valleys. Almost every tribe can point out those features of the landscape which mark the boundaries of their lands and tell how the people first knew that this was their country and that it was in exactly the right place. The more knowledge one has, the more significant do the various traditions seem, for the conglomerate taken together testifies to the uniqueness of the continent.

The white man, when viewed in this context, appears as a perennial adolescent. He is continually moving about, and his restless nature cannot seem to find peace. Yet he does not listen to the land and so cannot find a place for himself. He has few relatives and seems to believe that the domestic animals that have always relied upon him constitute his only link with the other peoples of the universe. Yet he does not treat these animals as friends but only as objects to be exploited. While he has destroyed many holy places of the Indians, he does not seem to be able to content himself with his own holy places . . . for his most holy places are cemeteries where his forefathers lie under granite slabs, row upon row upon row, strangers lying with strangers.

Insightful whites have intuited aspects of creation. Carl Jung remarked that the dreams of American patients generally held a special messianic figure cast in the form of an Indian. Franz Boas demonstrated that by the third generation of immigrants, the people had changed facially and were beginning to look like the Indians who preceded them. D.H. Lawrence noted that while the Indian would never again possess the continent, he would always haunt it and it would always find affirmation in his spirit. John Collier saw in the Indian folkways the solution to many of the pressing problems of modern industrialization. And song writers have long noted that natural features have a personality of their own. It is not for naught that we romanticize "Ol' Man River." The process of creation continues and will do so until everyone has a special place to live and relatives to enjoy.

It has always been this way. John Neihardt spent a great deal of time discussing the Indian tradition with Black Elk, the Sioux Holy Man. One day, after Black Elk told Neihardt about how the Sioux had received the sacred pipe which is present at almost all the tribe's ceremonial occasions, Black Elk remained silent for several minutes. Finally he turned to Neihardt and said: "This they tell, and whether it happened so or not I do not know; *but if you think about it, you can see that it is true!*" And so it is with the Indian understanding of the land and the coming of the people.

Her weathered face a reflection of the seared land she tills, a Navajo matriarch gazes beyond the far Arizona horizon. ". . . in the end we become part of the landscape," taking on the characteristics of a sacred place.

Origins

As the spectacular space voyages of the last decade have revealed the faces of our fellow travelers in the solar system, so we have come to appreciate the uniqueness of our own planet Earth. We are, we find, fortunate beyond any reasonable expectation. We are also reminded that the origins of this land—its composition and processes—are to be sought not only here on Earth, but also in the cosmic events of the remote past.

Just about all of the activity on the Earth, whether biological or volcanic and tectonic, is powered by two great sources of energy. The decay of radioactive elements locked within the Earth provides heat to drive the restless wanderings of the continents and earthquakes and volcanoes. From the sun comes the energy that powers weather, which through rain, ice, wind, and surf continually sculpts, erodes, and redistributes the surface of the land. These forces have shaped our continent into its myriad forms, including Utah's Delicate Arch, left.

Of the myriad forms of life that have evolved on Earth during the last three billion-odd years, we humans seem to be alone in wondering from whence it all came, what makes it work, and where it is going. A series of stunning scientific discoveries during the past 25 years has tentatively answered some of these questions, while posing many more. In the following chapters, certain aspects of the Earth's origin, driving forces, and future are portrayed.

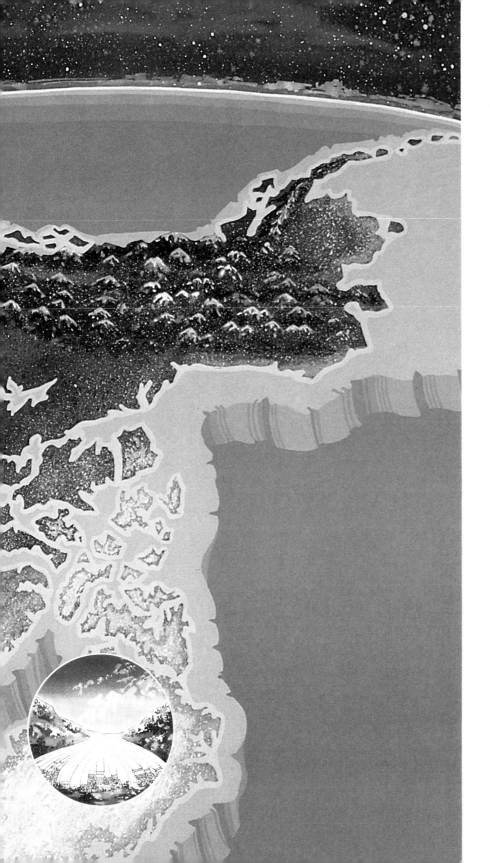

Small clues often speak to scientists of great events in the past. Smithsonian geologist William G. Melson takes us on a tour of Virginia's Shendandoah National Park to discover in the rocks evidence of a number of mighty transformations of our continent.

Shifting to a wider view, artist Pierre Mion illustrates the history of the Earth and our continent since the formation of the sun—concluding with the probable end of our planet billions of years in the future.

In "The Ephemeral Cape," transplanted New Englander Russell Bourne examines the shifting sands of Cape Cod and ponders the indifferent ease with which the forces of nature sometimes erase man's works.

Proving that paleontology is still a lively science (North America's first dinosaur eggs were discovered just this summer), the Smithsonian's Nicholas Hotton III takes us on an imaginary time trip to see what momentous changes have taken place during the last quarter-billion years of North American history.

Finally, botanist Sherwin Carlquist explores the volcanic origin of the Hawaiian Islands and its implication for the subsequent arrival and evolution of the islands' unique—and threatened—fauna and flora.

Face of North America: Central drainage system sandwiched between two ranges—the western one vigorously growing; in the East, a worn and gentle upland. Glaciers scoop out Hudson Bay and sculpt the Great Lakes. Erosion roughs out Grand Canyon. Inset circles, from lower right-hand corner: continental glaciation; oceanic erosion; aging Appalachians; sinkhole formation in limestone; delta formation; Hawaiian volcanism; seismic displacement; uplift of peaks at the Pacific strand.

59

Shenandoah Roots

By William G. Melson

During my childhood in the Washington, D.C. area, it was my good fortune to go on family drives to Shenandoah National Park for the day. It became a tradition to go up there each year to view the spectacular fall colors displayed against the beauty of the Blue Ridge Mountains and Shenandoah Valley. In me then was a growing and intense interest in nature and, in particular, in rocks, so abundantly and colorfully arrayed in the park.

What was at first a childhood fascination became a discipline that I now pursue as a geologist at the Smithsonian's National Museum of Natural History. Often over the years I have returned, as if still on that family pilgrimage, to the grandeur of Shenandoah National Park. Yet now my trips there are mainly with small groups of students from the Smithsonian Resident Associates. My objective: to share with them my fascination with the area's geology.

Shenandoah National Park encompasses about 193,537

Led by geologist William Melson, students hike a misty trail, having passed the gentle farms that lie east of the Shenandoah. One of the first phenomena they confront is a stream flowing through basaltic rock.

acres of Virginia's Blue Ridge Mountains, which in this locale mark the eastern edge of the great Appalachian chain. Between the Blue Ridge and the Appalachians proper lies the Shenandoah Valley, one of the loveliest parts of the country.

The Blue Ridge and the Appalachians are old mountains, once lofty, now worn by time and rain into gentle folds and fertile valleys. My students and I go to the Shenandoah not only to pursue geology in a setting of quiet beauty but, perhaps more importantly, to learn about the relentless forces that have shaped our land. Won't you settle down in your armchair and join us on one of our tours?

As we start toward the park, we travel north along the west lip of the Potomac River Gorge, a gorge which is like a deep incision into the Piedmont, the "foot of the mountains." The gorge exposes many secrets which are elsewhere buried beneath a thick mantle of soil.

The dramatic story revealed is one of 800 million-year-old seas and ranges, and the processes that created and destroyed them. Imagine, for a moment, the ancient setting revealed by the rocks of the gorge. Rivers and streams have been rapidly eroding a barren mountain range—land plants have not yet evolved—and carrying their burden of sediments out onto a nearby sea floor basin. As more and more sediment pours into the basin, the region we now see exposed at the surface becomes deeply buried, perhaps as much as several miles down. With burial, temperatures increase and heat and pressure gradually convert the sediments into rock. Then the layers of sedimentary rock are folded by mighty movements of the Earth's crust, and molten rock from the interior of the Earth invades, drastically changing the mineralogy of the rocks and obscuring their sedimentary origins.

As the layers of rock are folded and thrust up, they form a new mountain range, and the sea is pushed away to the west as the mountains rise. But they too are eroded and weathered

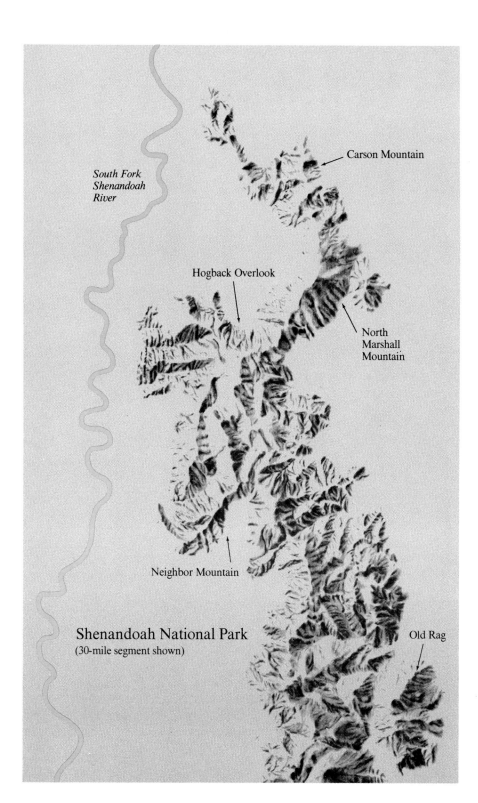

South Fork
Shenandoah
River

Carson Mountain

Hogback Overlook

North
Marshall
Mountain

Neighbor Mountain

Shenandoah National Park
(30-mile segment shown)

Old Rag

Virginia's Blue Ridge Parkway, south of Shenandoah National Park, offers vistas of Appalachians' weathered folds. Though much eroded, 225 million-year-old mountains are still rising, may reach new heights.

away even as they rise, their sediments settling to the bottom of the westward-retreating sea.

In the gorge of today, we find the eroded roots of that long-gone mountain range, now being eroded again, but by the Potomac. This time its sediments are carried *eastward* to the Atlantic Ocean.

In this series of episodes, we see the essence of the "rock cycle": Sediments are transformed into rock as they become deeply buried, only to be eventually uplifted, subjected to weathering and erosion, transported elsewhere by streams and rivers to become sediment again, recompressed into rock, weathered and eroded again, and so on.

As we leave the Potomac River Gorge and approach the misty ridge of Bull Run Mountain, we begin to see evidence of some of the most dramatic events in the history of the Earth. The soil color along the road suddenly changes from the buffs, yellows, and oranges of the Piedmont to reddish or maroon. These reddish soils and outcrops are mute testimony to the ponderous dance of the continents termed continental drift. This now-accepted theory holds that ancient continents came together to form one great continent, called Pangaea, which subsequently broke into today's familiar continental shapes. At the time of the breakup, about 200 million years

At the summit of Old Rag Mountain, 1.2 billion-year-old granite rocks are exposed. Below right, author Melson explains the granitic outcrops at Hogback Overlook, teaching geology the best way: on the hoof.

summit we perceive dark outcrops, appearing as high, vertical monoliths extending above the trees. The monoliths appear on both sides of the trail and continue on down each side of the mountain, as if defining a line. They are prism-shaped basalt columns which were originally long, vertical fissures up through the granite mountains, probably feeding molten material from the Earth's interior to overlying volcanoes. Such fissures filled by igneous rock—rocks once molten—are termed dikes and are common in the granitic rocks throughout the park. Here, on Carson's summit, these dikes are more resistant to weathering than their enclosing granite and thus have been etched out during the erosion of the modern Blue Ridge.

Leaving Carson Mountain, we continue south on the drive, stopping soon at Hogback Overlook, not only to view the Shenandoah Valley vista below us, but also to examine a spectacular road cut that gives us a look at fresh, unweathered, Pedlar formation rocks. The rock here is again granitic, and in this case is also termed an "augen gneiss." At one time, these rocks were under such intense pressure that their mineral grains were smeared out in the direction of movement, leaving a definite grain, or oriented fabric characteristic of the rock called gneiss. The original large crystals of feldspar

ago, our area was close to the Equator, and the maroon soils are typical of wet tropical climates in Equatorial regions.

Passing Bull Run Mountain, we enter Shenandoah National Park about two hours after leaving Washington. Ascending to the crest of the Blue Ridge, we proceed along Skyline Drive, the winding road that extends the length of the park. Our first goal is the summit of Carson Mountain, for here we find the oldest geological formation in the park.

As we ascend, natural outcrops of a light-colored granular rock, a variety of granite, appear, partly covered by lichens. Here and there rays of sunlight sparkle on rock surfaces, revealing crystals of feldspar. This formation was originated about 1.2 billion years ago when molten granite invaded the region. After that time the formation, termed the Pedlar, was involved in an epoch of uplifting and mountain building. Eventually, about 800 million years ago, its overlying layers of rock stripped away by erosion, the Pedlar formation was exposed in a mountain range with elevations similar to that of the present mountains. The character of the former roof rocks and where they were deposited remains a mystery.

As we continue up Carson Mountain, we see impressive evidence of what happened after those granite mountains of perhaps 800 million years ago had been eroded. Nearing the

are now eye-shaped (hence the term *augen*, German for eyes), stretched out during the deformation or shearing. This deformation can be found at every outcrop in the park and, in fact, at nearly every rock involved in the uplift and north-westward transport of the rocks accompanying the final and most intense folding of the Appalachian basin.

Herein lies the remarkable story of the collision of what may be termed proto-Africa and proto-North America during the formation of Pangaea about 250–225 million years ago. That convergence of continental plates had in fact begun much earlier, perhaps as early as 650 million years ago, and continued episodically, terminating here in the final folding of the Appalachian basin. Seemingly, the belts of deformation caused by the collision moved progressively westward behind the retreating Appalachian sea.

The effects on the life of this time were immense. Many seas disappeared as the continents came together, and their eventual drying up may have played a key role in the adaptations of what were then marine animals to survival on land. Indeed, the bloom in reptiles is traced to this time. And the destruction of so many shallow marine habitats may have led to many extinctions, for example, to the end of the trilobites. This master continent was to be short-lived because in Triassic time Pangaea was rifted, and the gradual opening of the Atlantic began. We find, then, a time span of perhaps 50 million years for the existence of the master continent here. During this time land plants and animals migrated over Pangaea, spreading similar species over much of the area.

In Triassic time, this area and Africa split apart, and the Atlantic Ocean basin began to form. Eventually the Atlantic and other newly opening ocean basins created barriers to migrations of land flora and fauna, leading eventually to the distinctly different life forms we find on each isolated land mass. It looks as if we can divide much of Appalachian geologic history into two vast phases: the time of the gradual closing of the Appalachian sea between Pre-Cambrian or Cambrian time and Permian time as Pangaea formed, and the breakup of Pangaea and the opening of the Atlantic. During the ongoing drift, North America carried our region from the Equator to its present latitude at about 38° N. But while this area was close to the Equator, the tropical climate supported the luxurious forests from which the great coal beds of Appalachia were formed.

So, in the single outcrop of augen gneiss at Hogback Overlook, we find arrows which point to startling changes in this region over the past 1.2 billion years. Yet, the Blue Ridge geology story is not complete. We must continue on our tour

*Remnants of ancient volcanism, basaltic
columns reach up among hemlocks, opposite.
Above, crystals of plagioclase in fine-grained
basalt. Birches reached this far south
at time of glaciers. These stayed.*

of Shenandoah to learn more about ancient volcanism.

We proceed still farther south along Skyline Drive, stopping at the Appalachian Trail where it ascends North Marshall Mountain reaching an elevation of 3,368 feet. Our vertical ascent is a short one—300 feet—yet some of the principal features of the ancient volcanism are revealed. Walking north we find ledges and then cliffs rimming the northern face of the mountain, cliffs of grayish-green, very fine-grained rock. At the summit overlook this rock contains roundish spots, sometimes filled with white quartz, in other places filled by the bright green epidote, in places by both minerals. These were once gas cavities or bubbles formed by gases escaping from lava flows. As such they reveal the volcanic nature of the formation, called the Catoctin formation. These gas cavities were later filled by new minerals during the deep burial of the lava flows under perhaps as much as 30,000 feet of sedimentary rocks. At such depths, temperature rises and

Old sledge and cabin, below, suggest that other things besides rocks change slowly in the Shenandoah, where there is often a peaceful coexistence between the works of man and mighty geological forces.

reactions occur between percolating water and the original black basalt, creating new minerals. All the lavas and dikes of the Catoctin formation have been through this "pressure cooker," more or less changing their original mineralogy and, to a lesser extent, their structures.

The chemical composition of the Catoctin lavas is like those that erupt over modern "hot spots," the lavas that form the Hawaiian Islands and the Snake River Plains-Yellowstone area, zones of large-scale partial melting of the upper mantle. The mantle is the concentric shell between the Earth's crust and its core from which lavas periodically rise and in which the convective motions occur that "drive" continental drift and sea-floor spreading. Here, in the Catoctin formation, we have the vast volcanic deposits left by a long dead hot spot, a hot spot which may have played a key role in the opening of the proto-Atlantic.

At the last stop on our tour, near the summit of Neighbor Mountain, we scan the forest and find a stand of white birch, conspicuous amidst the darker bark of the enclosing hardwoods. These birches do not exist today at lower elevations south of southern New York state. They were abundant, though, here in the Blue Ridge at all elevations during the Pleistocene, the ice age period of the last five million years. Their descendants can now survive only in the cooler climates that exist in the high parts of the park.

We look down on the Shenandoah River, and wonder what changes are still occurring in the park. Clearly, if we examine the Shenandoah River at flood stages, we see that our mountains and valleys are being carried away. At the present rate of erosion, we can calculate that the entire drainage basin of the Potomac River, of which the Shenandoah is the major tributary, joining it at Harpers Ferry, would be eroded to near sea level in about five to 10 million years, which, as we realize, is a geological instant. Yet, we have discovered too that the Blue Ridge province and its extension into the Great Smoky Mountains is continuing to rise at a rate more than adequate to maintain its current height and, in fact, outpacing erosion to create yet higher peaks.

As we leave the park, we may wonder that a single small mountain range can represent so much of our continent's history. The Shenandoah National Park is a detective story—the geologist the private eye. His clues are the structures and formations of the rocks. They reveal to his trained eye ancient origins, mighty transformations. It is a long tale that the rocks tell, and one that is never quite finished, for the same forces are still at work, here in the Shenandoah and everywhere else, building up and tearing down our land.

Evolution of a Continent

Illustrations by Pierre Mion

It seems that the universe began some 15 billion years ago with an inconceivably great explosion, the "Big Bang," which released all matter and energy from what cosmologists call the primeval atom. The matter quickly coalesced into swirling gas clouds, then into galaxies of stars.

Much later, perhaps five billion years ago, our own sun and its planets condensed from gassy dust clouds probably left over from the death of one of those early stars, as depicted in the series at left. As the gas clouds flattened into a spinning disc, the sun contracted into a sphere. In the tremendous heat and pressure of the sun's interior, hydrogen atoms began to fuse to form helium, releasing vast quantities of energy, and the sun became luminous. At a distance from the newborn sun a clump of matter orbited, condensing and agglutinating into what we call the Earth.

As the Earth consolidated, it swept remaining debris from its orbit and the resultant bombardment of meteoroids gave the solid sphere a pitted, moonlike surface. A period of extensive volcanic activity followed. Gasses vented from the Earth's hot interior to combine with those left over from formation to create a primordial atmosphere. This early mixture, consisting mainly of hydrogen, methane, ammonia, carbon dioxide, and water vapor, would be poisonous to most present-day organisms. But it seems to have been just right for the fostering of the first living things, which probably

Opposite, from debris of earlier star, solar system forms, sun becomes luminous. Top, primitive Earth is blasted by meteoroids, while, above, volcanoes release gasses. Below, continents join, then split.

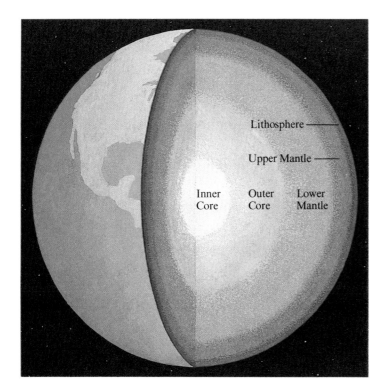

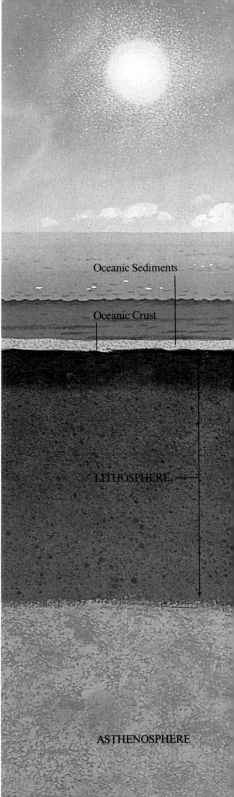

appeared in the shallow seas produced by condensation of water vapor released by volcanoes. As the primitive organisms achieved the ability to photosynthesize, they began to release oxygen, and the atmosphere gradually changed into its present composition, chiefly oxygen, carbon dioxide, nitrogen, and water vapor.

We have now skimmed over an immense amount of time and have reached about 600 million years ago, when a tremendous efflorescence of complex life forms took place, made possible, perhaps, by the maturation of the oxygen-rich atmosphere. While a parade of biological forms filled niches all over the Earth—with varying degrees of success— another great change in the face of the planet took place. About 650 million years ago, the ancient continents began to converge until about 250 million years ago when, in collision, they combined as a single master continent, today called Pangaea. Relatively short-lived, Pangaea broke up about 200 million years ago, and the continents, more or less in today's shapes, drifted to their present positions.

The theory of continental drift, first advanced by German meteorologist Alfred Wegner in 1912, was scorned for many years. But in the last decade, nearly incontrovertible evidence gleaned by oceanographers, geologists, and geophysicists has

Above, current model of Earth's interior. Below, in slice through northern U.S., North American plate carries continent west, colliding with Farallon plate and causing volcanic activity in Pacific Northwest. Opposite, California's coastal ranges are created as North American plate overrides Pacific plate (about 100 million years ago).

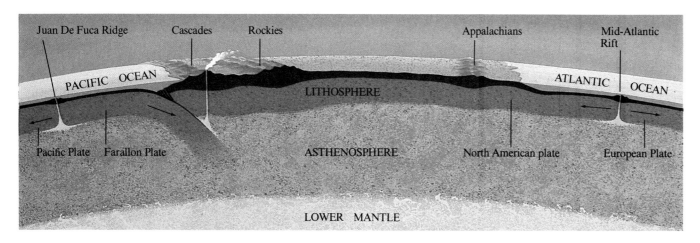

Below, Hawaiian Islands chain was probably formed when a "hot spot" underlying moving crustal plate punched through it to build up a volcanic island. As plate drifted farther northwestward, other islands were created in same way. But rain, waves rapidly reduced older islands, eroding them first into jagged spines, then into coral reefs.

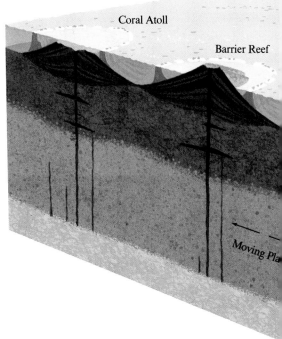

Coral Atoll

Barrier Reef

Moving Pla

Awesome power of water erosion is revealed by Grand Canyon, above. As Colorado Plateau was uplifted about 10 million years ago, Colorado River, carrier in modern times of 400,000 tons of sand, mud, and rock per day, began to cut canyon. River's jeweler's saw-like action—together with side streams, erosion, and weathering—produced canyon up to one mile deep, 15 miles wide. To geologists, canyon exposes slice of Earth's history going back two billion years.

Above, glaciers—frozen water—plane and gouge the land. California's Yosemite Valley was carved into distinctive U-shape by three successive waves of glaciation during Pleistocene Epoch, lasting from about 5,000,000 years ago to 10 to 15 thousand years ago. Ice age glaciers ground down mountains, cobbled New England, filled Great Lakes, left moraines of sand and stone: Cape Cod is one. Top right, composite map of maximum extent of glaciations in mid-North America.

given the theory widespread acceptance.

Often called "plate tectonics," the theory maintains that the Earth's outer layer, or lithosphere, is split by cracks or rifts into a number of plates. Molten rock wells up through these rifts from the asthenosphere, the next layer down, then spreads and hardens to form new sea floor. Continents, thicker but less dense than the sea floors, are embedded in them and are carried with them as they spread. If part of a continent lies across a rift, the continent may split apart, and a new ocean basin will be created as the formerly joined pieces separate.

Associated with tectonic activity are earthquakes such as those that bedevil California's San Andreas Fault area, which lies along a rift zone. Volcanoes are also concentrated along plate boundaries and rifts.

Though the mechanisms by which these complex movements take place are as yet poorly understood, the energy to power them comes from heat produced by the

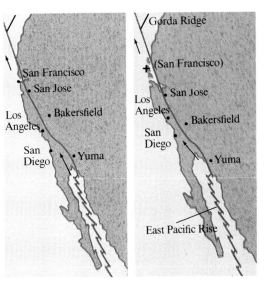

Above left, San Andreas Fault is boundary between two moving plates. Above right: In 5,000,000 years, western plate will carry Los Angeles 175 miles north, thrust San Francisco into Pacific Ocean.

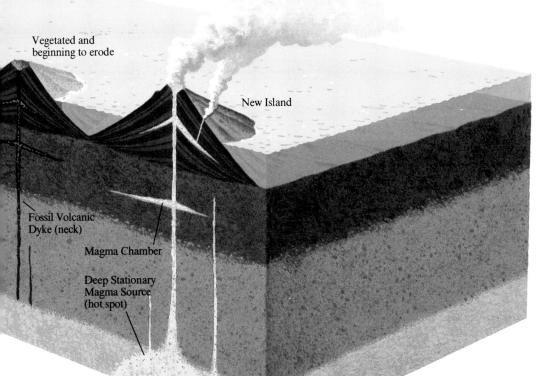

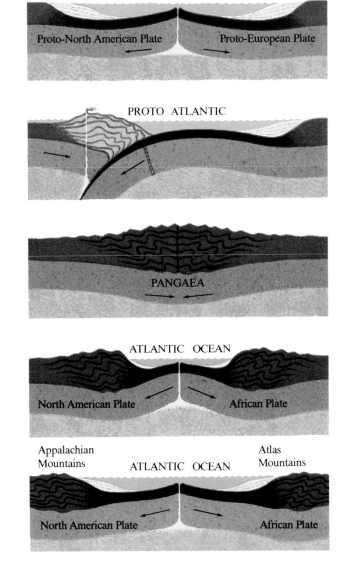

In Cambrian Period, 600 million years ago, North America, Europe, Africa are separated by sea. Continents converge causing volcanic activity during Ordovician, 425 million years ago. In Permian, about 250 million years ago, continents collide, creating master continent, Pangaea, and upfolding Appalachian, Atlas Mountains. Pangaea soon splits; about 165 million years ago Atlantic Ocean begins to form as sea floor spreads. Ocean still widens in modern time.

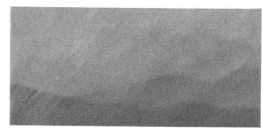

Berkeley hills, top, may be islets in 5,000,000 years as Baja California-Southern California coast slips north. In very distant future, above, Earth's atmosphere becomes more Venus-like, hot and dense.

decay of such radioactive elements as uranium and thorium, locked within the planet during its formation. This "endogenic" energy (so called because it comes from within the Earth) is one of the two great sources that power all activity on the Earth. The other major source is the sun. (A lesser source is tidal energy, produced by the interaction of the moon's and sun's gravitational attractions with the Earth.)

Without the sun's rays, the Earth would in all likelihood be a cold and lifeless ball. Some of the solar energy that reaches the Earth is absorbed by the atmosphere and surface and retained as heat. Variations in the amount of solar energy absorbed by different regions of the planet produce the Earth's climate and weather systems.

Over long periods, complex interactions between solar energy and other phenomena (see pages 204–211) bring about changes in the Earth's climate. But it is the forces of the weather—rain, wind, waves—that relentlessly nibble at the land. As fast as tectonic activity can raise a mountain range, erosion begins to level it. Water is the chief agent of destruction; even as it nourishes life, it wears away at the rocks and the soils, the mountains, meadows, and beaches.

So it is that energy from within the Earth and that from the sun have been at work for billions of years, continually reshaping the face of our land.

In some tens of billions of years, scientists believe, the sun's hydrogen "fuel" will become largely exhausted, and our star will enter a period of decline toward old age and death. Before it dies, it will expand prodigiously, its surface perhaps reaching out as far as the Earth's orbit. By that time, all of our water and atmosphere will have been boiled or driven off, and the Earth will be left, a charred, lifeless ball.

By then, if we humans have been intelligent enough to get along with each other, we will have long since gone off to find another fortunate home planet.

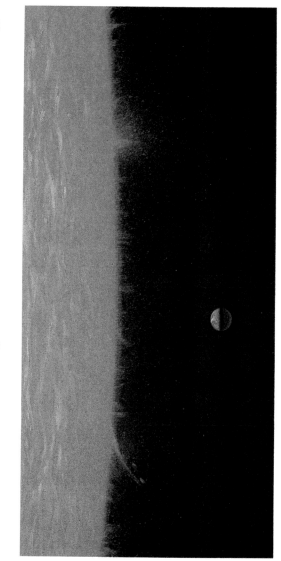

As Earth evolves into the future, left, continents drift, collide to form new combinations; ultimately planet dies, charred by enlarging sun. Right, hugely swollen sun, expanding as it burns the last of its hydrogen "fuel" and begins to convert heavier elements into energy, looms over the moon and lifeless, airless Earth, foreground. As a red giant, above, the sun may expand until it reaches or goes beyond the Earth's orbit. Sun will eventually shrink, burn out completely.

The Ephemeral Cape

By Russell Bourne

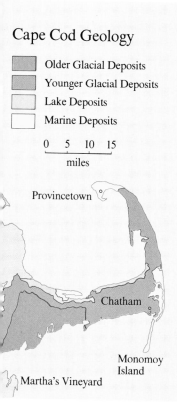

Cape Cod Geology

- Older Glacial Deposits
- Younger Glacial Deposits
- Lake Deposits
- Marine Deposits

0 5 10 15
miles

Provincetown

Chatham

Monomoy
Island

Martha's Vineyard

Friend of mine on Cape Cod told me about the first house he'd tried to buy there: weather-grayed shingles with white trim; from the porch you could see the blue bay beyond low dunes at the end of the grass. But then he went over to the real estate office to check out the plot plan and the lot shown as "his" didn't seem to be on the water. "Trouble is," the realtor explained, "the one shown in front of your lot isn't there any more."

The sea had claimed it. And of course my friend's putative lot would be the next one devoured. So he regretfully called off the deal. Yet, ever remembering it, as one will an old love, he went back to look at it last year. The new owner was standing disconsolately against a snow fence strung across the lawn; canyons cutting beneath it would soon undermine the porch. The man didn't wave back as my friend drove away.

Last summer my son and I sailed down Cape Cod Bay. Through binoculars we could see bulldozers at work scooping up sand in front of summer cottages south of Manomet, building bulkheads to replace vanished dunes. Further along, landowners had sunk heavy boulders in the face of an eroded cliff. Everywhere miniature people strove in the circles of my glasses to barricade property against the laughing sea. Valiant, I told my son, who thought it strange.

My grandfather had always thought there was something peculiar about Cape Cod, too. I remember his tales of the "mooncussers"—the midnight wreckers who would pull down warning lanterns from the Cape's Atlantic cliffs so ships would run on the shoals at the cliffs' feet and fall prey to marauders' knives. He also told of deep-draft ships sailing in and out of Bass River on the Cape's south shore, which, as I plainly saw through youthful eyes, was too shallow for anything but the lightest pleasure craft. Tales too of how the Cape had anciently been forested, but now the only stay against the denuded sand hills' blowing away was rows of pitch pines planted by "Roosevelt's damn lean-on-your-shovel boys."

As far back as 1850 the Cape struck observers as somewhat unearthly; villagers in Orleans complained that "a large part of the real estate was freely moving back and forth in the air." Numerous people liked to go there, nonetheless, to savor the tea-table quiet of English-named towns where lilac hedges led up from church green to windmill hill.

Grandfather's saint Henry David Thoreau had commented on the special quality of those who would live on the Cape. He also wrote, in 1855: "The time has come when this coast will be a place of resort for those New Englanders who really wish to visit the seaside. At present it is wholly unknown to the fashionable world."

Blown by Nor'easters, scourged by ceaseless tides, haunted by history, loved by generations of peculiar natives and particular summer folk, Cape Cod still faces the reality of its most severe problem: It seems to be disappearing. This is not merely a matter of a house or two falling off the dunes or of a harbor silting up; it's an epochal wipe-out.

Scientists concur that, at its present rate of retreat, the Cape may be swept away in a mere 10,000 years. Thoreau suspected that something colossal like that was going on, having noted that a cliff near Highland Light had been eaten away to a depth of some 40 feet in the eight months preceding June 1850. But, stepping back from the abyss, he judged that generally the cliff edge "was not wearing away . . . at the rate of more than six feet annually." Then, with a transcendental shrug: "Any conclusion drawn from the observations of a few years, or one generation only, is likely to prove false."

Graham Giese, an oceanographer at the Center for Coastal Studies out at the very clenched-fist-end of the Cape's gesticulating arm, prefers to talk in millimeters. And he prefers *not* to talk about the Cape's sinking but about the sea's rising relative to the land. He'll say that the rate of the sea's rise on

Cape Cod is three millimeters a year. If you insist on feet, he'll grant the Cape's giving up a foot or so every 100 years. He'll also concede that the Cape's oceanside cliffs are retreating at about two and a half feet a year—erosion being more of a threat, in truth, than land subsidence or sea rise. Yet, he claims, there's no cause for alarm.

On the contrary, Dr. Giese is excited about the cyclical process of upthrust and erosion, which he considers "as fundamental to the land as evaporation and precipitation." As a spokesman for rationalism, he sees more enlightenment than mystery in the mastodon teeth that scallopers dredge up from Georges Bank—the fossils demonstrate that those shoal waters were dry land 15,000 years ago. That was after the glaciers had deposited sufficient moraine to supply the Cape's backbone but before glacier melt had brought the waters up to near their present level. He finds cause for celebration, not frustration, in the strength of the Cape in defending itself against the continuous, millennia-long process of the storm-lashed seas rising and pummeling New England's coastal outpost. Admiringly, he charts the orderly retreat, the gradual dispersal of the cliffs' sands north around the tip of Provincetown and south along the strand of Monomoy toward Nantucket (admitting that some 20 percent of the land materials are totally lost in the process). He gives the Cape a fighting chance of surviving awhile, "if people would only leave it alone and stop disturbing the system with groins and bulkheads . . . if they'd understand that most attempts to 'save it' merely cause further wash-outs."

None of this is regarded as either very informed or particularly helpful by the fishermen who suffer most from the Cape's changing shape—and gradual disappearance. These men, who in the local idiom "beat the seas for a living," give no thanks to Graham Giese's Center or to the Woods Hole Oceanographic Institution for data or explanations. Instead they conclude their struggle is essentially against implacable, unpredictable forces. And I'm inclined to agree. Who can really say why the spit at Nauset Inlet grows about 300 feet in a northerly direction each year, adding to the taxables of Orleans, subtracting the same from Eastham, and foiling all attempts to make a decent fisherman's harbor? Who can say how soon Chatham Harbor—one of three still successful commercial ports, where there used to be many—will find its entrance channel completely clogged? What could I reasonably answer to the fisherman who wanted to know "what the hell kind of sense it makes to have only two feet of water at Chatham's lead-in bell?" Not that he was expecting that it should make any sense.

Breaking seas menace beach houses north of Chatham during '78 winter storm. Southward, Monomoy Island, below background, spills sand over shellfish beds through breach. Thus barrier beaches shift shape, change fates.

Dry-land conundrums trouble the fishermen even more than those encountered at sea. Real estate and recreational interests compete for harborside properties, their various representatives brandishing bankers' dollars and insurance-backed mortgages. In all the sweep of Provincetown harbor (known as "P-town" to the locals), where artists across the generations used to find forests of masts hung with nets and where gull-wreathed ships thronged the docks, only one commercial pier remains. Says Sherrill Smith of the Massachusetts State Fisheries, "Nothing that nature can do to us is as bad as what people have done."

In the past few decades there seems to have been little question whether the Cape's fishermen were cursed or blessed. Penny-wise investors declined to underwrite larger, more modern vessels; huge foreign factory ships and trawlers crowded the New Englanders' boats off the banks; prospects looked dismal. The over-fished cod, long-time staple of the fishery, was listed as a vanishing species. With rust-streaked hulls leaning forlornly against unrepaired piers, fathers urged sons to seek other employment.

But then either the gods relented, or the 200-mile fishing limit was passed by Congress, or natural forces reasserted themselves for the reconstitution of the cod population—or all of the above. Representative Gerry Studds, known as "the Cape Congressman," gives all credit to the 200-mile limit, the 1977 law which he, laboring forcefully and successfully, pushed down the throat of the U.S. State Department. He counts a 20-million-pound increase in the amount of fish caught off New England's shores in the year since passage of

the act. He sees the recovery of the cod as but one beneficial result of the legislation: "Before the 200-mile zone was created, foreign fishing fleets had severely overfished haddock, flounder, and a number of other species besides cod. But under the provisions of the new law, foreign fleets have been allowed to catch only fish that are surplus to the needs of American fishermen."

To all of which upbeat news a harborside friend of mine replies, "Nonsense. It's just a spasm of good luck. Look at the simultaneous recovery of the sea scallop— two million bucks last year, thank you. We're dealing with a two-year life cycle, you know, something that begins way back and that responds only slowly to what's happening right now. Does that have anything to do with the recent 200-mile limit? No, sir!" He feels that neither science nor politics should be taken seriously as cures for the Cape's ills. Yet the remarkably rich catch of 1978, which produced some $20 million worth of landings at Cape harbors, undoubtedly has affected the decisions of many who were hesitant until very recently about going down to the sea in ships.

Roaring forth from the harbor mouths in powerful new fiber-glass hulls fresh from the factory (as opposed to the old steel "Novies" built in Nova Scotia), the bold young men and women now take off down the Great South Channel to Georges Banks, following their fathers' wakes. Lobstermen from Harwich cruise out to set pots far down in canyons cut in the continental shelf, hauling up a catch totaling more than a million dollars a year. Line trawlers which had pocketa-pocketed out of Chatham at 4:30 a.m. return 13 hours later to

surfcasting

raking for quahogs

bullraking for quahogs

clamming

unload 30-odd fish boxes, each packed with 125 pounds of cod or yellowtail. The captain himself, who started out as a sternman sweating the lines and hoists of the net, now may earn $25,000 annually after paying off costs.

Perhaps hard work and native grit have something to do with the Cape's improved economy. A cartoonist might rightly depict the modern Yankee hiking up his overalls and spitting in the eye of the decades-long curse of underemployment and vocational disarray. Or perhaps the denizens' strikingly imaginative response to the rigors and opportunities of their changing land accounts for the momentary improvement in mood and money flow. In the ringing words of Congressman Studds: "the Environment *is* the Economy!" Something more creative than mere real estate canniness or fisherman's fortune seems to be at work.

There's the game, for example, of "Put 'n Take," which is a notably clever way to make the best of an environmental problem. My friend Ray Rogers, who owns a newspaper in Yarmouth, starts telling about the game by explaining that most years there's a crisis in Cape communities when it appears that there won't be enough quahogs (hard-shelled clams) to hook the tourists. The selectmen, warned by motel owners that a lack of happy quahog diggers means no money for anyone, demand that the shellfish warden *do* something. In reply, the warden first explains about the ravages of last winter's "anchor ice," a frozen-earth condition which begins at the harbor's sides, creeps under water along the harbor's bottom, and ultimately kills all creatures in the harbor's muddy matrix. Then, having explained why the local beds

have no quahogs, he pauses . . . and perceives that the only solution is to get some of the shellfish from elsewhere. Slowly a plot forms: He knows that Boston and Quincy have lots of quahogs in their polluted harbors and that he could pick them up at little cost. Then he could truck them back to town, plant them in the local beds of a moonless night, be reasonably sure they'd get flushed out adequately in the good local waters, and pronounce the situation OK when the season opened. The selectmen lean back, light cigars, tell him to get his truck gassed up. That's the game of "Put 'em in here now so they can take 'em out later."

Onshore, offshore, Cape fishermen—whether year-round commercial or summertime casual—net a rich harvest from life-giving waters. The fortunate angler trolling in cruiser below may catch 6,000 pounds of striped bass annually.

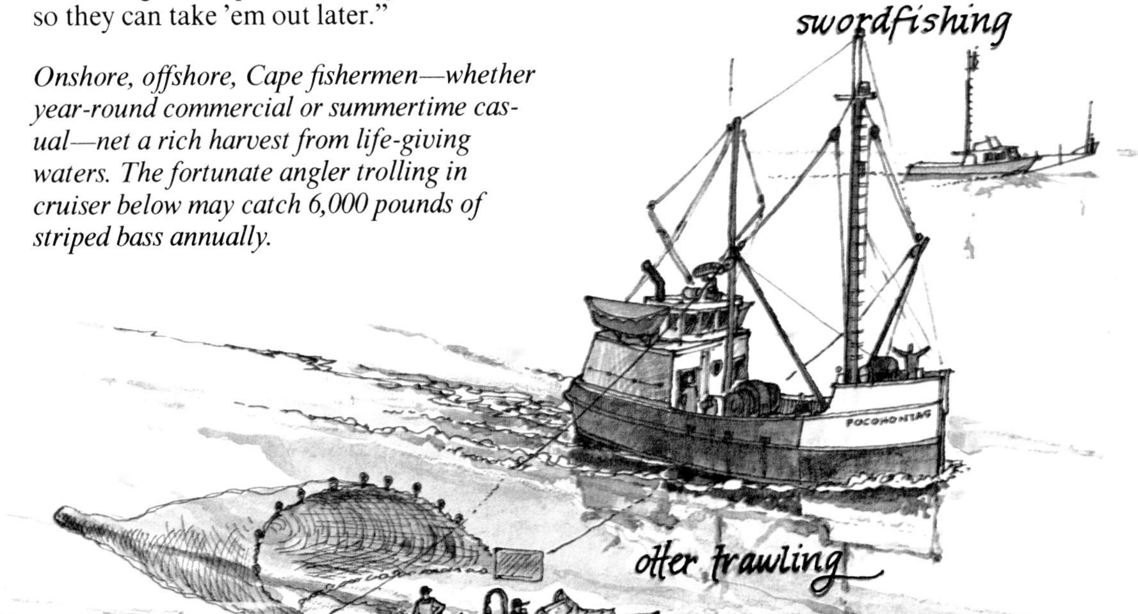

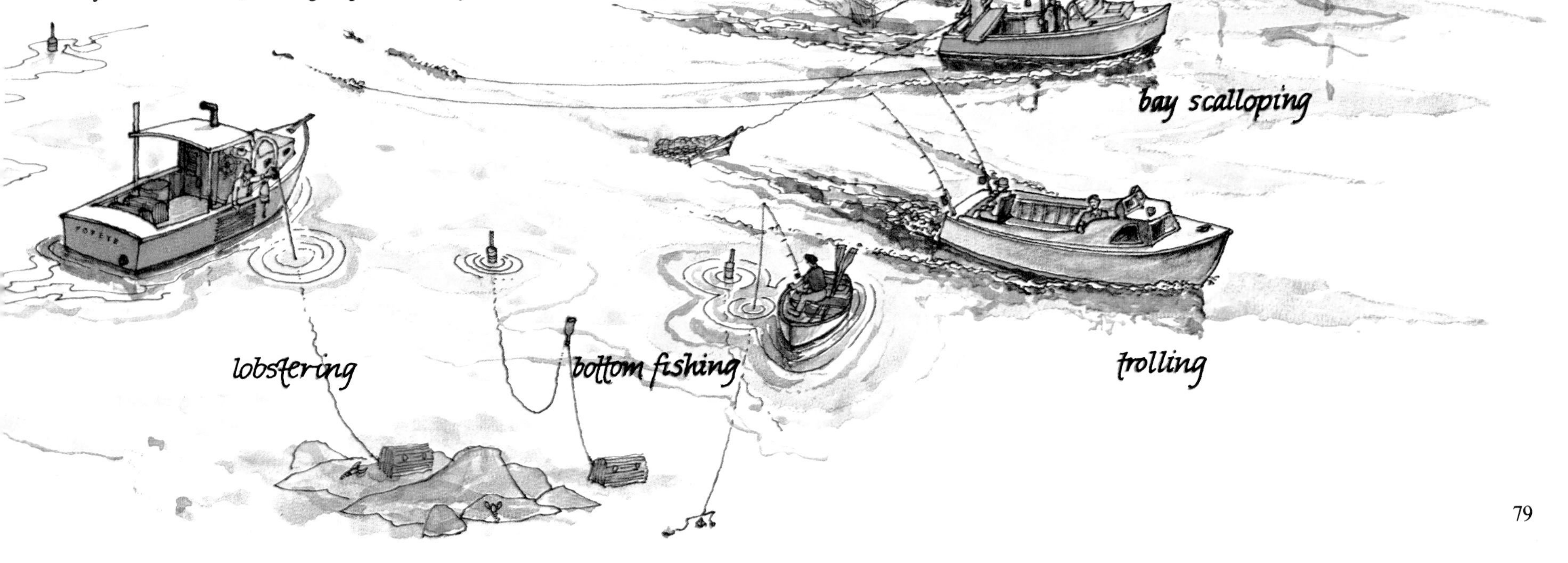

swordfishing

otter trawling

bay scalloping

lobstering

bottom fishing

trolling

79

Historic life-saving station on Cape's North Beach once launched countless rescues of threatened seamen, then faced sea's threat itself. Photos from '64 and '77, above, show the disappearing land.

What we call real estate—the solid ground to build a house on—is the broad foundation on which nearly all the guilt of the world rests.

–Nathaniel Hawthorne

Ray Rogers also reports that it's these local wardens who monitor the quality of the creeks' water flow and the reaction of shellfish to it, seeking ways to improve production. The trick is to keep the tidal current flowing in and out of the pond from behind the barrier beach, ensuring the growth of organisms within and the passage of wildlife to and from the bay outside at the proper stages. But with such a current, how to secure the delicate baby oysters so they can feed on the wetlands' nutrients? In process here is the larval development of the oyster; only after several weeks of free-swimming incubation in a watery surround can the oyster safely drop to the bottom to mature. Local conservationists have scored successes by collecting oyster spat on boxes made of slats and chicken wire; they then suspend the boxes beneath rafts anchored in the creek. The result: numerous well-fed oysters and another good, homemade oyster season.

Congenitally the Cape Cod fisherman has been reluctant to share information with others about his catch—where, how many, what kind. This secrecy has been justified by the well-known dictum that "the silent pig gets the most swill," a philosophy hard to refute. But in the pre-1978 depression, faced with overwhelming competition from landlubberly interests, the industry struggled to bring itself together. Fisher-

men started speaking to state agents, even cooperated with researchers of the Cape Cod Planning and Economic Development Commission.

The same cooperative spirit seems to have influenced the proudly independent Cape Cod communities. Strung like local cranberries on a thread, the villages along Route 6 from the mainland to Provincetown had traditionally vied with each other to see whose "Bide-a-While" cabins, fried clam stands, and drive-in movies could most effectively prevent the tourist from getting through the gauntlet with a dollar in his pocket. Now that form of excessive development is viewed as counterproductive, even by the most unreconstructed old-line Yankees—not only because it does nothing to increase real property values, but also because of possible overload of the Cape's fragile soil and drainage system.

The rising cost of houses on the Cape, stalled briefly while developers learned how to live with the conservationists' demands, is again mounting. Recognizing at last that, since the Cape is not only fragile but actually disappearing, they'd better address themselves to its care, builders have accepted some previously unthinkable restrictions: limited construction of waterfront bulkheads; no building on floodplains or in wetlands, strict oversight of septic tanks. Nonetheless,

Cape Codders determined to save station from hurricanes and winter storms, lifted it onto barge for voyage to retirement. Below, barge rounds light at Provincetown where Pilgrims found haven three centuries earlier.

good drinking water is threatened both by incursion of salt water and by pollution's seepage. Glacial moraine is hardly the foundation rock of which the Bible speaks; the natives are looking to high ground (what there is left of it).

An engineer acquaintance of mine who rents a P-town house whenever he can get it reports the occasional, unnerving sight of *fresh* water rising out of the front lawn. Ducks play, children splash, town fathers (who worry perpetually about sin and drinking water) blame it on the summer theater riffraff. What's actually happened, as the engineer explains it, is that the rain water, collected in various subsurface channels and generally regarded as the sacred "water table," floats on top of the denser salt water which rises and falls with the tide. At summer's apogee, when the theater folk and all others consume so much water for car washing and sundry purposes that the weight and amount of the fresh water is decreased, the salt water floods into the subsoil channels, forcing the slight skim of fresh up through the greensward when the moon is full. Normalcy returns after Labor Day, the lawns wither as sandal-wearers retreat, and natives reassure themselves that the situation is basically OK.

Of course, the era of cooperation between real estate and fishing interests, and the current spasm of good luck, may run

out one day, just as blue sky (in Yankee terms) serves generally as a "weather breeder." Planners may succeed no better than scientists or politicians in holding the sand castle together as the tide rises. Storms like the dreadful February '78 blast that broke through the barrier strand at North Beach and that split Monomoy in two may so destroy the land as waters rise that the end will be hastened. But meanwhile, one can take joy that the Cape still has its peculiar integrity and still stands as a kind of first line of defense for the northeast coast against the Atlantic's rampages.

A young woman I know participates in that joy. She grew up on the Cape, graduated from Bennington recently, and plays a cello like Roger Staubach plays quarterback. She and a group of fellow musicians came back to the Cape for a visit a few springs ago, lugging their instruments with them up to the top of the cliffs near Truro. When (and if) the whole structure of the peninsula finally gives way, these spectacular cliffs, themselves the creation of wind and wave, will be among the first to go but perhaps the longest retained in memory. There is, therefore, a kind of eternal beauty about them, recognizing as one must that eternity is, in Graham Giese's phrase, cyclical.

The young people sat there for a while, hugging their knees, contemplating the golden sweep of the National Seashore's beaches, sensing the surge of the ocean's gusts and breakers. Then they took up their instruments and played, singing out into the incredible blueness. And to their amazement, their tune was answered by another melody. They looked down into the water and saw a vast pod of whales migrating south, huge black bodies rising and falling beyond the surf line. Their tails beat the waters, their cries and snorts hung on the wind.

If the Cape's curse is that the land, despite all efforts, will be swept away, perhaps the blessing is that what comes next will be more astonishingly beautiful.

Four Moments in Time

By Nicholas Hotton III

Maps accompanying illustrations indicate areas of continent above sea level at specific times. Dots mark locales.

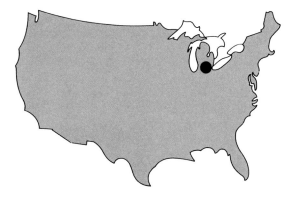

Illustrations by Eleanor M. Kish

Imagination can take us millions of years into the past. This means the creation of mental pictures, an important part of the Smithsonian's work. Scientists eventually entrust their scholastic images to artists, in this case to Eleanor Kish, who can transform our thoughts into paint on canvas as she does here with great drama.

Such a trip, like a visit to Dearborn or Williamsburg, is subject to limitations of record; the farther back we go in time, the less certain we are of details. In this brief time trip, we see what the fossil record shows as most probable—a few of the largest and most common organisms in an environment dictated by continental movement and climatic change.

That last somewhat cryptic phrase has a practical translation: What is now our land once lay far to the south. It has since drifted to the north. The farther back we travel through time, the closer the continent will lie to the Equator, and the warmer the climate will be.

Our view on this imaginary jaunt is limited by the telescoping effect of time travel, and stops are scattered in time and place for maximum diversity. Since we travel backward through time, some scenes seem more familiar than others.

Our ultimate destination: a time not only before any people lived on the land now called the United States, but before the mammalian ancestors of humanity even existed. Let us embark!

First stop, the site of Ann Arbor, Michigan (see map), about 10,800 years ago, 11 a.m. of an autumn morn. We have come but a short geologic step from our own time, yet the elephants are startling evidence that things are different. These two are Jefferson's mammoths, *Mammuthus jeffersoni*, named for an eminent paleontologist who among other accomplishments became President of the United States. They are grazers, inhabitants of open country. Their southerly relatives, the better-known Columbian mammoths, are very like the European animals depicted in cave paintings by the men who hunted them.

We encounter no people, but this is a rather out-of-the-way place, not far south of the retreating continental ice sheet.

For several million years prior to the time we are visiting, various elephantine mammals have been conspicuous. They probably first crossed from Asia, like man himself, via the Bering land bridge. In addition to the grazing mammoths before us, there are at this time the mastodons, which being browsers tend to be confined to the forests.

As we think these thoughts, we recover from our initial shock and fascination with the exotic, to become aware of much that is familiar: the gold of the autumnal foliage of the birches against the green-black of the spruce forest, the beaver, and moose. All are much as they would be in October 1979 in northern New England, southeastern Canada, or the Upper Peninsula of Michigan.

Early Oligocene Epoch, Casper, Wyoming

Next stop, Casper, Wyoming, about 30 million years ago, nearly 3,000 times as far back as our first jump took us. Perhaps 25 million years will pass before creatures resembling man will appear on Earth.

It is midafternoon, high summer. On the slope below us are two titanotheres, herbivorous mammals that look rather like rhinoceroses, but are as big as elephants.

Like the rhinos of our era, the prehistoric titanotheres were derived from browsing, horse-like ancestors, and have remained browsers in their prime. The smaller, slender animals in the distance are camelids, primitive members of the line that led to the camels and llamas of our own time.

Today, the world's most complete fossil record of horse, rhino, and camel lineages can be found near Casper. It is preserved in sediments plastered against the lower slopes of these hills and in the river valleys. The animals pictured in this specially commissioned artwork seem exotic to us, for their descendants are no longer native to North America. In the perspective of geologic time, however, they are more typical of the United States than we are.

Despite the great length of our second leap into the past, much is still familiar. The scenery is grossly similar to that of the present, and the river may well be what we call the North Platte.

The kinds of trees are familiar: oaks, willows, sycamores, and cottonwoods. Their trunks show growth rings indicating seasonal climate, though the alternation of wet and dry conditions in this era would be more striking than the change between warm and cold seasons, those that characterize our own time.

The most impressive differences, aside from the mammals, are the thicker stands of trees and the rarity of grasses. The climate is wetter, and grasses are restricted to the drier hilltops and slopes, not yet having spread to form prairies at the expense of the forests.

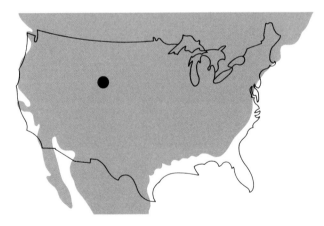

Skull of titanothere, top, yields anatomical details for artist's reconstruction, left. Elephant-sized beasts lived 30 million years ago.

Early Cretaceous Period, Washington, D.C.

Here we go again, this time near Washington, D.C., about 110 million years ago. It is about 7 o'clock of what looks like a typically muggy summer morning. However, we can no longer tell seasons from appearances, for this part of the continent is much farther south than it will be in our time. The trees show no evidence of seasonal alternation of growth and quiescence, for there is little difference between summer and winter in temperature, rainfall, or length of daylight. The climate is very similar to the weather of Washington, D.C., in the month of August, but it continues that way the year 'round, monotonously hot and humid.

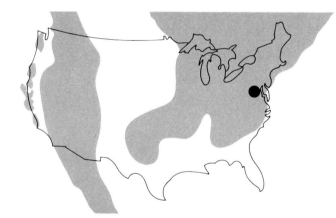

The only animals we see are dinosaurs; about 30 feet long, they are half-grown individuals of the small (!) sauropod *Pleurocoelus.* Unlike the reptiles we know, these stride ponderously about on vertical limbs like so many elephants, and like elephants tend to gather near water. Their abundance is perhaps as unusual as their form. Only five are visible at the moment, but their presence is all about us—smashed vegetation, tracks, droppings, noises in the forest.

How can the environment support so many very large animals, especially as they seem as active as mammals? Some dinosaurs were quite active; they could obtain great mileage from a little food. Mammals generate heat even when inactive, and so require a much larger fuel supply, and a given environment can support fewer pounds of mammals than of dinosaurs.

Plant life is little more familiar than the geography and animal life. The trees are conifers, but they are most closely related to redwood and cypress, forms that survive far from Washington, D.C., at the present time. Undergrowth is mostly ferns. We have been told that the earliest flowering plants are in existence, but none are visible to us, for they are largely restricted to disturbed areas along the water courses, as where creek banks have caved in.

Fossilized seed-bearing cones of ancient sequoia-like trees. Around area that would become Washington, D.C., trees thrived 110 million years ago.

. . . the bones came together, bone to his bone . . . . lo, the sinews and the flesh came up upon them, and the skin covered them . . . and the breath came into them, and they lived.

—Ezekiel

Early Permian Period, Wichita Falls, Texas

Last stop is Wichita Falls, Texas, about 270 million years ago. As at our previous stop, we can't identify seasons by appearances, because this part of Texas is too close to the Equator. The rain is probably seasonal, because the trees show growth rings, but whether it's winter or summer is certainly anybody's guess.

We are now so far back in time that the familiarity of anything we see should be viewed with suspicion. The animals, for

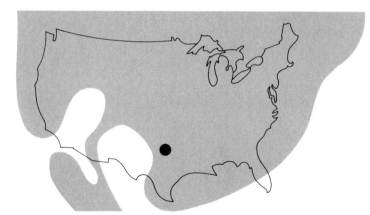

example, are neither crocodiles nor six- to eight-foot lizards, nor are they dinosaurs. They are pelycosaurs, members of a lineage contemporary with but distinct from the remotest reptilian ancestors of lizards, crocodilians, *and* dinosaurs.

Because the pelycosaur lineage leads ultimately to mammals, we call pelycosaurs mammal-like reptiles, but functionally they are very reptilian at this stage. The predator, *Dimetrodon,* has seized its prey, a small individual of *Cotylorhynchus,* by a short rush and a snap of the jaws, and will simply hang on until the victim dies of shock and loss of blood. So also feed the 10-foot-long Komodo lizards of our time, the "dragons" of Southeast Asia, which like *Dimetrodon* take prey as large as they are.

Nor do pelycosaurs approach mammals in their control of body temperature. The fin on the back of *Dimetrodon* serves to increase surface area relative to body volume, and functions as a solar panel or radiator. This is clear evidence of a high degree of dependence on the external environment as a source of heat, a conservative lifestyle in terms of energy, more like that of most living reptiles than that of mammals.

Few plants resemble those of our time— some ferns, and, through the mist in the right background, a spindly early conifer, *Walchia.* Of the other trees, some (clubmosses and scouring rushes) are represented in our day by low, herb-like forms, and others (seed-ferns) have long been extinct.

Cotylorhynchus, *being bitten, right, was similar to* Edaphosaurus, *skull, below. Skull was distorted during 230 million-year-long burial.*

Beachheads
for Life

By Sherwin Carlquist

Unique, isolated, delicately attuned to their island habitats, the plants and animals of Hawaii are being threatened with extinction even as we begin to appreciate their highly specialized adaptations. Descending from the original wind- and seaborne settlers of these lava islands, the wildlife of Hawaii evolved for millions of years until man arrived with his pets, pests, and domestic animals. The story of the rise and population of the Hawaiian Islands is clear and dramatic, but still unfamiliar to most.

The Hawaiian Islands are not just the major islands of Hawaii, Maui, Lanai, Molokai, Oahu, Kauai, and lesser islands near them (see map, p. 95). Beyond Kauai to the west lie small rocky islands: Niihau, Nihoa, and Necker. Then there are coral atolls representing the last vestiges above water of worn-off volcanoes: French Frigate Shoals, Laysan, and Midway, for example.

Westward from Midway lies Wake Island, beyond which there are no islands or remnants before Japan. Along the bottom of the northern Pacific between Midway and the Kamchatka Peninsula of Siberia lies a series of underwater mountains, the Emperor Seamounts.

If our present ideas are right, the Hawaiian Islands represent the most recent episodes in a long history of volcanic activity, the evidence of which stretches across the Pacific. Geologists find that the Earth's crust, in the form of gigantic plates, is constantly in motion. The largest of these, the Pacific Plate, has been moving northwestward. Suppose that a "hot spot" of lava underlies this plate, perhaps 100 miles beneath the surface. Material welling up from the hot spot punches a hole through the plate and may build up to form a volcanic island.

If the plate moves after a volcano forms, but the hot spot remains at the same place beneath, a chain of volcanoes will form, the most recent one still above the hot spot. In the North Pacific, the Emperor Seamounts, about 75 million years old, may be the oldest products of the hot spot. Midway may be as many as 45 million years old. Of the "high islands," the islands still well above the surface, Kauai has rocks dated at about five million years, and the island of Hawaii is only one million years old or less. The newest land in the Hawaiian Islands is exactly where one would expect: at Kapoho, on the eastern tip of the easternmost island, Hawaii.

An equally perfect part of this picture is the fact that the higher volcanoes, Mauna Kea (13,796 feet) and Mauna Loa (13, 680 feet), are farther east in the Hawaiian chain. These two smooth-faced volcanoes are almost untouched by erosion. Kauai, on the other hand, is worn into steep cliffs, deep valleys, and knife-edge ridges.

If Hawaiian land is wholly made up of lava, how can it support a diversity of life? We usually think that a variety of rock types is required for a variety of plants and animals. However, hundreds of species of flowering plants, insects, ferns, and land snails have originated on these islands. Pockets with distinctive ecology must have occurred.

If all of the Hawaiian Islands had been low, pockets of special ecology would not have happened. A low island like Kahoolawe, with few plants and animals, proves this. A few big winter storms would drop rain on such an island, but the rest of the year would be dry there. So little erosion would occur that the island surface would change only slightly. An island with a peak more than 1,000 feet high, however, would tend to condense moisture from wet air. The trade winds, which come from the northeast, blow most of the year. These masses of air, saturated with moisture during their passage across the North Pacific, can be triggered into showers by a mountain. Thus mountains which rise to crests ranging from about 2,000 to 7,000 feet would tend to be wet in this part of the Pacific. At about 7,000 feet, rising clouds have lost most of their moisture, and alpine areas of the Hawaiian Islands are virtual deserts.

Windward sides of the higher islands are wet, leeward sides dry, lying in "rain shadows." The crests of mountains tend to be covered with trade-wind clouds much of the time. Leeward sides of mountains may be wet near the crest because the wind blows showers well beyond the crests. The wettest place in the Hawaiian Islands, Mount Waialeale, may receive over 600 inches of rain annually; valleys leading to the summit are like funnels which condense rain. The driest place is Kawaihae, with about 12 inches of rain annually. It is in the rain shadow of Mauna Kea, and ridges shelter it from rains coming from other directions.

Because lava tends to erode rapidly, deep valleys and steep ridges are produced in the wetter mountains in less than a million years. Coral reefs thriving in warm seas near the islands are wave-eroded into salty beaches. Winds blow the coral sands inland where they are converted into nonsalty soils. Very quickly, as geological time goes, wind, rain, and waves produce a rich variety of habitats from simple volcanic cones. All that is needed for the development of hundreds of kinds of plants and animals is . . . a few arrivals.

Although the Hawaiian Chain may have arisen long ago, and high volcanoes may have stood where now there are only undersea mountains, none of the islands was, as far as anyone can tell, ever connected with a continent. The easternmost point of the islands is about 2,300 miles from California. Such distances pose formidable obstacles to the natural transport of plants and animals from continents to islands. Two factors which rule out most successful transport are the inability of most land plants and animals to survive

Aerial view includes Honolulu, in the distance, and Pali Highway on Hawaii's Oahu Island. Nuuanu tunnels, at right, take highway through one of the twin volcanic ranges that formed the island 4,000,000 years ago.

91

Eroded face of Kauai Island's Na Pali coast gets sidewise blast from constant trade winds. Inland lie such habitats as verdant Waimea Canyon and 5,000-foot Mount Wialae, special opportunities for isolated life forms.

Sticking to the feather of an obliging bird, fruit of the Pisonia, *above, prepares for an aerial voyage to Hawaii.* Bidens pilosa, *above left, equips itself to snag a ride to the islands by means of its seeds' sharp barbs.*

immersion in seawater, and the tendency of the new locality to have a different ecology from the old one. A seed can cross thousands of miles unharmed, be deposited on a clear piece of land, germinate—but fail to grow because the land is too sunny. Or it may grow successfully and flower, but fail to set seeds because a pollinating insect is absent. Difficulties like these would seem to rule out all but a very few events of immigration unaided by man. However, the very variety of Hawaiian habitats has favored a few chosen arrivals, and of these, the plants were probably first.

Some kinds of plants can disperse over much longer distances than others. Large size is not necessarily a hindrance—coconuts, the fruits of some palms, can float—and extremely small size is definitely an advantage, because very small objects can be carried long distances in several ways. Spores, much smaller than seeds, are the reproductive cells of ferns, mosses, and fungi. Some spores are so small that 1,000 of them laid in a line would be an inch long. Updrafts can lift spores into the upper atmosphere where the jet streams, super-rapid air currents, whisk them far away from their points of origin.

The same method of travel can apply to very small seeds although even the smallest seeds are relatively large—at the very least 10 times the diameter of spores. When seeds are carried aloft in air currents, the fallout is quicker; nonetheless, one Hawaiian tree, the ohia, probably reached the islands via the winds.

Many seeds are carried far afield by ocean currents, and one can often find quantities washed up on beaches. Some, like coconuts, may float for months and still germinate upon arrival at a suitable landing place. Oddly enough, though, only a few of the progenitors of the islands' flora drifted there in the ocean currents. Plants that travel by sea tend to be beach dwellers, having dropped their seeds where the surf could pick them up. The adaptations for sea travel and beach life are often linked, and "once a beach plant, always a beach plant" is usually the rule.

Inland from the beaches, the Hawaiian Islands are mostly covered by dry or wetland forests. These forests hold clues pointing toward another agent of seed transport: varieties of colorful, fleshy fruits, attractive to birds. Only rarely can fruit-eating birds retain seeds throughout long migratory flights, but rarely is not the same as never. Significantly, if such events of transportation were common, the plants of the Hawaiian Islands would be the same as those of tropical regions around the world. Instead, at least 95 percent of native (also called "endemic") Hawaiian plants occur nowhere else on earth. The 5 percent or less which do occur elsewhere are those which can disperse easily, like the beach plants which are indeed spread over much of the world.

Many land birds such as pigeons like to eat fruits, but few fly to remote islands, while marine birds, albatrosses for example, almost never eat fruits. However, shore birds (curlews, plovers) do eat fruits sometimes, and they do make regular migratory flights to the Hawaiian Islands. Under experimental conditions, at least, shore birds can retain their seeds for as long as five days.

Terns, boobies, gulls, and shearwaters—migratory birds which cross seas in great numbers—would be ideal agents for seed transport if the seeds could hitch rides on them, and many can. If one looks at areas where seabirds nest, one can find seeds and fruits covered with barbs, bristles, hooks, and stiff hairs. Other seeds and fruits are covered with viscid, sticky substances, or become slimy when wet and adhere to whatever they touch. Hooked, barbed, sticky, or viscid seeds have a great advantage for travel over long distances. They tend to stay on a bird indefinitely, so that the length of flight is not a concern. The birds preen on arrival, dislodging seeds in places suitable for their growth.

Animals cross large spans of ocean no more easily than do plants. Many species of insects, the largest group of animals in any area of the world, can fly, but very few are able to fly for more than a few miles nonstop. Migratory behavior could account for the presence of one butterfly and one dragonfly on the Hawaiian Islands, but most insects are, at first glance, mysterious arrivals. We do have some hints: Hawaiian insects are smaller than continental insects, suggesting again that diminutive size aids travel.

Some groups of insects common on continents are missing on Hawaii, an obvious indication that some do travel better than others. Entomologist J. Linsey Gressitt devised a test to determine if insects could travel by air to Hawaii and which groups of insects were most likely to do so. Using net traps on aircraft and boats, he sampled areas far from any land; the catch showed that smaller insects can and do float in the air at great distances from land. Furthermore, the insects he caught belonged to the same assortment of families found in the Hawaiian and other islands.

Gressitt also caught spiders, and not surprisingly, since spiders are also endemic to the Hawaiian Islands. By virtue of their light bodies and parachute-like webs, some spiders can float on the winds; for them as well as for insects, spores, and small seeds, the jet streams appear to provide the mechanism for travel over long distances.

Land snails might seem to be poorly adapted to transoceanic travel, but they are present on many volcanic islands. Very small land snails could stick to birds; snail eggs certainly can, and some may be resistant to drying.

Lizards might also seem unlikely voyagers. In fact, zoologists thought until recently that no lizards were endemic (i.e., pre-human) to the Hawaiian Islands. Now a gecko and a skink are regarded as endemic. Experiments on lizard eggs have shown they are not harmed by immersion in seawater, and lizards do lay eggs in logs that could float long distances. It is even possible that an egg-carrying female might survive for days or weeks on a floating log.

Birds themselves, one might imagine, would have no trouble reaching the Hawaiian Islands. This is true for migratory seabirds and for shore birds, as banding programs have shown. They visit the Hawaiian Islands on a regular and predictable basis. However, most land birds do not instinctively fly for more than very short distances and many are not physically adapted for long flights. Consequently, very few land birds became established in the Hawaiian Islands in pre-human times.

The unlikelihood of dispersal over long distances has often been appreciated, but unlikely events become likely when given enough time. Even if something can only occur once in a million years, that something ought to occur in the Hawaiian Islands, where Kauai is five million years old and the islands west of Kauai are much older. Of the few immigrants, some clearly flourished. Estimates show that approximately eight flowering plant species have originated from each original immigrant, about 16 insect species, some 50 snail species, and about seven bird species. Clearly, conditions suitable for establishment—conditions like those the immigrants had left—were present in the islands. However, other previously unexploited niches were also present, providing opportunity for diversification into numerous new species. Many of the arrivals probably established themselves in moderately wet-to-dry areas—environments not too different from those of the continents. But Hawaii's truly wet forests—much wetter than most others found around the Pacific—offered the immigrants challenging new habitats to exploit. And evolutionary adaptation to a wetter area is just one example of the myriad opportunities for diversification offered by the varied ecological zones and pockets of the Hawaiian Islands. So many and so little-known are these examples that no single article, or book for that matter, can contain them all. I have chosen a bird and a plant, the honeycreeper and the tarweed, to stand for the rest.

The land is the simplest form of architecture.

–Frank Lloyd Wright

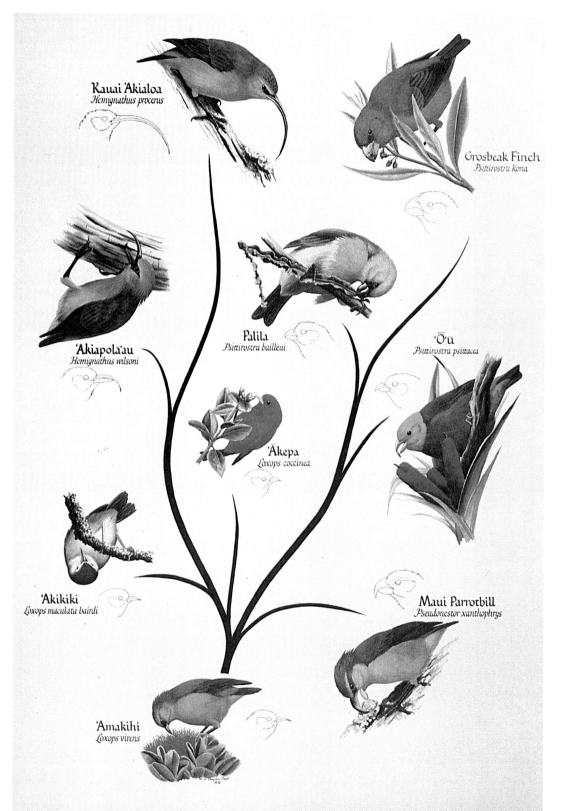

Kauai 'Akialoa
Hemignathus procerus

Grosbeak Finch
Psittirostra kona

'Akiapola'au
Hemignathus wilsoni

Palila
Psittirostra bailleui

'O'u
Psittirostra psittacea

'Akepa
Loxops coccinea

'Akikiki
Loxops maculata bairdi

Maui Parrotbill
Pseudonestor xanthophrys

'Amakihi
Loxops virens

The Hawaiian honeycreepers are members of a single family (Drepanididae) restricted to Hawaii. However, to find in other birds the different types of beaks and adaptations evolved by honeycreepers, one would have to look at several quite distinct families, from parrots to nectar eaters.

The ancestral honeycreepers which gave rise to such varied descendants are thought to have been nectar-feeding birds of unknown origin. We have no way of knowing what the early Hawaiian honeycreepers were like, but they may have resembled the relatively unspecialized amakihi (*Loxops virens stejnegeri*). The amakihi has a moderately short, curved beak ideal for reaching into shallow flowers. As would be expected of an old type of honeycreeper, the amakihi takes nectar from those flowers, but it also probes shallow bark crevices and sheathing leaves for insects, the untapped food source that provided an evolutionary opportunity for the early honeycreepers. Other slightly shorter-and-straighter-beaked *Loxops* species feed exclusively on insects—but on small ones found on leaves or near the surface of the ground.

Psittarostra, with its stout, parrot-like bill, may represent a close relative of *Loxops,* but with marked differences. If bill shape is a lever for exploiting the environment, we might guess that *Psittarostra* feeds like a parrot. The grosbeak finch (*Psittarostra kona*), apparently extinct since 1896, crushed seeds and ate their protein-rich storage material, a vegetable substitute for insect protein.

The rare Maui parrotbill (*Pseudonestor xanthophrys*) looks like a "non-missing link" between *Loxops* and *Psittarostra.* Like the latter, it has a heavy beak, but long and curved—the upper portion longer. With this bill, the Maui parrotbill crushes stout twigs containing boring insects or insect larvae, an ability which could be exaggerated into the seed-eating habit of *Psittarostra.* Such an intermediate adaptation might be the reason for the parrotbill's rarity.

Evolving toward another extreme, *Hemignathus* presents a totally different kind of bill: long, slender, and much curved. The Kauai akialoa (*Hemignathus procerus*), last seen in the early 1970s, appears by virtue of its very long bill to be adapted for nectar-feeding. Seek nectar it does, but it also feeds on the insects it finds in the nectar of long, tubular flowers. It winkles insects out of leaf bases, deep borings in stems, and other difficult-to-reach places. Thus it really is not a nectar-feeder, but a mixed feeder.

Halfway between the long, sickle-beaked Kauai akialoa and small-beaked *Loxops* is the very rare nukupuu (*Hemignathus lucidus*). The beak is slender, the lower half much shorter than the upper. The nukupuu apparently uses

Main Hawaiian Islands
Spanning 388 miles

The Hawaiian Islands, stretching 1,900 miles across the Pacific, yet only 6,450 square miles in area, provided new opportunities for the many species, opposite, that evolved from the original honeycreepers.

the lower portion as a chisel, the upper part as a probe. In this way it can work through large amounts of rotten wood quickly in search of insects. The nukupuu also seeks nectar, but apparently in shallow rather than deep flowers.

The story of these and other Hawaiian honeycreepers is remarkable because it shows us how great leaps in adaptation take place. The various species of honeycreepers occupied many new realms and became adapted to narrowly localized habitats and insect prey, thereby reducing competition amongst themselves to a minimum. If the islands had been occupied by many other kinds of insect-eating birds, it is doubtful if the honeycreepers could have occupied insect-eating niches at all.

The honeycreepers' adaptation to a variety of habitats and food sources is closely paralleled in the plant kingdom by the story of the tarweeds and their Hawaiian silversword relatives. Here I must admit to something of a personal interest. As a graduate student in botany a number of years ago, I hiked into Maui's Haleakala Crater to visit the fine colony of silverswords dotting one of the crater's cinder cones.

There is a stark magnificence about these silverswords of Haleakala, with their gigantic crystalline rosettes, so perfectly adapted to this harshly beautiful, volcanic-cinder desert, and

I was deeply impressed as I approached. Examining the maroon flowers, I noticed the sticky covering on the outsides of the heads. This substance, obviously produced by hairs, exuded a familiar and pungent scent in the clear, warm summer air. I recognized the scent from summertime field trips I had taken in California as the resinous smell of the tarweeds, which flower in the summer heat on dry hills and weedy roadsides. Botanists of past decades had believed that tarweeds and silverswords were closely related, but by the time I was a student the relationship was in doubt. Nonetheless, the scent and the hairs that produced it made me suspect that in Haleakala, 2,500 miles from California, the silversword was indeed a much-altered kind of tarweed. To be sure, I pickled samples of the plants and took them back to my laboratory for study later that year. Examination of their anatomy and chromosomes proved that the scent from the silversword flowers that day in Haleakala was, in fact, a reminiscence of an ancestry that led back across an ocean to California's mountains.

The tarweeds of continental America being, in the main, inhabitants of dry and sunny places, the original tarweed immigrants to Hawaii probably established themselves in similar areas. Such habitats include recently deposited, bar-

... the psychological basis of the home-feeling that Hawaii develops is as deep as human nature ... engendered by equability of climatic conditions.

—Stanley D. Porteus

95

ren lava flows like some of those found on the island of Hawaii. On these dry flows grows *Dubautia scabra,* a small, sprawling shrub with diminutive, narrow leaves, well formed to restrict evaporative water loss.

But the Hawaiian tarweeds have also become adapted to a variety of wetter, shadier, or higher zones. The Kilauea area of the island of Hawaii is a center of recent volcanic activity and is the home of *Dubautia ciliolata.* Kilauea is somewhat wetter than the areas favored by *D. scabra;* with more water available in its zone, *D. ciliolata* grows a little larger than *D. scabra* and can afford longer, broader leaves. In the cloudy forests above Honolulu *D. plantaginea* grows to a height of six feet and sports leaves longer and broader than its drier-area relatives.

A tree-sized tarweed, *D. knudsenii* reaches a height of up to 20 feet in the very wet rain forests of Kauai. In this moist habitat 3,000 feet above sea level, evaporation is low, and *D. knudsenii* spreads its narrow, shade-adapted leaves over a wide area to expose them to as much light as possible. Its flower heads hang down so they will not fill with water during Kauai's frequent showers.

The silverswords (*Argyroxiphium*) are closely related to *Dubautia.* What *Dubautia* is to lower elevations of the Hawaiian Islands, the silverswords are to the higher mountains. The Haleakala silversword (*Argyroxiphium sandwicense*) is perfectly adapted to the "alpine deserts" of Maui. The leaves are slender and thick and can store water, as do leaves of the succulent plants of other dry parts of the world. New leaves of the silversword are sheltered deep among the older leaves, well protected against the island's alpine frosts. The leaves are a brilliant white, covered with felty hairs which reflect the intense, high-altitude sunshine and perhaps slow evaporation. The gigantic cone of flowers blooms in July, during alpine Maui's brief warm season.

The various Hawaiian tarweeds are remarkable in the ways they match the environments they occupy. In no other single area of the world can one find a single group of plants occupying such a wide range of places with such diverse forms. The mainland tarweeds, mostly annuals, are small plants inhabiting rather dry places, and these characteristics were probably the keys to the tarweeds' success in Hawaii. They are the very characteristics that would enable the tarweeds to grow in such disturbed areas as recent, dry-climate lava flows—areas discouraging to most other kinds of plants. Disturbed areas are often stressful environments, and only hardy plants, capable of rapid adaptation, can exploit them to the fullest. This the tarweeds were able to do, and, by virtue of these same attributes, spread into other zones as well. Beautifully in tune with their habitats, the tarweed family could withstand most natural onslaughts, but, like many of Hawaii's animals and other plants, they were not prepared for competition with man and his co-invaders.

By the eighth century A.D., waves of Polynesian sea travelers had peopled the islands, bringing with them plants and animals that disrupted the endemic species' harmony. The arrival in the 19th and early 20th centuries of the Euro-Americans further increased the strain. Today, housing, logging, farming, and other interests, to say nothing of the hosts of introduced plants and animals, compete with the endemics, and the endemics are losing.

The recently compiled Smithsonian Institution list of extinct, endangered, and threatened plants in the United States contains over 1,000 entries from the Hawaiian Islands. This is well over half of the native flora! What is so unusual about

Hawaii's famous silversword finds a foothold high in Maui's Haleakala Crater. Early farmers found rich soil for their taro plant; later plantations prospered from imported pineapple and sugar cane, opposite.

the Hawaiian Islands that their species are so vulnerable?

Unless one is well acquainted with the nature of island organisms, one may consider lava islands merely as small bits of land basically like mainland areas. They are emphatically not, and the difference can be put in a few words where plants are concerned: Hawaiian forests in pre-human times existed without herbivores. No sheep, horses, pigs, goats, or even smaller herbivores like rats or squirrels or rabbits touched the plants of these islands. By contrast, the mainland U.S. contained numerous herbivores, and mainland plants developed thorns, poisonous substances, unpalatable or stinging hairs, or strong-smelling oils to be resistant to them. Hawaiian plants are not resistant, lacking such defenses. They are all-too-easy prey for cattle, pigs, goats, and other animals introduced by humans. Moreover, when these animals trample the forest floor, they create pathways ideal for the establishment of competitive weeds.

Weeds in Hawaii are not at all what weeds on continents are. Such beautiful, even delicate mainland flowers as rex begonias, fuchsias, hydrangeas, passion flowers, nasturtiums, and watsonias are intrusive pests in the Hawaiian Islands! Far more serious are plant pests which animals will not eat readily: blackberries, gorse, lantana, all of which are protected by prickles or thorns.

Guavas, bayberry, Brazilian pepper—the list of plant pests could go on and on. Plants were introduced by gardeners unaware that their favorite vegetables and other plants from back home could escape and create havoc in the island environment. Though some of the less noxious ones may vanish, many are now in Hawaii to stay at the expense of the natives. This has confounded those ecologists who thought that weeds would disappear when man-damaged forests were allowed to regenerate, as had been observed in most mainland areas. And even worse, the likelihood is high that once established, each pest species may displace and force into extinction more than one endemic species.

Why? Remember that the ancestors of today's threatened island plants (and animals, of course) were settlers on an essentially empty land and since have had hundreds of thousands or even millions of years to learn to coexist. On the limited land area of the islands and the even more limited areas of particular habitats, many of the endemic species have become so highly specialized that they can reproduce only within those habitats and cannot spread to others. They also tend to become inbred when they exist in small numbers— and inbred plants are easy prey, or may even "extinguish" themselves, when defects are exposed. This does not hold true for introduced weeds, however. Many are generalists which can invade several adjacent habitats and spread to all the islands.

There are other reasons why the native plants compete less well. Plants which have evolved with little competition (which is true of those in Hawaii) tend to have lowered levels of resistance to disease, particularly new diseases. They have lower rates of reproduction and lowered ability to disperse. Unable to disperse, if they vanish from the Hawaiian Islands, they will vanish completely.

In addition to the difficulties plants face, there are other problems for survival that confront the endemic animals of the Hawaiian Islands. Birds require larger areas for survival than do plants. An area sufficient to maintain silverswords would be too small to maintain honeycreepers. There are five kinds of flowering plants on Necker Island, but the island is too small to support a population of land birds.

Island animals are susceptible to parasites and diseases introduced by man and his animals. Bird malaria, an introduced disease, is spread in the Hawaiian Islands by mosquitoes (also introduced) and fatally infects honeycreepers even in areas not penetrated by people.

Animals depend on food sources. If their food sources disappear, they must also. Prior to human occupation, the native animals not only had no competitors, they had few predators. That is no longer true, both Polynesian and later peoples having introduced all manner of predators and competitors. Moreover, island animals are characteristically fearless and thus are even easier prey.

Can zoos save Hawaiian animals, can cultivation or botanic gardens save Hawaiian plants? Not for long. In cultivation, plants tend to hybridize with certain related plants; they may become inbred if they do not hybridize. The former ruins the identity of the stock, the latter makes for vulnerability and eventual extinction. Although animal species rarely hybridize, problems of inbreeding do occur, and a naturally reproducing colony is hard to maintain in a zoo. As most ecologists would now concede, there is no substitute for the natural habitat for long-term survival. If that habitat is ruined, the results are predictable. Furthermore, when large numbers of individual species in a given habitat are threatened, a few more conspicuous ones may be selected for conservation, but others (inconspicuous insects or plants) rarely are.

Some timely action can prove successful. On Haleakala, the National Park Service fenced an area; goats were excluded, and within the fence, silverswords thrived. Shouldn't goats be killed off altogether? Certainly, but dense and diffi-

cult terrain makes hunting only partly successful, and when only part of the goat population is killed, the effort is useless for the goats soon regenerate. Those interested in conservation must concede that the Hawaiian situation is drastically different and more difficult than most conservation problems on the mainland United States.

Though the future of Hawaii's life forms remains gloomy, a stroller through the islands' forests can still enjoy moments of miniature discovery and revelation. On an ascent of the boggy slopes of Puu Kukui on Maui one time, I stopped to rest and noticed the sedge tussocks on the bog. In these tussocks I saw the inconspicuous leaves and wiry foliage of ferns I might never have seen otherwise; there were mosses I might have overlooked. Catching my breath, I took the opportunity to try to figure out why the minute wispy leaves of that particular moss went with the misty, soggy surroundings. Certainly the only way to understand such adaptations is to know the environments in which plants and animals exist.

Stopping on a hike through a rain forest near the crater of Kilauea Crater, I discovered an *Astelia* plant in flower. This Hawaiian lily has inconspicuous white flowers, seemingly a poor way to attract a pollinator. But close observation showed that although small, the flowers were filled with nectar and had a strong fragrance, almost a caricature of a lily's scent. These devices were, in fact, serving to attract flies which busily pollinated the plant, despite its location in the shady recesses of the forest.

A walk along the rim of Kalalau Valley, where cliffs drop 4,000 feet into the sea, is one of the great experiences available to a naturalist. One can see the orange strata representing about five million years of lava flows framed by stunted and twisted ohia trees. In midsummer, many of the shrubs within this rain forest by the precipice of Kalalau Valley are in flower. Naturally I stopped frequently to observe these shrubs. After a little while, I realized that at each stop I was being observed. Silently, but with wry, twitching motions of its head, an elepaio was perching close to me, bent on absorbing all the details of my appearance and what I was doing. Most native Hawaiian birds are very shy and difficult to find. The elepaio finds *you*. In doing so, it is a lovely example of the uniqueness and fragility of Hawaiian life.

Couple walking Kauai beach at sunset find few shells amid churning surf that sculpts the lava cliffs. Kauai will eventually be reduced to a reef, its drowned pinnacles serving as base for another Pacific coral atoll.

... fragrance of forests growing out of wet, wild earth, the tang of salt water breaking on clean beaches and lava headlands ....

–Armine van Tempski

Wild Things

Less dramatic than some other creatures, the land snail shown here is as good an example as any of the state of wild things. It single-footedly, and sometimes upside down, treads a blade of Everglades sawgrass, moving almost imperceptibly in and out of the sunlight and, more often than not, departs its slow-moving existence into the gullet of a big bird. In fact, one bird, the Everglades kite, is endangered precisely because it feeds only on a particular kind of snail that is found only in particular parts of the Everglades and, as that unique ecosystem comes under increasing human use . . . it is all connected, as biologists regularly remind us.

Herein, S. Dillon Ripley details the ways of some American birds, chronicling their patterns of migration across the land. These patterns may change—in fact, they are bound to—and often it is mankind's doing. Sometimes, he finds, it is not. Edward S. Ayensu, also of the Smithsonian, traces the interweaving of plant and animal habitats across the American land and notes how often the fabric can tear. Where, these days, can you find a patch of tall-grass prairie? There are a few, but they are going fast.

Yet another kind of endangered species is a group of people caught in a difficult, and perhaps disappearing, way of life that pits wildlife against domestic life—the Basque sheepherders of Nevada where the cold, high rangeland becomes stained with blood in the war between the coyote and the

sheep. The battle, it appears, will be won not on biological but on economic grounds and by government policy.

Elsewhere the government has retained for our use and delectation acres of some of the most monumentally beautiful wildlife habitat in the world, the national parks. How should they be structured? Should they preserve monuments and recreation areas or unique and fragile ecosystems where irreproducible species can continue to exist?

Pondering these matters, it is perhaps well to begin modestly with naturalist John Hay and let one's mind dwell on a single tree—the object of a boy's delight, and a world unto itself—a member of a tribe that helped to found the nation.

Land with many habitats: Florida, America's tropics, nurtures bizarre birds and reptiles; south-central region holds armadillo and prairie dog; the pronghorn ranges northward, one of the few U.S. species without an Asian counterpart; Pacific states harbor redwoods, condors, and cacti; along the northern tier wolves almost vanish; Atlantic Seaboard sustains deer, migrating waterfowl, birds of prey. In both East and West species unable to live with urbanization slip toward extinction.

The Founders' Tree

By John Hay   *Illustrations by Alan E. Cober*

"For untold ages Maine had been one unbroken forest, and it was so still. . . . This waste of savage vegetation survives, in some part, to this day, with the same prodigality of vital force, the same struggle for existence and mutual havoc that mark all organized beings from men to mushrooms. Young seedlings in millions spring every summer from the black mould, rich with the decay of those that had preceded them, crowding, choking, and killing one another, perishing by their very abundance—all but a scattered few, stronger than the rest, or more fortunate in position, which survive by blighting those about them. They in turn, as they grow, interlock their boughs, and repeat in a season or two the same process of mutual suffocation. The forest is full of lean saplings dead or dying with vainly stretching toward the light."

That dark and eloquent passage from Francis Parkman's *A Half Century of Conflict* mirrors the feeling the early colonists must have had when facing the wilderness. If it was savage, malignant, and misanthropic toward its own, how must it be toward them! But in the next century, until they began to disappear, the original forest trees of New England were to provide the resource that helped timber-starved Europe to rejuvenate itself. The white pine, *Pinus strobus,* undoubtedly the "great pine" mentioned by Parkman, once occupied vast stretches of coastal and interior New England from Maine down to what is now

Rhode Island and Connecticut. Its stands were complexly associated with hardwoods, and it originally seeded into open meadows, as it still does today.

The white pine was the king of these forests, mature specimens growing from 150 to 200 feet tall. But there were giant sugar maples with trunks of 15 feet in circumference; magnificent 350-year-old hemlocks; and white and red oaks 100 feet tall with branches spreading 150 feet.

These splendid trees are a memory. The present forest, returning after the decline of farming, is only a pale reflection of its former self. At the same time, for anyone like myself who was brought up in New England, the nature, substance, and dimension of the land can be seen as inextricable from the trees. Their roots, their shape, their striving give the land life and, unless we are becoming too spaceless in ourselves to receive them, trees can still provide us with the signals we need in order to recognize the fundamental character of where we live. The trees are continually striving to return to their original stature, to state the complex struggle of life in their own terms, and the effort cannot be ignored.

The crown of England attempted to reserve white pines of a special girth and height for the Royal Navy's masts and spars, which was conservation of a sort, but in time the King's Broad Arrow with which these trees were blazed became a symbol of tyranny and injustice, thus materially contrib-

uting to the Revolution. What the pioneers wanted, and always wanted, was to exploit the seemingly inexhaustible resources ahead of them without interference. Because the white pine grew in areas that were rich in rivers, they could make their way through the primeval forests, cut the trees down, work them toward the water, and float them downstream to be sold. Enormous white pine stands became open clearings. Farms and settlements were established. The wood itself, light and strong, could be used not only for ships but for houses. It could be made into boards and timbers, as well as shingles—a process in which there was enormous waste—and carved into fine woodwork. The brawling lumbermen had their way, helping to fill the American spirit with a wonderfully spontaneous and lusty folklore. The Republic moved toward fortunes in railroads and manufacturing, and after a while there were no more virgin stands of *Pinus strobus* in view.

Since the white man arrived, this great wilderness country has been taken advantage of on a scale that must never have been equaled. Its exploitation has led us from rags to riches and here we are trembling on a precarious height, regarding the ground where the white pines used to flourish, and wondering how far we may have to back down. It is easy to say that our progress is based on American ingenuity and knowhow—but this is not to give enough credit to their sources. If we want to look back and

3 to 5 inch blue green needles 5 to the bunch

4 to 8 inches

Winged Seed

80 to 110 feet in height. Sometimes to 150 feet.

alan E. Cober '79

up to our original strength, there is no better way than to find a white pine.

To the original inhabitants, of course, the wilderness which we set about clearing and taming was not a wilderness at all. Nor did the Indians ever gain power and riches from it in the sense that the white man did. It was their spiritual home in which they lived mutually with all other life, power enough for the long term, in a sense that we have been violently neglecting.

New Hampshire, where I spent much of my boyhood, is tree country, and the white pine, which favors regions of heavy snowfall, is one of its dominant species. I remember one stand, bordering a wooded road, which had been left to grow to considerable height. The pines formed vaulted ranks and aisles like a Gothic cathedral. I looked up and they sang in my spirit as the wind swished through their fine, long needles swinging in the light.

The great hurricane of 1938 (see page 198) cut a swath through inland New England and hit our lakeside area head on. All these cathedral pines and others pluming by the lake shore for a hundred years or more went down like so many matchsticks. My father, who loved trees, came up from New York where he was working to view the damage, sat down by the road and cried. But since this is a land of trees—in the character and quality of the light they are adapted to, and in the cold and stony soil which the old-time farmers cleared and plowed—it is also an irrepressible land.

In some areas where white pines had grown in on abandoned fields and then been knocked down by the hurricane, they were succeeded by an understory of beech trees, with smooth, silvery gray trunks reminiscent of marine fish or shining white birch or sugar maples and ash. Following their pattern, the pines seeded in open clearings and unused pasture lands, taking the opportunity to reclaim thousands of such acres for themselves.

Either as farmland or original forest, these northern hills have exacted their tribute from human beings, certainly their respect. They forced a hard life and cantankerous natures on the natives. The long, dark, snowy winters and the short growing season, to which the trees were to the manner born, are not easy on human dispositions. But at least the people were molded by the place they lived in. As Wendell Berry puts it in his book, *The Unsettling of America:* "If we do not live where we work, and when we work, we are wasting our lives and our work too."

One fall afternoon, I was walking down the lower slopes of a minor mountain. It was toward sundown, and getting much colder. Behind me a screech owl wailed in the shadow of a belt of brilliantly white birch that lay between mixed evergreens and hardwoods. Otherwise the air was still. I walked out into a clearing where there had once been a small farm, with nothing left but a cellar hole, and an open field before it that was crowded with white pine seedlings. Below that, a long stone wall descended by a cold, clear, rocky brook perpetually sounding. I could feel the edges of an overload of freezing air that was about to fall and turn the grasses white. The ground too seemed withheld, waiting in silent strength.

The original house, I knew, had a sometimes grim understanding with the North. A combat had been waged here between life and its limits. People had become close-

mouthed in the process. "Nothing to recommend," I heard them say. But they were centered in time and place, and there was a tall sky and long hills to look out on and remember. Give them credit for the way all seasons indentured them.

They had left their doorstep behind them, a great slab of granite, and a big sugar maple. Its broad beamed trunk, covered with shaggy, deeply ridged, gray bark, stood over their cellar hole like a reliable ancestor and descendant. The field where they had grown corn or vegetables was returning to its original symmetry. The wilderness air had its way. A chorus of crows responded as the cold, rushing waters fell toward the base of the hills. Soon, blue stars would shine out in the well of night. I listened to a silence that followed me away.

There are occasions when you can hear the mysterious language of the Earth, in water, or coming through the trees, emanating from the mosses, seeping through the undercurrents of the soil, but you have to be willing to stand and receive. And there is a planetary silence behind it that defines the unseen quality of existence, as on a day when the New Hampshire white pines —the founders of the United States—are loaded with snow and nothing stirs. They seem to say: "What more do you want to know?" What more, indeed, can we know? We are obligated to greater principles of unity than the ones we impose on "man's" environment.

There was a white pine of fair height standing on a knoll over a little ravine that cut the hillside slopes above the lake, an area where my father introduced many species of rock plants between the granite boulders. It was in that tree that I built a platform from which to view the world along with the red squirrels. I inhaled its resinous scent. The wind blew through the branches, sounding like the sea, and what distant worlds I imagined there I can no longer remember, but the tree sheltered and

encouraged them. White pine wood, soft and clean and easy to cut, also sent me on other voyages. I built a houseboat of it, a flat-bottomed boat with uptilted bow and stern and a cabin. It was powered by a Johnson outboard, or a long oar when the motor failed, with which I drove it slowly forward, and from it I fished for black bass and explored all the inlets and corners of the 11-mile-long lake.

Having the mind of a mole, I built tunnels in the hillside below my tree house. I built trenches there too, being war-minded, and awaited attack. The fringe of woods along the water's edge sounded with the liquid notes of thrushes in the twilight. The lake itself made music with its wavelets most of the year around. They slapped at the timbers of our boat dock, or at the rocks along the shore, and they lipped at the edge of the ice in early winter. At times a stiff wind sprang up to chop the lake's surface to pieces, while at others the waters were wide, limpid, and glassy. I watched thunderstorms come in from the direction of Blue Mountain to the north, and the gathering noble blue-blackness would suddenly roll in overhead and the rain splashed across the lake, which ran with corrugated ripples, while the gods let loose their thunder and their bolts of lightning. If I was caught in the open and there was no time to reach the house, I would go in under the pine for shelter. It is an unfortunate man or woman who has never loved a tree.

I go back to the white pine for its truth, its great architecture of living on. When I used to climb its ladder branches I was only following after. It accommodated me, as it still accommodates the squirrels, the nuthatches, and finches that feed on its seeds, and the airs that invade it whisking off snow in wintertime or, in other seasons, making its needle-loaded branches shake and swing like the plumes of a running ostrich. I shared my original climbing with all trees, and with experience I began to see them as part of the

common community, competing, growing, and dying. (Trees never told you life was easy.) The basic nature of their growth and survival has the closest parallels with all other terrestrial systems. Their ability to survive unending stress shows in engineering that is no less governed by cosmic limits and the laws of attrition than our own. They spiral into adjustment. That the white pine still seizes New Hampshire as its own means it knows the winds of those northern latitudes—that freezing and thawing are built into its endurance, and that its roots know the acid, stony soil as beach grass knows the sand. All its descendants inherit these great attributes. We can be grateful to trees for an incomparable patience.

Keeping the Wilderness

By Edward S. Ayensu

Not long ago I made a botanical search along a portion of Maine's St. John River in the vicinity of Allagash, a village of 456 people that lies between the settlement of Dickey (consisting of some 10 buildings) and the Lincoln school. I was looking for a modest plant, Furbish's lousewort, which is distinguished chiefly by the fact that it is an endangered species. The Army Corps of Engineers seeks to build a dam in this area—the Dickey-Lincoln Dam—and conservationists have cried out that the project would inundate most, if not all, of the plants and they would be lost to us forever.

Feelings about this conflict run high. In a letter to the editor of *Time* magazine, someone wrote, "Imagine the gall of this preposterous plant to halt the construction of a $668 million hydroelectric project like the Dickey-Lincoln Dam in Maine. For heaven's sake, the species was thought extinct anyway—let's make it official and drown it under a few billion gallons of water."

Approval of Dickey-Lincoln project would mean flooding of St. John River, far left, probable extinction of already endangered lousewort. Opposite, aborted development in central Florida creates lonely landscape.

How do you weigh the value of a single plant species against the need for electricity in Maine? Suffice it to say here that Furbish's lousewort is a useful symbol to focus the attention of Americans on their dwindling natural plant and animal resources.

When I left the shores of West Africa for the United States, I was already familiar with the carelessness with which my own people were handling the land. Even as a nature study student in high school, I could see the splendor and fecundity of the tropical vegetation being reduced. I held passionate views about what was being done to the African environment by developers, both foreign and domestic. I was compelled to rationalize that the exploitation of natural resources in developing countries often created unavoidable pressures on the environment. But when I arrived in America and had the opportunity to travel extensively, I instantly became overwhelmed by the extensive and intensive denudation and devastation of this infinitely blessed land. I began to wonder if the inhabitants of this country were really aware of what was being done to their land and souls.

Although I was not born in this country, I feel compelled to offer a thought: You have a beautiful country that is rich in natural and human resources. For two centuries, you and your ancestors have progressively plundered the environment in the name of progress. Lack of sensitivity to the other forms of life that share the environment has resulted in the extinction of many plant and animal species in recent years. A large number of plants, perhaps 10 percent of the native species, are highly vulnerable to extinction and others are daily becoming extremely rare. If progress continues to be measured by the increasing mutilation of the land, we definitely will be condemned by future generations. It is in this context, perhaps, that one might consider the Dickey-Lincoln Dam and other like projects, past and future.

Nature has its own way of maintaining balance in the ecosystem. The long, slow geologic and climatic changes that have taken place on this planet have resulted in the development and migration of new plant species, and favored the extinction of others, leaving associated changes in patterns of distribution and abundance. Among the major natural occurrences that affect plants are the uplift and sinking of land to form mountain ranges and islands, volcanic eruptions, floods, erosion, glaciation, hot and dry periods, droughts, expansion of deserts, succession in lakes and ponds to exclude pioneer and aquatic species, and lightning fires. In addition, natural biotic factors such as newly evolved competitive species, plant diseases, insect

damage, and animal damage from overgrazing and destruction of edible fruits and seeds have played their role. Another factor that should not be overlooked is that when a species becomes very old or senescent, and is reduced to small populations of relicts from floras of older geologic periods, it may suffer genetic depletion or loss of genetic variability and become inbred and unadaptive, or develop narrow specialization that results in its rarity and perhaps extinction. All these factors interact over a very long time and result in some sort of a natural balance and stability within an ecosystem.

Unlike the original inhabitants of this country, today's technologically motivated man has drastically changed the landscape by building great cities, huge dams and power plants, and increasing irrigation, expanding agriculture, draining wetlands to make way for more human settlements and polluting the atmosphere, all of which further threaten

to destroy or modify more of the natural environment.

These large-scale activities have affected plant populations by causing instant death and severe reductions in the number of available plant communities in which a species may survive. Plant habitats are often destroyed outright by the indiscriminate use of bulldozers, flooding, the lowering of water tables, and drainage. Clear-cutting timber operations have produced unfortunate cases of erosion and have rendered original landscapes useless and unsightly.

There are some regions in the United States that have experienced a variety of transformations in unison. One case involves the environmental problems associated with the interior wetlands and saline tidal areas of South Florida.

In the mid- and late '60s, when I taught advanced studies in tropical botany in Florida, I became aware, first hand, of the changes in vegetation that were taking place there. In the Everglades, man has tampered with the natural vegetation despite the establishment of the Everglades National Park. Systematic observations by scientists have shown that, as a result of water level fluctuations, there have been shifts in the location of some species and the loss of others. "Tree islands" of mixed species within the grassy basin have been alternately flooded and burned almost out of existence. Species such as dahoon holly and sweet bay are still to be found in places, but cocoplum, red bay, and wax myrtle have disappeared from many of these islands.

Manipulation of the Everglades has also had a particularly dramatic impact on the animals that occupy such an environment. For example, the alligator populations have been driven into artificial lakes and canals in and around development sites, and it is not uncommon to find 'gators these days on lawns and in swimming pools in residential areas as well as in sewers and even in school yards. As a result of the many pressures on this reptile, game officials in Florida receive well over 8,000 requests annually to remove stray alligators from private property.

In the coastal areas, particularly most of the eastern coast, natural vegetation has been altered drastically—principally through beach erosion. The beach shoreline of the Hobe Sound National Wildlife Refuge near Palm Beach is eroding steadily. The sea has encroached on the land nearly 250 yards since 1940. The strand flora is reputed to be virtually nonexistent, and the stabilizing mangrove forest is being covered by sand and ultimately washed out to sea.

The Big Cypress Swamp system, supporting a major *Taxodium* forest (some of the trees have girths of six feet and reach over 100 feet in height), has been cut over until

the trees are nearly wiped out. The few stunted (though still fairly sizable) cypress trees that remain exhibit reduced growth due to the lowering of the water table caused by overcutting. In other areas that support cypress growth, drainage projects have permitted the development of human habitation and the spread of agriculture to a degree which conservationists question. Some parts of the drained areas have been invaded by slash pine, willow, maple, water oak, and cabbage palm. In the Big Cypress Prairie areas, drainage created excellent conditions for the invasion of persimmon, red bay, oak, and maple into the grass-dominated environment.

The pineland flatwoods in the northeastern and northwestern parts of southern Florida have been severely reduced to a secondary succession pine forest through heavy harvesting, stumping, and fires. Today much of the area, especially the coastal pineland, has been subjected to urban development, and the frequent, hot fires in many suburban pinelands have resulted in the retardation of the native sand pine and slash pine. Efforts are being made to manage what is left, but it is not the same!

By all standards, the hammocks are among the most attractive and interesting areas of South Florida. A climax community, the flora is largely of West Indian origin with representatives of sub-temperate zone species. There are altogether some 150 species of trees as well as many shrubs and vines that inhabit the understory. The high ground of the hammocks attracted human encroachment from the earliest times, and many have since suffered from severe impact to the point of total destruction. Several investigators have reported that fire has caused more irreparable damage to the hammocks than any other agent. A trip through the hammocks in the Everglades National Park will give any nature lover a disquieting knowledge of the destructive powers of fire. For example, the hammocks in western Monroe and Collier counties and those in the Fahkahatchee Strand have been ruthlessly fired and mercilessly vandalized to such a degree that many rare orchids such as the inconspicuous, miniature *Polyrhiza lindenii*, and other plant species have virtually disappeared. Today, a few places on Indian sites in the mangrove areas, a few mahogany hammocks, and the southern end of Paradise Key are the only remaining sites that resemble the original virgin forests. But even in these areas many of the original species are wanting.

Equally disturbing is the condition of the woodlands of the state of Tennessee. Originally this state was heavily covered with forests, and "explorers" not only shot or trapped the wolf, fox, lynx, otter, mink, and beaver, but subjected the flora to equivalent abuse. More recently, in the middle of Tennessee within the open cedar glades, a number of plant species have been destroyed by the flooding of Priest Lake. Others in the surrounding areas have largely disappeared because of development projects including housing schemes and industrial complexes. Today there are at least 19 plants in central Tennessee that are rare or endangered because of the destruction of their natural habitats. The most unfortunate aspect of such wanton destruction is that threatened plants such as the cedar-glade fameflower, Tennessee milkvetch, Gattinger's prairie clover, and Nashville breadroot constitute a unique plant assemblage that occurs nowhere else in the world but the Central Basin of Tennessee.

In the Southern Appalachians, a region harboring numerous rare species peculiar to the area, a tree was found in 1975 that since 1915 had been thought to be extinct. The Virginia round-leaf birch was located, after repeated searches, in rural Smyth County, Virginia. There a population of 15 plants exists mostly on privately owned land adjacent to the Jefferson National Forest. The initial publicity of discovery resulted in successful attempts at theft and vandalism, but the trees are now officially protected under the Endangered Species Act of 1973 with the eager cooperation of the local landowner, and they are being propagated by the National Arboretum in Washington, D.C.

To proceed westward to the mid-United States, one may say with due reverence to all the amazing landscapes in America that none is so imposing—and entirely different in composition and history from the eastern environment—as the prairie. At one time, about one-third of the United States was dominated by a cover of tall, medium, and short prairie grasses. When I first saw the prairie about 13 years ago, the seeming emptiness between the blue sky and unbelievable

Endangered round-leaf birch, Betula uber, *below, survives behind seven-foot fence on ranger-protected Virginia forest land. Rangers' wars on poachers in 1960s helped ensure alligators' recovery in Everglades National Park.*

stretch of grassland invoked a feeling of monotony. This, I found out in my later readings, was not a unique experience. When the *Boston Courier* journalist J.H. Buckingham traveled by stagecoach from Peoria to Springfield with then-Congressman Abraham Lincoln, he described the prairie as follows: "For miles we saw nothing but a vast prairie of what can compare to nothing else but the ocean itself. The tall grass, interspersed occasionally with fields of corn, looked like the deep sea; it seemed as if we were out of sight of land, for no house, no barn, no tree was visible, and the horizon presented the rolling of waves in the afar-off distance. There were all sorts of flowers—as if the sun were shining upon the gay and dancing waters."

But the prairie is not as monotonous as it first appears. Mixed into the surviving pure examples of each kind of grassland are several species of other original grassland plants known collectively as "forbs." Today a selective trip through Illinois will give you the pleasure of seeing what the prairie was like many years ago. This is because several prairie conservationists are now trying to salvage these unique communities. For example, Robert Betz, a biology professor at Northeastern Illinois University, and his colleagues have been working to conserve the Gensburg-Markham Prairie, a 100-acre undisturbed tract of land lying between the Tri-State Tollway and south suburban residential development in the Chicago area. Betz points out that 200 years ago, when the first settlers arrived in that area, much of the vegetation and landscape was prairie. There are other preserves near Chicago, such as the 80-acre Wolf Road Prairie in the suburb of Westchester, which has been given special attention since 1974 by volunteers of the Save the Prairie Society. The many conservation groups working with the Illinois Department of Conservation have helped create various prairie parks for public viewing. Some noteworthy ones include Belmont Prairie in DuPage County, Fults Hill Prairie in Monroe County, Goose Lake Prairie in Grundy County, Harlem Hills Nature Preserve in Winnebago County, Peacock Prairie in Cook County, and Ayers Sand Prairie in Carroll County. Within these preserves one is likely to see several species of orchids, orange lilies, blue gentians, pink phlox, yellow sunflowers, and many prairie grasses. The

buffalo grass and *Spartina* grass that form continuous turfs may literally be direct descendants of an organically united clone-line from the very plants that took possession of the Great Plains when the great glacial retreat occurred thousands of years ago. These grasses, which propagate by stolons or rhizomes, may be characterized as a physically "eternal" plant-to-plant lineage that forms large colonies covering extensive areas of the Great Plains. They are contemporaneous with the giant redwoods (*Sequoia gigantea*) of the Mariposa Grove in the state of California.

The major effort that the state of Illinois is making to conserve and preserve some of the original prairie lands is unfortunately not being repeated in other states. Much of the prairie in the United States, particularly tall grass prairie, has been converted into agriculture; there are no representatives of this type of tall grass prairie within the national park system. However, there are areas, such as the Flint Hills of Kansas, that still have examples of tall grass prairie consisting of tall bluestem grass, Indian grass, and switch grass. Found among these grasses are such wildflowers as the downy prairie phlox, larkspur, bird's-foot violet, wild indigo, black-eyed Susan, and verbena. Ironically, the Flint Hills represent ideal grounds for the fattening of cattle. Kansas state conservationists have always contended that cattle grazing, and not farming, has been the major factor in the destruction of the tall grass prairie.

Many of the cattlemen, and those who own land coveted by gas and oil producers, have opposed any moves by the Kansas legislators and the Congress of the United States to convert any prairie grazing grounds into nature preserves. It seems disquieting to think that of over 52.5 million acres of land in the state of Kansas, nearly 20 million acres are used principally for grazing. Yet the slightest encroachment on the remaining land for the establishment of nature reserves is vehemently opposed by the cattlemen.

Al Bohling in *National Parks & Conservation Magazine* reported that, of the remaining tall grass prairie in Kansas, perhaps the finest examples can be found in parts of Chase, Lyon, Butler, and Greenwood counties. However, during the mid-1950s, the development of the Kansas Turnpike, running from Kansas City to Wichita and Oklahoma, made inroads into this once undisturbed region.

The story of the disappearing prairie and the loss of other plant life through excessive grazing has occurred elsewhere in the United States, including in the state of Texas. The once abundant grama grass that covered many ranges is now substantially reduced and has been replaced by inferior

No living man will see again the long-grass prairie, where a sea of prairie flowers lapped at the stirrups of the pioneer . . . .

—Aldo Leopold

In the foothills of the San Juan Colorado Mountains, not yet touched by the plow, grasses thrive at an altitude of 9,000 feet.

species such as needle grass. Studies begun in the early 1920s reported the disappearance of the tall bunch grasses and their replacement by short grasses, woody plants, and less palatable or even toxic forbs.

It is not only the prairie grasses that have been subjected to destruction and subsequent disappearance. Many forest trees and shrubs have suffered similar abuses. When Columbus and his men saw the forests of the Caribbean for the first time, he could not help but make a note in his diary that described the forest sites as "stretching to the stars with leaves never shed." Much of what the original settlers of different parts of the United States saw has been cut down, and the once astounding stands of natural vegetation have now been reduced to patches of disjointed secondary forests inundated with the results of human "developments" established in the name of progress. Many of the most familiar types of forest trees throughout the land are represented by endangered and threatened species, including among their number species of cypress, birch, chestnut, oak, walnut, willow, maple, holly, magnolia, ash, cottonwood, alder, and plum.

The animals that coexist with forest vegetation are also obviously affected. The whooping crane, the California condor, and the bald eagle, which are among the rarest birds in the world, suffer because of the clearance of their nesting and roosting sites and are therefore endangered. Recently the U.S. Forest Service was able to acquire a 240-acre stretch of private timberland in Klamath County, Oregon, representing the largest known eagle roosting site in the United States outside of Alaska. It is used nightly by nearly 300 bald eagles. Such acquisitions will naturally encourage the population levels to increase. The condor's situation is more precarious. So far gone is its wild canyonland environment that attempts will be made to capture some of the remaining handful of birds and breed them in captivity. This is, of course, a measure of desperation.

The revelations of the destruction of what was once the splendor and grandeur of the forests can be equally matched with the destruction of one of the most marvelous spectacles in the land. These are the vernal pools, pools of water that occur sporadically in grasslands of California's Central Valley and no other place in the world except Oregon and the Cape Province of South Africa. In early spring these pools are ringed with beautiful flowering plants exhibiting most of the colors of the rainbow. They teem with waterfowl. Some of the plants that ring the vernal pools include species of goldfields, meadowfoam, and popcorn flower, as well as unusual

grasses such as *Neostapfia* and *Orcuttia*. In their study of California's vernal pools Robert Holland and Thomas Griggs observed that some pools are large and deep enough to support the growth of perennial species such as *Eleocharis macrostachya* and rarities such as *Legenere limosa* and *Orthocarpus succulentus*.

The survival of the vernal pools has been a major concern for both researcher and conservationist. It has been estimated that 40 percent of the valley has the potential to support vernal pools. But the continuous agricultural development program in the Central Valley has taken over millions of acres of land for the production of over 200 different kinds of crops. Currently most of the pools are found on the older terrace soils along the eastern side of the Great Valley. Besides the threat of agriculture, some vernal pool sites have been taken over by urban and industrial development because such sites are considered unprofitable for agriculture due to the closeness of the hardpan layer to the surface soil. More insidious forces of destruction are the numerous flood control projects which dot the foothills of the northern California mountains. Though some vernal pools have been officially preserved, the new reservoirs, built to increase the efficiency of water distribution systems for irrigation, will certainly affect the last remaining stands of native California grassland and their pools.

Another distinctive ecological entity that has been under constant threat and danger is the desert habitat of the cactus. Lyman Benson of Pomona College says that of the 268 taxa of native cacti, 27 "are so rare or restricted in occurrence as to be vulnerable to extinction." There are some cacti, such as the prickly pear, that are hardy and adaptable, but most species are highly specialized in their requirements for soil composition and slope of the land; as a result, they can only survive in "narrowly limited habitat niches that provide the exacting living conditions they require."

The major threats to the survival of these curious plants are commercial exploitation of the rare species, the over-zealous collecting of low-growing species, the construction of housing projects in areas where rare and elusive species occur, the conversion of cactus habitats to agricultural farmlands, and to some extent grazing and fire. Benson postulated that because the effects of housing construction, agriculture, grazing, and fire are difficult to control except on rather limited bases, the only feasible avenue to assure the survival and the preservation of especially the small, rare species, is to prevent or at least reduce commercial exploitation and indiscriminate collecting.

The harsh shriek of the panther's mating call still echoes in the Everglades, now home of only a dozen or so. Opposite: Another haven for wildlife disappears as clear-cutting ravages redwood forest in central California.

The insatiable appetite of those who have been changing the complexion of the environment in the United States has not been confined to the lower 48 states. The Alaska environment has recently been under heavy attack (see page 252). The state of Hawaii, on the other hand, has been subjected to untold abuse since 1778, when Captain James Cook discovered the islands. The native vegetation, representing more than 2,500 flowering plants, of which 96 percent are found nowhere else in the world, has been reduced by nearly half. Substantial portions of the major islands, once resplendent with native vegetation, have now been upholstered with concrete and steel, and much of the rest has been reduced to agricultural farmlands. What represents the lush, tropical vegetation in Hawaii today is, for the most part, not native. The famous orchids, plumeria, and flowering ginger are all introduced as are many of the islands' birds. Efforts are now being made to preserve the vanishing native species, but the uniqueness of the islands will continue to diminish if current developmental and forestry practices continue. A major change in Hawaiian attitudes is necessary (see page 90).

One can perceive, however, behind the dreary fugue of habitat destruction, a tentative melody of hope. On the whole the United States is developing a conservation mentality, committing itself to the preservation of some of its remaining landscapes, to the perpetuation of what took millions of years to create. Recently an insignificant fish, the snail darter, caused the Tennessee Valley Authority to pause in a headlong rush to build a new hydroelectric dam in Tennessee. And in *pausing* to reflect on the project, the builders found that the dam was after all uneconomic. Perhaps Miss Furbish's nondescript lousewort and other insignificant creatures—now that we have found them on the brink of vanishing—will serve to make us pause and reflect in similar ways on our present course.

Dame Sylvia Crowe, a former President of the British Institute of Landscape Architects, said in 1962 that the attempts being made to save the American landscape are a discouragingly small "effort compared to the vast forces of destruction, but because it is a positive ideal as opposed to a negative, it has a cumulative strength of all living things which must in the end prevail against inertia." In concluding she noted: "If this present civilization does not perish, it will be because it has found the way to create a new ecology combining the emanation of men's skill and brains with the ecology of organic nature and has learned to fashion from this new landscape a world within which men can function not merely as economic units, but as men."

Men now begin to realize what as wandering shepherds they had before dimly suspected, that man has a right to the use, not the abuse, of the products of nature . . . .

–George Perkins Marsh

Rare red pitcher plant, Rubra saracenia, *above, unfolds in bogs, savannas of Georgia and Carolinas. Conservationists fear disappearance of California's vernal pools, opposite, which flourish with life after rainfalls.*

The Ebb and Flow of Species

By S. Dillon Ripley

Autumn weather on our bird farm in the rolling Berkshires of Connecticut brings crisp evenings, the early reddening of the maples, and a sense of restless movement in the air. I have a love-hate feeling about the autumn, a wistful sense of nostalgia for the summer inexorably past, but a renewed sense of briskness, even of purpose. Now, in the late 1970s, skeins of Canada geese appear early each evening—15 or more flying low, raising a matching hubbub from our own geese on the ponds below. Often a small group of passersby will circle and drop in, sideslipping with startling acrobatic grace to land and yelp and shout and stretch necks and flap wings with our resident birds.

But most of the geese are higher, often in much larger groups, their ululations ringing wildly, echoing through the hills. Sometimes in the deeper blue haze long after sunset, we cannot really see them, but only hear the wild calls that trail away faintly, stirring the blood, evoking thoughts of times long past, of other days and distant places on the land.

It was not always so in our corner of northwestern Connecticut. When I started keeping wildfowl there in the 1930s, there was only one resident flock of 50 or more geese on nearby Bantam Lake, descendants of captive-reared birds put out by the White Foundation. By the 1940s, these birds had drifted away to join the feral flocks on Long Island Sound. The winters were harsher then for a spell of years, and winter feeding had stopped on the lake. But now we have a quantity of geese, coming and going over Connecticut, far more, I suppose, than in the last 100 years. Flocks of Canadas may be seen on golf courses in the summer, occasionally husbanding their young over the greens—much to the dismay of golfers who often complain of skidding on the fresh droppings. So the fish and game people must spend a good deal of their time these summers answering complaints and even live-trapping geese to move them to some more remote body of water where they will not contaminate suburbia.

What is interesting is that there is no real stability in all of this. Growing up in one part of the country, you might have supposed that Canada geese, if they passed through your land, were a fixture. If you had grown up in parts of North Carolina or near the St. Mark's Wildlife Refuge in the panhandle of Florida, for example, you might assume that Canada geese in great numbers were still a winter phenomenon, their flocks passing over in the hundreds if not thousands. But it would not be so. The shift from spring plowing to fall and early winter plowing for corn in the coastal lake areas of North Carolina in the 1950s meant that dropped cobs and corn kernels all but vanished from the winter fields from there down into northern Florida. The result has been that although a few thousand birds still linger, the vast majority, well over 1,000,000, winter along the shores of Chesapeake Bay, Maryland, Delaware, and Virginia, where spring plowing still prevails, and abundant kernels and dropped cobs lie on the autumn fallow fields. There is a local cycle everywhere. In colonial times these birds had other patterns across our land. In nature nothing is fixed, nothing is static. Change is all around us, although the changes may be imperceptible in the course of a generation. It is human nature to like things to stay the same, even if it is not a fact of nature.

Gregarious purple martin, left, stakes out claim to efficiency apartment. Originally nesters in tree and cliff cavities, martins seem to prefer man-made shelters, return to same each spring. Opposite: Canada geese glean Connecticut field near Secretary Ripley's home, en route to the Chesapeake Bay.

The chestnut-sided warbler, now a familiar migrant in the eastern states, breeding in the northern third of our country, was a rarity in John Audubon's time. We do not know exactly why. Birds that today like thickets and hedgerows might not have found as many a century and a half ago. I do not know. But it is evident that conditions change continually and not always because of the hand of man.

Climate shifts inexorably. Birds and other vertebrate animals shift too, even the warm-blooded migratory species whose mobility and thermal insulating powers give them an opportunity to exploit environments opened up by the retreat of the ice and glaciers of the northern latitudes in the past 10,000 years. The whooping crane is a good example of a powerful species with a potential for exploration of new habitats. Never very common, even in such records as we have of the time before the incursion of the white man, these huge, splendid birds, white with black flight feathers and a splash of red on the forehead and face, were scattered sparingly across our land in savanna country, open prairies, and shallow swamps along the southern tier of states and from the Gulf to the Canadian prairie provinces.

With the arrival of the white man in the southern and central states and the prairies, the range of the whooping crane began to shrink all but imperceptibly. On the other hand, the smaller sandhill or "Canada" crane, which Audubon confused with the whooping crane, has apparently been far more abundant than its large cousin throughout our recorded knowledge of the continent. It did not suffer, therefore, from the relatively marginal effects of modern man's agriculture and the hunting pressures brought when guns replaced bows and arrows. (Wary to a fault, neither species could be shot in numbers as could ducks and geese.) Why then did the whooping crane gradually dwindle away? We know only that its numbers began to decline. Agriculture and incidental shooting combined must have taken some toll by reducing available nesting areas and driving the wary birds away from former ranges. In any event, at the beginning of this century, whooping cranes were already uncommon—rare enough to become an early symbol of vanishing species, though not necessarily one to be ascribed to man's intervention.

Two remnant populations survived through World War I. One lived along the marshes of the eastern edge of the Texas Gulf Coast and in western coastal Louisiana. The other group wintered in mid-Gulf coastal areas of Texas and seemed to vanish each spring somewhere into the blue—as we now know, into the far north via the Platte River and Saskatchewan. Only recently, with the advent of small pros-

pecting airplanes, was that remnant's secret destination revealed in the muskeg pools north of Great Slave Lake. This population was indeed a *remnant*. Being exploratory, this small group had instinctively edged itself as far north as a brief summer cycle would allow. This must be a very recent development, placing the birds at the very limit of tolerance for nesting, egg laying, hatching, and fledging their young—so much at the limit that both eggs laid in each nest can seldom ever be reared. Climate alone would see to that, in addition to the innate hostility expressed by the chick of the first egg to hatch for its smaller, later sibling. The race in that climate is, indeed, to the strong: The second chick virtually never survives.

Birds tend to evolve constantly toward economy; it pays off when migration is a fact of life. Lightness, quick absorption of fat supplies for flight—everything about a migratory bird must be fine-honed for survival. Why then should the northernmost remnant of whooping cranes still cling to the tradition that each pair, having managed to fly to the farthermost tundra having the most marginal nesting and growing season, still lay two eggs when one would do? Only, I think, because this surviving population is at risk. They were farthest north virtually by accident. If the weather changed and the first egg to be hatched froze or the chick starved, there might still be better weather in a week or so, permitting the second to hatch successfully.

By World War II the survival of the whooping crane was a matter of considerable concern. Then in 1949 a coastal hurricane killed all of Louisiana's resident population except for one wing-crippled survivor, which was rescued, christened "Josephine," and placed in the New Orleans zoo. In subsequent years concern continued to mount, bird experts were consulted, and now a full-fledged campaign to save the whooping crane, largely under federal U.S. and Canadian supervision, is showing results. There are at present close to 100 whooping cranes at liberty and in captive breeding programs, giving an early promise for the future. This is one example of man's ability to pull a species back from the brink.

Other cycles across the land have been different. Some species pass over an invisible threshold and become extinct. Some are only thought to be rare and may reappear without apparent reason. The passenger pigeon, whose annual flights darkened the sky in Audubon's time in the south central states, and whose corpses, killed by market hunters, supplied meat for major cities of the eastern and midwestern states, suddenly dwindled at the end of the 19th century. The market for the birds as food had vanished by the early years of this century, but instead of recovering, the species became extinct, even though individuals could be bred in captivity as can any other dove or pigeon. None of the theories of why this happened has been proven so far.

One theory is that it was a mass phenomenon: The population could not survive unless the nesting colonies were enormous, thus providing the mutual enhancement of noise and the group hysteria necessary for mating. Flamingos, for example, like to breed in clusters where the squabbling and mating-display sounds and visions seem to enhance the process of nest building and egg production. But this can also be accomplished in small groups of flamingos. Collective sexual excitement may be generated by a dozen or more birds in a colony. So it would seem illogical to assume that a colony of a few hundred passenger pigeons might not keep the species going, once human hunting pressure had evaporated. No real explanation for their decline appeared. The passenger pigeon, under pressure, was fated to keep on going down even after the pressure was removed. The last survivor died in the Cincinnati Zoo in 1914, a mournful reminder of the dwindling riches of America's land, one of some seven North American bird species now gone from us.

As some species go, others may survive by accident. Eighty years ago egrets, the lovely white marsh birds with delicate plumes and trains of lacy feathers carried over the back and rump in the breeding season, were on their way out. It was the era of ladies' fancy hats, and the plume trade stretched around the world in a hysteria of high fashion. Nesting in the southern and Gulf states, the egrets seemed doomed. Breeding colonies were decimated; adults were killed just as their young were in the nest, thus killing off two generations at a time. Eventually public opinion turned against the plume trade as society became aware of the profligacy that it represented. Today, egrets and herons of all kinds have made a comeback, nesting along our coasts and rivers in more northern latitudes than were recorded 100 years ago.

Meanwhile, in the last 30 years a new heron has arrived in the United States, the cattle egret, a smaller white heron about the size of our native snowy or lesser egret, with a brownish suffusion of feathers, particularly about the head, in the nesting season. This is an Asian and African species and there is no sure evidence of how it arrived here. First seen in 1950 in the Everglades, it was noticed in fields near cattle, the birds' preferred habitat in its African and Asian homelands. Presumably it reached South America on favorable trade winds from Africa via the Canary Islands in the 1870s,

Sluggish waters, sawgrass flats, and mangrove thickets in Everglades National Park form an ecosystem, Grand Central Terminal, for diverse subtropical bird life. Black skimmer, opposite left, and egret, opposite above, fish in the tea-colored waters. Right, cattle egrets feed on flies that pester beasts.

for there had been a few records from the Guianas, thought at the time to have been escapees from a zoo or tropical botanical garden. But how can we explain the species' sudden explosion? In the last 30 or 40 years it has spread all over the South and seems to march farther north each nesting season, already reaching the Canadian border. What has it found to like about our land?

Why are there such cycles of abundance and scarcity? The whole history of the land—and the constant succession of forms in which its users appear—is involved. Plant life of all kinds plays a part, creating intricate mosaics of successive stages for insects, which in turn provide new opportunities for foragers, from the small to large, all intertwining in their degrees of dependence one upon the other. All we know is that the appearance, decline, and sometimes reappearance of species of animals is a direct function of the natural environment. But what is "natural"? The definition of the word eludes us. Taken together, the cycles of the land, as pointed out elsewhere in this book, represent a continually developing series of events over millennia, over recent centuries, over the last 300 years of man's *effect* upon those cycles, and now finally over the last decades of intensive exploitation.

The saga of recent times has been told over and over. In the past 30 years most of us in America have been made aware of the dangers implicit in unmeasured use of chemicals, thanks to the foresighted writings of William Vogt, Fairfield Osborn, and Rachel Carson. The last named especially, with her elegiac prose, stirred up Americans in a manner perhaps not equaled since the turn of the century. This awareness found public expression in the outpouring of environmental protection legislation during the 1960s. There is a general sensitivity to the dangers to our environment which has become endemic in us. For the better, I think, we are all alerted to the necessity for controls and qualitative testing of new techniques of land use and development, and to the dangers of exploitation without regeneration. Measure for measure, the land is used and must be used for productive purposes if we are to continue to support ourselves. But we know now that it must be done rationally and with foresight. Planning comes hard in our lives. Prudence has not been a virtue in the history of this country.

Something of what birds tell us about our own lives is encouraging for the future. The use of pesticides has come under regulation in America; many of the most toxic have been abandoned. The decline in uncontrolled pesticide use has shown that species once threatened with extinction can come back. Predators like falcons, eagles, and ospreys are particularly vulnerable, as we learned nearly too late in their case. As pinnacles of a food chain, they absorb DDT residues that accumulate in the liver and fat deposits of individual birds and render them relatively sterile, if not killing them outright. But they can make a comeback with time! How miraculous it is to find an eagle's nest with living young along the coast of Maine, when for 15 years before that pair of eagles may have faithfully continued laying infertile eggs. The decline of pesticide use has allowed such long-lived birds to weather the cycle and outlast it.

Not all species will survive, however. Only recently we have had the sorry truth brought home to us that many of our North American birds, beloved by those who love the land, do not really belong to us, nor can we preserve them even if we have the mind to. Perhaps two thirds of the breeding pairs of birds of many North American forests migrate elsewhere a good part of the year. The Smithsonian Institution has held two seminars on the subject of bird migration into adjacent countries to the south of our own land, in 1966 and again in 1977. Ecologists and ornithologists have gradually compiled evidence that the "silent spring" of which Rachel Carson wrote is likely to happen to our own land because of what is happening elsewhere. John Terborgh of Princeton University has shown that more than 150 landbird species of our forests leave an area of some 16,200,000 square kilometers (6,250,000 square miles) of territory in North America south of the tree line, and funnel into a combined area of only 2,175,000 square kilometers (840,000 square miles) in Mexico, the Bahamas, Cuba, and Hispaniola, wintering in an area about one seventh the size of their northern breeding zone. More than half of this available land in Central America and the Greater Antilles has already been denuded of forest and converted to cropland and pasture. The remaining forests are being cleared at a rate of a few percent a year, so that woodland habitat for these arboreal birds will have disappeared by the end of the century.

Availability of food is, of course, the dominant aspect of such birds' survival. As one travels south in the forest and savanna of Central America, the evidence indicates that insect food occurs in woody habitats, northerly in the lowlands and more southerly in the mid-level highlands—the very areas preferred for cattle and agriculture. Thus 32 warbler species including the Blackburnian, black-throated green, and cerulean will be the first to disappear. Along with the warblers, Terborgh lists six species of flycatcher, three thrush species, the blue-gray gnatcatcher, and four vireo species known to winter in mature tropical forests. These all are typical and major features of our forest bird life. There is little hope for halting their decline. The demands for firewood, charcoal, building materials, and even range for goats seem relentless. Some countries such as El Salvador, Haiti, and Jamaica have already reached a human population density of 150 per square kilometer (390 per square mile) in the rural areas. This is a threshold at which all semblance of forests soon disappears. Nor is reforestation an answer unless it is undertaken at a level of sophistication which has not so far been reached. Practically all reforestation in the tropics today consists of the introduction of single species of trees, a system termed "monoculture" by planners. Such environments are typically barren of birds, presumably for the reason that they are lacking in insect variety. Only a revolution in forestry techniques can hold any promise for the future.

This does not mean that, in time, no species of birds will be found in our woodlands. There will probably be as many birds in the foreseeable future, but the composition of species will change. Versatile types will survive; other less adaptable species will decline or gradually disappear. A number of ornithologists have recently studied bird populations in forest remnants in Delaware, Maryland, and selected tracts in the District of Columbia. Since the 1950s, migratory species

have declined steadily and year-round resident species have declined slightly. There are a variety of reasons: housing development; cutting down of undisturbed woodland; high-density occupation of parks by tourists, resident bicyclists, horseback riders, and picnickers; reduction of undergrowth; and general urban untidiness and overuse. The same is true of any American metropolitan area.

What is to happen to our land? It has been a dilemma for generations, ever since the end of the last century when John Muir and John Burroughs sounded the alarm over the endless felling of forests. Since that rallying cry, millions of acres all over our land have been set aside as forests, national parks, reserves, wilderness areas, and wetlands. Much of this land is safe, though much has been eroded in the passage of time by compromise decisions on use, ranging from the search for forest products and mineral exploitation to outdoor recreation. Much of this happens gradually so that the erosion, like the gradual disappearance of robins on our lawns, is simply not noticed. Memory is fleeting, and conscience becomes onerous even for those who hold responsibilities for the land.

Ecology is still little understood as a science. To many, it seems inexact because of the complexities of the quantifi-

Martha, left, the last passenger pigeon, died at the age of 29 in 1914. Screech owl, far left, has nocturnal habits, acute hearing and vision, and protective coloration, which add up to survival. Opposite, Blackburnian warbler by Robert Ridgway, Smithsonian curator of birds, 1880–1929.

123

cation process. Most other branches of the biological sciences are governed by procedures of analysis which are well defined, quantifiable, and follow set patterns. Ecological experiments and the gathering of the necessary evidence take too long. A plant succession study and the measurement of all the chemical and physical changes involved may take 15 years. No government agency or business corporation wants to make an investment of time or money in such a monotonous and prolonged process. We like a "quick fix" in America; a 15-year experiment totally lacks charisma.

If there is one thing certain, however, it is that we are going to have to live with ecology as a science. We are capable of learning many ways of redressing the balances which we have upset. In due course we shall find many ways of improving our lot. Progress in development must go hand in hand with the preservation of as much of our natural environment as possible as a program of protection for mankind itself in the future. The more species irreversibly counted out, the more chance there is that we have reduced some of our own necessary "surround," the complex of environmental factors which makes for human survival.

At present there is a movement in ecology to study what is called the minimum critical size of environments. How *much*

Bald eagle, left, endangered symbol of America, finds respite at Blackwater, Maryland, wildlife refuge. Sandhill cranes, above and opposite, against New Mexico sky. Captive breeding of cranes holds high priority at Smithsonian's Conservation and Research Center, Front Royal, Virginia.

of a particular habitat is required to produce living space and food for a group of species which can then survive genetically? When does inbreeding, for example, destroy the viability of a population? Much of the pioneering work in this line of inquiry has been carried out on tropical islands such as Barro Colorado in Panama where the Smithsonian Tropical Research Institute is located.

Interesting experiments are now being conducted in tracts of woodland in the Atlantic states to determine what the minimum critical size can be for a breeding population of forest animals. As is true of islands in the ocean, there appears to be a direct correlation between successful breeding of woodland species and the existence of forest fragments which can be as small as 35 acres in extent—*if* (and the "if" is crucial) such small areas are subsidized by nearby larger forests connected to the fragments by corridors of forest, or only separated by short distances. Thus large tracts of forest are critical to the preservation of maximum biotic diversity.

Bird species will continue to wax and wane in numbers and kind just as they have over millennia of natural change. Speeding the process of change with unplanned technology is unfair, dangerous to ourselves in the long run, and unnecessary to boot. We owe it to the glorious evidences of successful life around us to show that we are ingenious in saving such unique creation.

Listening to the calls of the geese in the evening, I can visualize the ebb and flow of life in its cycles of abundance and change. I would have it so. If Canada geese decline in Connecticut in the next years, I will be content if I know they have moved, but not if they have ceased to exist. Let them go from my sight if need be, but not from the world's sight. There is poetry in the evidence of creation, the sounds and color, the kaleidoscopic variety of species. Their diversity is evidence that we, too, are alive and, we may hope, that the world is a better place because of our presence as well.

Photographs by William Albert Allard

Numbered among the inhabitants of the land must be the singular people who seek a life for themselves where range animals and predators contend for survival. This story by William A. Douglass, also author of the following story on ranching, recounts a decisive day in the life of a fictional, but nonetheless real, Basque sheepherder.

—Editor's Note

A Sheepherder's Tale

It was late spring as Joaquin, a Basque sheepherder from Vizcaya in the Spanish Pyrenees, cinched his horse's saddle and whistled to his sheepdog Beltza. The first rays of morning sun splashed across the foothills of eastern Nevada. In the distance there was the tinkling of bells, the high-pitched cries of frantic young lambs and the deeper answering calls of ewes temporarily separated from their offspring.

He shouted *aurrera!* to Beltza, and the dog flashed by him into the undergrowth. Shortly, the bleating of the lead ewes, startled by the nipping and barking, told Joaquin that the band would soon be under control.

His task completed, Beltza stood to one side, panting slightly and eyeing Joaquin expectantly. Joaquin spoke with the dog about the plan for the day—rather than at him as the city dweller might address a pet. His conversation with Beltza made him aware that he was once again adjusting to a sheepherder's life of solitude.

He was pleased to note that his mental transition from the world of men was almost completed, for even after 12 years as a herder it was a painful process. Yet he was disturbed by the thought that it had been almost too easy. With each passing year it was becoming more difficult for him to leave the mountains in autumn than to enter them in the spring.

The thought startled him, and he forced himself to recall his reactions to the presence of people during this year's lambing, shearing, and docking. The April lambing had left little time to reflect. The outfit was shorthanded and the weather had been treacherous. Weary from lack of sleep, Joaquin, the little Peruvian herder Manuel, and the boss and his wife had worked 'round the clock to save as many lambs as possible.

Shearing was a more relaxed occasion, one of easy activity for the herder. The shearers were Mexicans who removed the fleeces in no-nonsense fashion, as they were

Snow lingering on Nevada highlands at end of April—one month before Joaquin's story takes place—supplies moisture for range. Sheepherder, opposite, rides out early to "chause 'em," keep track of flock.

paid on a piecework basis, and the whole operation seemed to be measured more in terms of seconds than minutes.

Engaged in such thoughts, Joaquin realized that for some time he had been aware of his boss's approach. The boss, Michel, a French Basque, greeted him curtly with *kaixo,* hello. He was a large man, powerfully built, and with stamina and quickness that belied his 75 years. He had first come to the American West to herd sheep in 1921 and liked to belabor his favorite subject—life in the old days before pickup trucks made the herder's lot more tolerable.

Joaquin's interest quickened when Michel spoke again. The Echeverrias had just sold their ranch, disgusted by their years of dispute with the Bureau of Land Management over their winter range rights on the public lands. The Iturrolas had sold their three sheep bands because of last year's severe coyote kills. They planned to convert to cattle.

Michel decided that it was time to count the sheep, so Joaquin and Beltza bunched them tightly. In the open, without benefit of corrals, it was a delicate and difficult task. Joaquin knew from a daily check of his 40 blacks and 30 belled sheep that he had not lost any stray bunches along the way, but there had been coyote kills.

As the last animal flashed by, Michel's face contracted into a frown. Two ewes and 138 lambs were unaccounted for! He complained loudly, almost argumentatively, that the situation was becoming impossible. Expenses were going up, grazing fees were increasing, lamb and wool prices were the same, and now this. Last year the outfit had lost over 500 animals to predators and this year promised to be worse. He could no longer meet his mortgage payments—the hell with it!

That afternoon Joaquin was troubled as he trailed his sheep deeper into the mountains. Preoccupied, he scarcely noticed the passage of time, and he was almost startled

to see the familiar grove of cottonwoods that would be his base for the next few days. For the first time that he could remember, his own camp seemed forbidding to him. So he walked among the cottonwoods looking at the Picassoesque figures that earlier herders had serrated into the trunks. One tree in particular held his attention. Crisply delineated in the soft bark was the surname Iturralde. Below it was carved a series of dates, 10 consecutive years, a living record of an annual sojourn in this grove of trees. The last entry was not numerical, but rather the simple statement *Nunca más,* never again!

Joaquin ran his fingertips over the rough scars of Iturralde's carvings, and then realized that he had made a decision. He whistled to Beltza and headed for camp to prepare supper. Despite his uneasiness with town life and his lack of English, next fall—after his lambs were shipped—he would move to Elko and look for a job. It was over.

The Last Range War

By William A. Douglass

When one speaks of endangered species it is common to think solely in terms of wildlife. However, if the definition is broadened to include lifestyles, then there is probably no "species" on the western range in more imminent danger of extinction than the Basque sheepherder and the way of life that he represents.

Open-range sheep husbandry is essentially a frontier activity, requiring access to vast amounts of rangeland. As the frontier matures and becomes something else, the sheepman finds it increasingly difficult to operate. If in 1970 there were still 1,500 men under contract to the Western Range Association, a sheep ranchers' organization which imports foreign herders, by 1976 their numbers had been halved to 750.

These statistics mask two trends of interest to the region's heritage. First, sheep husbandry is itself declining as sheepmen switch to cattle or get out of ranching altogether.

Second, Basques, long the ethnic mainstay of the industry, are disappearing from the ranks of the remaining herders. Of the men under contract in 1970 over 90 percent were Basques, whereas of the remaining 750 herders about one in six is a Basque (Peruvians now predominate, followed by Mexican nationals).

Joaquin's story is, of course, a "point-of-view" description

Sheep straggle down hill to Indian Creek camp of IL Ranch, opposite; total spread embraces 1,500,000 acres. At left, ewes gather around recently born lambs. Licked free of afterbirth, one finally rises on wobbly legs.

of these trends. Today's sheepman sees his position as almost untenable. The increase in his income from wool and lamb sales has not offset his growing operating expenses. But of particular concern to the sheepman are the recent developments which affect his access to the federal lands (which in Nevada, for example, constitute 86 percent of the total area). Stated succinctly, the rancher finds himself in a state of near perpetual confrontation with officials charged with administering the public domain. Hollywood movies notwithstanding, there has never been as much conflict over the western ranges as at present.

Hot in summer, cold in winter, and nearly waterless, the harsh interior regions of the American West were largely ignored by the first whites to view them in the mid-19th century. However, as the California gold fields played out, the search for mineral wealth spread into the Great Basin and the Rockies. The mining camps created a demand for agricultural produce, and one kind of agricultural lifestyle, ranching, proved adaptive to Great Basin conditions.

If water was scarce, wherever a small stream coursed out of a high mountain range the supply was dependable enough to establish a home base. If forage was sparse, land was abundant. Furthermore, ranching lent itself to permanent settlement in a way that mining did not.

And so it began. During the second half of the 19th century the ranching frontier was extended into every corner of the region capable of sustaining an outfit. However, the process was fraught with growing pains since establishment of a livestock-based economy brought the rancher into resource competition with others: the aboriginal population, the defenders of the region's natural environment, and other livestockmen contending for the same range.

The sad plight of the American Indian, which culminated in the creation of the reservation system, is beyond the scope of this review. However, the external pressure brought to bear on ranching by conservationists on the one hand and the competition that developed internally among livestockmen on the other, are not.

Regarding the former, the highly touted "winning of the West" was not without its detractors in the eastern United States. As the westward expansion progressed, conservation-

The Lord *is* my Shepherd; I shall not want . . . . Yea, though I walk through the valley of the shadow of death, I will fear no evil . . . .

−Book of Psalms

Crook at the ready, sheepherder wades into milling throng, small portion of ranch's 4,600 sheep. Skilled hands join him for springtime tasks of shearing, "docking" (cutting off tail tips), and castrating to help fatten males.

sequently liberalized and by 1916 the Stock Raising Homestead Act increased the allowance to 640 acres (a full section, or one square mile).

However, given the ecological realities of much of the American West, even the full section formula provided insufficient basis for a self-contained ranching operation. By an estimate made in 1881, under Nevada conditions it took 160 acres of rangeland to support a single cow! Consequently, some ranchers filed for homesteads in the names of relatives and employees, thereby acquiring private ownership of several thousand acres. However, more commonly they simply established one or a few homesteads on a water source, thereby gaining *de facto* control of vast tracts of contiguous grazing areas. On the other hand, any United States citizen could file for a homestead, and the ranchers had little defense, other than coercion, against the so-called nesters with their fences and plows.

Popular notions to the contrary, the reputed schism within the ranks of the livestockmen between sheepmen and cattlemen has been much overblown. Sheep are browsers, preferring bushy plants, while cattle are grazers, preferring grass. The real source of irritation to the settled ranchers, cattlemen and sheepmen alike, were the itinerant sheepmen—

ists became increasingly vocal concerning what they regarded to be spoliation of the western natural environment, particularly the destruction of beaver and buffalo. Deforestation, too, was attracting their attention. Whole mountain ranges had been virtually denuded of their timber reserves with no subsequent reseeding.

The creation of the national park and national forest systems in 1872 and 1897 had considerable impact upon western ranching since they came to encompass most of the suitable summer range on the public lands. The National Park Service adamantly prohibited grazing, but the parks were few and their impact was highly localized. The national forests were, however, another matter. After an initial period of hostility in which forest officials tried to exclude graziers from the national forests, a suitable arrangement emerged between federal authorities and one sector of the livestock industry. We shall return to this point shortly, but to understand why this was the case it is first necessary to consider the third source of competition for resources that the rancher faced—that posed by other agriculturalists.

The Homestead Act of 1862 allowed a settler to obtain title to 160 acres of land after residing on it for five years and providing evidence of cultivation. The provisions were sub-

usually former herders who invested their savings in a band, a burro, and a camp outfit and then roamed freely about the public domain. They neither possessed nor needed a home base. That most were foreigners, in the main Basques, did not further endear them to the predominantly Anglo-American settled ranching population.

The result was that a marriage of convenience began to emerge between eastern conservationists and settled western livestockmen. The ranchers were successful in ensuring that grazing would continue to be permitted upon the national forests, albeit under a federal quota system. On the other hand, individual allotments within a particular district would be made by a board of local ranchers. Aliens without land were declared ineligible for grazing permits.

The itinerants, far from being put out of business, became concentrated in mountain areas that afforded adequate forage but were too sparsely forested to be included in the national forest reserves.

It was in 1934 that the issue posed by the itinerants was finally resolved. Under the provisions of the Taylor Grazing Act all public lands outside of the national park and national forest systems were to be organized into grazing districts administered by an agency (presently the Bureau of Land Management) of the Department of the Interior, under essentially the same conditions pertaining to access of livestock to the national forest reserves.

In retrospect, many ranchers believe that this federal intervention into the chaotic situation of the itinerants was necessary. However, the rancher was accustomed to independent decision making, so though the hand of federal control initially rested lightly on his shoulder, from the outset there was friction between the regulators and the regulated.

With the maturing of the American West and a dramatic increase in its population, the demand for recreational uses of the public lands has accelerated. A myriad of interest groups, including hunters, fishermen, motorcyclists, four-wheel vehicle advocates, skiers, and campers have organized to promote their points of view. Conservationists, themselves frequently at odds with the recreationists, similarly lobby to preserve the region's environment and wildlife. In the ensuing debates the rancher is often portrayed as the villain, and may respond with hostility. There was a time when most ranchers welcomed, or at least tolerated, the weekender. However, a recent sad history of vandalism, littering, fence cutting, and the occasional shooting of livestock has prompted many a rancher to close his private lands to the public, a particularly disconcerting development for the

hunters and fishermen. As for the conservationists, most ranchers regard them with extreme resentment, suspecting that the ultimate goal of conservation groups is to convert the public lands of the American West into one vast wildlife preserve on which all grazing of livestock would be prohibited.

In the past and particularly at present, then, two key questions lie at the core of the general public's attitudes toward ranching: the impact of stock grazing on the range, and the impact of stock grazing on wildlife. These issues are obviously not unrelated, but may better be treated separately.

If one asks was/is there overgrazing in the American West the best answer is probably yes for the past and no at present. The particulars, of course, differ from area to area and from period to period. However, it seems clear that toward the end of the era of uncontrolled grazing much of the American West had suffered considerable environmental damage.

Today the same winter range that once supported 100,000 sheep is probably used by less than 10,000. Added to the sheer decline in livestock numbers are improvements in range management techniques, which have served to lessen the pressure of stock grazing upon the public domain.

The question of the impact of domestic livestock upon wildlife must be asked and answered on a species-by-species

Amadee Minaberry, like a pickup-driving Biblical shepherd, seeks the single, lost sheep, saving it from cold, starvation, and the river, opposite. Possibly he can sell the "leppie" for $125 to a ranch short on survivors.

basis. Prior to the introduction of ranching in the Great Basin, grasses were more abundant and the bushier sage and other species more interspersed than at present. The seemingly endless supply of grassland proved to be a deceptive attraction to the region's first ranchers, who found that though their cattle could thrive even through a winter on the bunch grass, closely cropped it required years to recover. As the stands of native grasses were distressed in this fashion, sagebrush and other bushy varieties spread at their expense.

This development affected the various wildlife species differently. Antelope, as grass feeders, declined in numbers and even disappeared from many areas of their former habitat. Conversely, mule deer and elk were greatly benefited by the conversion of the virgin range to a ranching ecosystem. Both species are browsers, and therefore require brushy feed rather than grasses. The tilt toward a sagebrush-dominated ecology and the deforestation of the adjacent mountain ranges favored the spread of brushy scrub plants, creating ideal deer country. Ultimately, the formerly rare mule deer emerged as the region's premier big game animal, and thereby became the object of a multimillion-dollar industry.

Several species of game birds, including quail and sage hen, benefited by the ranching ecosystem, and the successful introduction of pheasants was almost entirely due to the existence of agriculture. Ranching also generally favored the fisheries of the region, although some major natural lakes and streams and their native species have declined as agricultural demands for water increase.

It may be argued, then, that most, although not all, of the species considered thus far have been benefited by ranching. However, some of the most heated debates regarding management of the public lands center on the disposition of so-called varmints, species that until recently were defined as detrimental to both man's purposes and the region's natural

Perhaps the sheepmen are right and the coyote will outlast us all. And I sometimes feel that he may deserve to.

–Francois Leydet

environment. These included wild horses and burros on the one hand and predators on the other.

Efforts to protect the wild horse have received considerable attention in recent years. Possibly no other issue has served more to polarize opinion regarding the disposition of the public lands. Introduced by the Spaniards in the American Southwest and used by the Indians and white settlers alike, the horse has played a prominent role in the region's recent history. Escaped or deliberately released animals became the foundation of bands of feral horses. Similarly, burros that escaped or were abandoned by 19th-century prospectors were able to survive and proliferate on their own.

The ranchers viewed the wild horse and burro as a pest. Horses require considerably more forage than a cow or sheep, and the unchecked increase of the mustang population on his range threatened the rancher's very livelihood; consequently, he periodically conducted roundups. From his viewpoint the main idea was to control the mustang population; mustanging was a dangerous business, and the methods were none too gentle.

Beginning in the late 1950s, there was increasing concern by horse lovers and some conservationists over the plight of the mustang. The debate was acrimonious and characterized by irreconcilable claims. Protectionists depicted the horse in noble terms as a symbol of the frontier itself. For their opponents, the wild horse was a nasty, inbred, exotic (i.e., non-indigenous) interloper that posed a major peril to the ecological balance.

After an intensive lobbying effort by protectionists resulted in passage of the Wild Free Roaming Horse and Burro Act of 1971, there have been further difficulties. Freed from hunting pressure, the mustang has demonstrated remarkable fecundity, a capacity to increase by about 20 percent annually. Such increases have occurred recently despite the fact that 1976 and 1977 were two of the worst drought years in Nevada's history. The lamentable condition of both the rangeland and the wild horses themselves served to underscore for all concerned the need to institute effective management of the region's mustang population. However, the wild horse issue is far from resolved and promises to provide future copy to the newspapers and litigation to the courts.

The danger to domestic livestock posed by predatory animals is as old as ranching itself in the American West. Until recently, however, the ranchers' efforts to control and, indeed, to exterminate the predators were favored by the defenders of other forms of wildlife, aided and abetted by state and federal officials, and regarded indifferently by the gen-

"The foxes are out," sheepherders say when ewes have lambed and predators caught scent. Victim above was taken by coyote like leaper opposite; after devouring lamb, coyote regurgitates food at home for pups.

eral populace. Creation of the national parks and other wildlife preserves was felt to provide adequate area in which a few surviving examples of each predatory species could be maintained for posterity. Outside the confines of such reserves rapacious animals were, in every respect, treated as "fair game," unprotected by hunting seasons or the licensing requirement for hunters.

Under such pressure some predators, notably wolves and bears, disappeared over much of their former range. Cougars have proven somewhat more durable, and their predilection to inhabit extremely rugged country partly removes them as a serious threat to livestock. Eagles are felt to constitute a danger to newborn lambs in at least some areas of the West, but their impact on domestic stock is minimal.

From the ranchers' standpoint, then, to say "predator" is to mean "coyote." Of all of the wildlife species of the American West there is a sense in which the coyote is the most magnificent, if only for his adaptability. The coyote has proliferated and prospered, even extending his range, despite more than a century of concerted effort to eliminate him. His nocturnal howl is today the *nachtmusik* of the residents of the outer suburbs of many a western city.

The campaign to exterminate the coyote and the resources

mobilized to do so are impressive. As each new method of control is introduced there is a period of initial success, followed by a time during which the coyote population "goes to school," then by renewed frustration for his persecutors.

The coyote has not been totally without his apologists. Prompted in part by the belief that nature should be allowed to strike its own balance between predators and their prey, dismayed by the cruelty of the methods used to control the coyote population, and disturbed by the side effects of the predator poisoning program, some defenders of wildlife have lobbied against predator control.

Efforts to place the coyote on the protected species list have failed completely, and nowhere in the American West is he regarded as a legitimate game animal. However, the major achievement of the protectionists regards the use of toxicants. Studies demonstrated that poisons introduced into the ecology for the purpose of removing coyotes resulted in the inadvertent destruction of many other species as well. Consequently, in 1971, to the dismay of western ranchers, the use of toxicants was banned by Presidential order.

The effects of the ban were felt immediately. Between 1971 and the present a number of sheep outfits have either gone out of business or converted to cattle, ascribing the decision directly to the coyote problem. There has also been a notable shift in the attitudes of cattlemen.

Even those favoring predator control do not agree on the significance of livestock losses to predators. The U.S. Fish and Wildlife Service compiles its statistics on the basis of "verified" kills, i.e., actual carcass counts. The sheepmen, as in Joaquin's account, calculate losses by subtracting the number of animals shipped in the autumn from the total that is docked and marked in the spring. Recently, the U.S. Fish and Wildlife Service conducted a study of the problem designed to take into account all points of view in order to formulate an as yet undetermined new policy.

After considering the evidence from ranchers and other sources the studies concluded that the ranchers' figures were inflated. However, they further noted, ". . . average loss rates do not adequately portray the nature of coyote depredation on sheep. The losses are unequally distributed both geographically and among producers. Losses vary between and within states. Most producers suffer no or minor losses, while some 20–25 percent of producers suffer losses that are significantly higher . . . Harassment of livestock by predators and non-fatal injuries also result in economic loss to producers." They concluded that predation rates were higher in the 1970s than in the 1960s.

In conclusion, the future of ranching in the American West is at best clouded. If the 19th century was a period of expansion of the ranching frontier and the early 20th century one of entrenchment, the last three decades have clearly witnessed its retreat. Ranching makes extensive rather than intensive use of the natural environment, and is a frontier activity in the sense that it is predicated upon sparse human settlement of vast land areas. The maturing of the American West and the emergence of contending claims upon the public patrimony have all underscored the tenuous position of the region's ranchers.

Morning at ranch begins with strong coffee, satisfied look at bagged coyote—a sad sight for conservationists. Evening ends with jug of wine, weary recognition that though ranching wanes, tomorrow will be much the same.

Legacy of the Parks

By Alfred Runte

America's environmentalists, for all their praiseworthy passion and splendid impatience with those who would treat the land less sensitively, might do well to set their campaign into historical context. They—or perhaps I mean we—wage a struggle not only against vested economic interests but also against the deep-seated national attitude about the protection of our land.

From the beginning, that attitude tended to be defensive (with all the psychotic overtones which that word usually carries). It stemmed from the 18th- and 19th-century search for a distinct American identity: Early nationalists, though confident in their new-found freedom from England after the Revolution, faced understandable frustration in defining American culture. Thomas Jefferson, rising to the challenge, pointed out the rugged beauty around Harpers Ferry as proof that the environment of the United States portended cultural greatness in the future. He opened his *Notes on the State of Virginia* with the comment that "The passage of the Patowmac through the Blue Ridge is perhaps one of the most stupendous scenes in nature. . . . This scene is worth a voyage across the Atlantic."

Yet doubts lingered in the American breast that we had much grandeur to offer visiting Europeans. Not until the mid-19th century when the U.S. had annexed the western portions of the continent did fellow Americans discover a topography which seemed worthy of Jefferson's admonitions. Still, Easterners felt abashed in comparison to the allurements of the Rhine or the Alps. James Fenimore Cooper wrote in 1851 that "As a whole, it must be admitted that Europe offers to the senses sublimer views and certainly grander, than are to be found within our own borders, unless we resort to the Rocky Mountains, and the ranges in California and New Mexico."

Nonetheless, it was in that very year of 1851 that Yosemite Valley was discovered; by the close of that decade a veritable

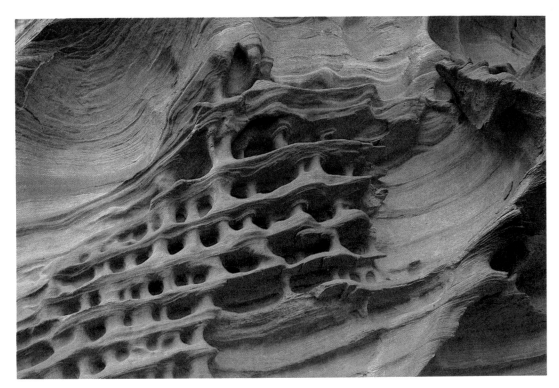

Centuries of water erosion honeycombed rock face at Utah's Capitol Reef National Park. Opposite, Harpers Ferry National Historical Park, West Virginia, recalls John Brown's raid to raise slave revolt in 1859.

tide of enthusiastic observations swelled forth. "No one scene in all the Alps" could match the valley's "majestic and impressive beauty," proclaimed one commentator. All America agreed—but skeptics awaited evidence that the United States would be prepared to interfere with private interests to preserve such treasures of the land for posterity.

The fear that confiscation of Yosemite Valley by private claimants would prevent its becoming a national monument was very influential in convincing Congress to grant the gorge to California as a state park in 1864. Simultaneously Congress extended the same protection to the Mariposa Grove of Sierra redwoods, approximately 20 miles south of the valley. From the time of their discovery during the early 1850s, the big trees had gained notoriety, not only because of their huge circumference, but through publicity that many specimens predated the birth of Christ.

As yet little had been said about the "ecology" or the "environment" of the West; those terms were not publicized until the 20th century. Throughout the 1860s and 1870s Americans were preoccupied with identifying and promoting the natural "wonders" of the western regions. Explorers, tourists, artists, and correspondents alike embraced the land's curiosities as substitutes for the man-made monuments so absent in the American scene. The *Springfield* (Mass.) *Republican*'s Samuel Bowles, for example, took comfort in his fantasy that two formations in Yosemite Valley, Cathedral Rocks and Cathedral Spires, recaptured "the great impressiveness, the beauty and fantastic form of the Gothic architecture. From their shape and color alike," he concluded, "it is easy to imagine, in looking upon them, that you are under the ruins of an old Gothic cathedral, to which those of Cologne and Milan are but baby-houses."

It is unfortunate from our point of view that Bowles and his contemporaries were in no real position to judge how

Grand Prismatic Spring sparkles like an emerald in Yellowstone National Park, a land born in volcanic fire and sculpted by glacial ice. Exotic coloration is caused by microorganisms that thrive in hot spring waters.

their eagerness to overcome America's cultural limitations would exact limitations on the national park idea. True, their bias for "freaks" and "curiosities" of nature evolved into an inspiring and magnificent series of parks, but most of the reserves, because of their restriction to focal "wonders," were badly designed for the management of natural environments.

Such a critical comment could only be made after the fact, of course, by a knowledgeable Monday morning quarterback—someone like myself who represents academic disciplines unknown then. Before joining the Smithsonian in 1978, I had spent 10 years or so learning enough environmental biology and cultural history to serve as a social scientist in this lively area of scholarship and applied theory. During those studies, I found it important to respect the level of sophistication in the natural sciences of those pioneers who were instrumental in establishing the national park system. Today's insistence that national parks respect ecological boundaries is admittedly new; it calls for a readjustment in priorities so that the parks protect such entities or systems as watersheds and animal migration routes rather than simply highlight unique geological formations.

The inclusion of an entire watershed within a national park ensures some degree of control over substances entering and leaving the ecosystem. Some species of plants and animals depend on the characteristics of an entire watershed for their subsistence. For example, Redwood Creek, in Redwood National Park, California, has illustrated the futility of trying to preserve this kind of forest area without extending protection to its headwaters. Loggers have so denuded the slopes adjacent to the corridor of parkland bordering Redwood Creek that groves within the park itself have been jeopardized by mudslides and flashflooding. A classic exception to this parks policy is Isle Royale National Park, Michigan, just off the Canadian shore in northern Lake Superior. Because the entire island was preserved as a park, all of its watersheds were retained intact, allowing the persistence of the island's ecosystems and their biota.

Yellowstone and Grand Teton National Parks, in the northwest corner of Wyoming, have long symbolized the struggle to modernize the national park idea in accordance with ecological needs. Although both parks share common biological units, especially wildlife migration patterns, each reserve was created separately. Yellowstone, established in 1872, seemed the perfect encore to the theme of monumentalism. Advocates of a grand and monumental national park at Yellowstone reinforced their arguments by pointing out how that other national treasure, Niagara Falls in New

York, had fallen victim to tourist sharks who charged fees for viewing that wonder. Surely, they contended, such a sight should be "as free as the air or water."

Congress responded with uncharacteristic promptness, and on March 1, 1872, President Ulysses S. Grant signed the Yellowstone Park Act into law establishing the world's first national park. Right from the beginning the reserve was huge—more than 3,300 square miles in area. Yet throughout history its size has been misleading. In fact, Congress had not paid any attention to its importance as a wilderness and wildlife preserve. But after the explorers and natural scientists were able to impress upon Congress the necessity of extending protection to Yellowstone's hinterlands (where, they believed, closer inspection would reveal additional "freaks," "curiosities," and "decorations") Yellowstone was recognized as a sort of super "wonders" park—a celebration of the nation's newfound heritage of geysers, hot pools, and bubbling mud. In a country ever searching for uniqueness in its landscapes, these were the features of irrefutable distinction.

For any idealist hoping to find in the origins of the national parks a combination of statesmanship, altruism, and science, the truth here is somewhat disillusioning. Indeed, a major reason for the House and Senate's decision to approve Yellowstone as a park was that they deemed it otherwise worthless. Government geologist Ferdinand V. Hayden had reported to Congress: "The entire area comprised within the limits of the reservation contemplated in this bill is not susceptible of cultivation with any degree of certainty, and the winters would be too severe for stock-raising." Settlement would therefore be "problematical unless there are valuable mines to attract the people." Even opportunities for mining were remote because of Yellowstone's "volcanic origins"; volcanic formations suggesting that no "mines or minerals of value will ever be found there." With regard to agricultural possibilities in Yellowstone, here again, Hayden wrote, the region suffered "frost every month of the year."

The expansion of the national park system, as well as its conception at Yellowstone, has been due to this fortunate compatibility of negative biases. The nation's determination to seek out its boldest, most "monumental" landscapes invariably led enthusiasts to idolize precisely those features—mountains, glaciers, canyons—whose capacity for profitable exploitation was indeed doubtful from the start. Today more Americans realize that ecological conservation, as opposed to mere scenic preservation, demands the protection of ecosystems in their entirety. Still, it is hard to admit that landscapes as inspiring as Yosemite, Yellowstone, the Grand Canyon,

Mount Rainier, and Crater Lake, among others, owe their existence as national parks above all to their "worthlessness."

The Teton mountains, immediately to the south of Yellowstone, were spectacular landforms bypassed by the park. Their exclusion was partly unintentional. The explorers and naturalists, having observed the Tetons from a distance, felt moved to comment about their intriguing, stark outline. Beautiful—but what about minerals or ranching up there? Maybe the mountains had riches too real for the territory to become parkland. Delays followed delays, but eventually the nation realized that Yellowstone Park should have included the Teton mountains and their environs. Jackson Hole, a long valley just east of the range, was especially important as a winter habitat for Yellowstone's southern elk herd. Other mammals, among them deer and antelope, were also dependent on a far larger range than the national park originally included. In winter Yellowstone was too cold and its

Park Service stipulates that natural conditions of plant and animal life must prevail in protected areas. Nocturnal tree frog naps in Everglades, changes color depending on mood, temperature, surroundings.

snows too deep for the animals to find forage; food and shelter had to be sought in valleys outside the park boundaries. These lowlands, of course, were also primary areas for ranching and farming. Following the settlement of Jackson Hole in the late 19th century, the seasonal migration of the elk to their wintering grounds became a perilous undertaking. First the animals encountered sport hunters and poachers who shot out the herd by the hundreds. Beyond this gauntlet lay the physical barriers of fences, farms, ranches, and towns. The elk, predictably, did not flourish.

The high Tetons, long hailed as "the Switzerland of America" and "our wilderness park of Matterhorns," received park status in 1929. In vain observers and government scientists warned that, without the valley, the elk were still being squeezed off their winter range. Not until 1950, following one of the longest and most emotional conservation battles in American history, did environmentalists—then a new breed

Golden Gate National Recreation Area's 34,200 acres provide close-in getaway for harried San Franciscans. Independence National Historical Park in Philadelphia, opposite, preserves Carpenters Hall, Liberty Bell.

on the cultural scene—secure Jackson Hole as an addition to the national park system. Even then protection came only to the northern half of the valley, that portion determined to have the least potential for competitive farming and ranching. Notably, Congress now also restored the northern third of the range to the reserve since it had been determined that the region contained no significant asbestos deposits.

Shaped by the country's prejudice for spectacular, "world class" scenery, the national park idea foundered when finally caught between the dwindling romantic ideals of the 19th century and the dawning ecological realities of modern America. It remained for Everglades National Park in Florida, authorized in 1934, to break down the traditional assumption that only landscapes of supreme ruggedness are qualified for national park status. In the Everglades preservationists learned to express the importance of protecting wildlife and plant life, regardless of their physical backdrop. Indeed how else could the park be justified, asked Ernest F. Coe, the Miami activist who spearheaded the park movement—"it has no mountains, its highest elevation being less than eight feet above sea level." The "spirit" of the park, indeed the very reason for its inspiration, "is primarily the preservation of the primitive."

Thus for Coe and his allies the reserve marked a momentous evolution in national park standards. Shorn of all monumental "wonders," the wetlands of southern Florida epitomized the nation's growing respect for "natural ecological relations"—for "that balanced interlocking relation between the animate and the inanimate world."

The creation of Everglades National Park broke with the national bias for the monumental. Perhaps this occurred because the historic insecurities about American grandeur had been eased. Perhaps it represented a new understanding of the land. Whatever the cause, it was both an expression of a different perception and a life-giving precedent to the destiny of the parks. Now it was possible for Congress to consider the qualifications of seashores, lakeshores, and riverways for national park status. Still, Americans as a whole have never lost their special fascination for unique scenery. As late as 1974, in a survey sponsored by the U.S. Department of Commerce, for example, tourists ranked the Grand Canyon, Yellowstone, and Niagara Falls as the nation's preeminent natural landmarks. Yet to be determined is the extent to which the public has been educated to appreciate that all landscapes, not just scenic wonders, are essential to the integrity of the American land.

From the standpoint of ensuring the protection of environmental diversity, the question has never been more important. History has shown that past efforts to expand the national parks have always encountered the greatest opposition whenever the inclusion of so-called commonplace landscapes has been at issue. Commercially speaking, the lower the elevation of a particular topography, the greater the likelihood of developing its timber, grazing, or agricultural wealth profitably. This, of course, has been the traditional point of contention between preservation groups and resource interests. But there have been cultural biases to overcome as well, some unknowingly shared among environmentalists themselves. The gentler components of the American land—its prairies, plains, hills, and valleys—have not inspired the same emotional attachments as mountains, waterfalls, or canyons. Instead, as the naturalist John Muir observed in 1875, "Tourists make their way through the foot-hill landscapes as if blind to all their best beauty, and like children seek the emphasized mountains—the big alpine capitals whitened with glaciers and adorned with conspicuous spires. In like manner rivers are ascended hundreds of miles to see the water-falls at their heads, because they are as yet the only portions of river beauty plainly visible to all."

Indeed so-called nontraditional parks, including lakeshores and seashores, have often been advanced as recreation areas rather than as ecological preserves. The nation's preference for dramatic scenery may also explain why some states have stronger conservation programs than others. The historian Samuel P. Hays, for example, has noted that New York and California, traditionally two strongholds of environmental concern, have provided activists with "visible" goals to protect, such as the Adirondack Mountains and the Sierra Nevada respectively. New Yorkers also derived inspiration from the Catskills and Niagara Falls, and Californians from San Francisco Bay. Over the years such imposing natural features, in addition to great lakes, harbors, and rivers, provided the basis for a strong conservation heritage. This has stood out in obvious contrast to some states in the Midwest and South, for example, where conservation programs, in keeping with the subtleties of the prairies and pinelands, have generally been more diffuse. In fact, Congress itself has yet to approve a national park devoted exclusively to the protection of America's grasslands and their fauna.

In any case, little remains of the grasslands that greeted the pioneers. If and when such a national park is established—with three sites in Kansas under consideration—it will be relatively small in comparison to existing reserves. For the remainder of this century, Alaska looms as the focal point of

Unexpected contrasts awe visitors to Mount McKinley National Park. Sunrise at 1:30 a.m. in June illuminates cerulean glaciers, 20,320-foot peak, the brilliance of polychromatic volcanic cliffs, and blossoming tundra, opposite.

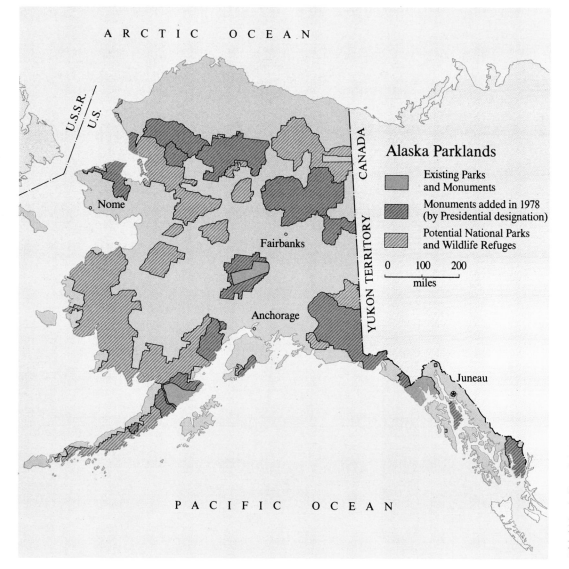

ARCTIC OCEAN

U.S.S.R.
U.S.

Nome

Fairbanks

CANADA

YUKON TERRITORY

Alaska Parklands

Existing Parks and Monuments

Monuments added in 1978 (by Presidential designation)

Potential National Parks and Wildlife Refuges

0   100   200
miles

Anchorage

Juneau

PACIFIC OCEAN

environmental issues, especially because it represents the nation's final opportunity to protect natural environments in their total diversity. Nearly a half century ago scientists consulting for the National Park Service summed up its basic management problem: "It is utterly impossible," they noted, "to protect animals in an area so small that they are within it only a portion of the year." National parks that had once seemed large now often prove to be inadequate for the protection of their "living landscapes."

The attempt to correct this deficiency in Alaska has continued to meet the resistance of the old prejudice. And when coupled with economic sanctions, tradition becomes an even stiffer opponent. As early as 1972, for example, the Conservation Foundation found it necessary to warn environmentalists to be on guard against proposals to restrict parks in the 49th state to "lands covered with ice and snow."

Because Alaska's proposed parks would contain unprecedented amounts of dramatic scenery, again their major deficiency as ecological units might go unnoticed by the American public. Indeed "for many of their keenest supporters," wrote E. Max Nicholson, a British ecologist, "parks are still viewed as the living embodiment of romantic values." This "delicious dream," built on a foundation of imposing scenery, not only must be reconciled "with an ever less romantic and more crowded world, but with the realistic tasks of park acquisition and park management."

To date a mere 1 percent of the American land has been set aside as national parks; the addition of enough territory to ensure their ecological integrity—including major watersheds and animal migration routes—should barely double that figure. Our reluctance to make this investment in the national parks can only undermine our image as a world leader in conservation. The national park idea is an American original; we alone conceived it and presented it to global civilizations. It therefore seems all the more incumbent upon the United States, with its great wealth of land, to set the example for the world both in the management of natural environments and scenic wonders.

The Smithsonian Institution is helping to meet this challenge in a variety of ways, from the environmental studies program of the Woodrow Wilson International Center for Scholars to actual fieldwork in the physical and biological sciences. In the final analysis, however, the future of the national parks depends on the wisdom, maturity, and generosity of the American people. Certainly the time has come to look upon the national parks not only as artifacts or leftovers, but as our eternal gift to posterity.

Shapers

Unsheathing his sword, a Spanish knight scratched the sunbaked mud with the steel point. A plan for an encampment appeared, straight sided (curves being hard to scratch or to build) and thick walled. Somewhere north of the Rio Grande, a foreign shape was thus imposed on the land by a newly arrived American. Other shapes would follow—shapes as tiny as your first garden, as large as the California marigold plantation at left.

Before such 16th-century invaders as the Spanish and French, however, the Indians had done their share of searching, settling, and land shaping. The distinctive marks of these ancestral people are still visible, not only in woodland trails but also in sophisticated communities with plazas and religious structures. The first story in this section, written by Bruce Smith of the Smithsonian's Department of Anthropology, reveals one such site.

In a curious way, those who have imposed designs on the American land have found themselves as much in the position of being shaped as shaping. The great architects and designers in Paul Spreiregen's historical essay on the traditions of land planning learned—like Jefferson on his own hill outside Charlottesville—to make the best of magnificent opportunities. The sodbusters, described in Joe Goodwin's subsequent journey west with three pioneer groups, had to respect the realities of the territories they ventured into . . . and to work hours beyond

reason. With pride in his accomplishments and recognition of the soil's unfailing abundance, one immigrant rhymed "... the land was sweet and good. I did what I could."

Suburbanites seek their share of the countryside, too, creating new landshapes in the process. As Ogden Tanner's essay shows, this passion for a special plot is a peculiarity of Americans, demonstrating perhaps their affection for the land but their frustration in trying to possess it in a limited way. Frustration and even despair have also characterized the urbanites introduced in Peirce Lewis's final story on the remarkable growth of cities and mega-cities. Yet this unique design, "the unprecedented American city," is by no means a cultural or commercial failure; it prospers as an imposed but dynamically evolved form on the land.

Cities, routes, and countryside: Three components change and change again as the people shape the land and the changed land in turn shapes the people. Communication corridors and a traffic network unify the economy. Held in the grid, horizon-filling farms spread across the entire heartland. Pacific Northwest states hold a lion's share of wilderness, and citizens there vow that as long as possible they will keep the land as nature shaped it.

The Temple Mound Builders

By Bruce D. Smith

Illustrations by John Douglass

One July day not long ago I stood at the edge of the steep bluffs just south of Memphis and looked west across the broad expanse of the Mississippi Valley. My vantage point was Chucalissa, a prehistoric mound center occupied, perhaps continuously, from around A.D. 1000 to A.D. 1600. Below me the river passed close to the base of the bluffs, and I could see barges moving slowly against the current. Beyond the river the flat floodplain stretched away into the afternoon haze, a manicured patchwork of soybean, corn, and rice fields.

Looking out over the hundreds of square miles of rich delta farmland, I was both awed and angered by the changes that modern technology had brought to the valley. Large-scale drainage projects, begun over 100 years ago and continued up to the present day by the Army Corps of Engineers, had opened up large tracts of low, swampy land to farming. More recently, within the last 20 years, enormous earth-moving machinery had rolled over much of the floodplain, methodically transforming a gently rolling topography into the pool table-flat fields needed for optimum crop yields. To many people these machines are massive symbols of progress, testimony to modern technology's mastery of the environment. They evoke much different feelings in archeologists like myself who have made the prehistory of the Mississippi Valley their life's work.

It is hard to express the mixture of helplessness and loss we feel as we watch a prehistoric settlement disappear beneath a bulldozer's blade. The simple truth is this: By the end of the 20th century virtually all evidence of prehistoric occupation of the Mississippi Valley will have vanished, swept away by the machines of progress. And it is not only the archeological record that is being erased, it is the landscape itself. The vast old tracts of bald cypress and tupelo have dwindled to small, isolated stands, clinging to existence along drainage ditches. The oxbow lakes, feeding grounds for the millions of waterfowl that travel the Mississippi flyway each year, are being filled in and farmed.

In A.D. 1300, the view of a vast floodplain forest stretching away to the horizon would have been quite deceiving. Beneath the apparent green uniformity of the forest canopy, the Mississippi Valley supported a complex intermingling of

Recreation of southeastern Missouri Powers Fort center in about A.D. 1300 includes, at upper right, figures preparing for ceremony. Participants may have worn copper falcons like that at left as badges of high rank.

quite distinct natural communities. The land itself presented a confusing topography formed and reformed by the constant shifting of the Mississippi River. These frequent meanderings, abandoning whole sections of the former channels, resulted in a complex landscape of remnant oxbow lakes, natural levee ridges, and backswamp areas. This floodplain world of cypress swamps, lakes, and levee ridges proved to be quite resistant to settlement by Euro-Americans. However, this seemingly impenetrable swampland was the setting for the highest level of prehistoric cultural development attained north of Mesoamerica. It was the heartland of the temple mound builders, so-called to distinguish them from other, earlier cultures such as the effigy and burial mound builders. Who were these temple mound builders? Where did they come from? What eventually happened to them?

It was not until 1882, when the Smithsonian Institution established a Mound Exploration Division within the Bureau of American Ethnology, that these questions were systematically addressed. A decade of exploration of the prehistoric mounds of the eastern United States followed, culminating in the 1894 publication of the monumental 12th Annual Report of the B.A.E.

Although refined somewhat as a result of subsequent archeological research, the basic conclusions of the Mound Exploration Division still stand. These temple mound building cultures were not, as earlier armchair speculators had imagined, a vanished race of giants, nor were they Mayans, Toltecs, Phoenicians, Egyptians, a lost tribe of Israel, or any one of a number of other colonizing ethnic splinter groups. They were indigenous Amerindian groups—the descendants of earlier eastern North American cultures, and the ancestors of later Indian tribes encountered by such early European explorers as Hernando de Soto. The research revealed that the lower Mississippi Valley had been continuously occupied by prehistoric human populations from about 9000 B.C. until the Europeans arrived. The temple mound cultures, which existed in the valley during the time period A.D. 800 to about A.D. 1600, represented the culmination of this long sequence of cultural development.

There are many aspects of the initial emergence of the temple mound cultures that are not as yet fully understood. Within a very short time span, at about A.D. 800–1000, profound changes took place in the way of life of some prehistoric groups occupying the Mississippi Valley. Agriculture became much more important in their economy, there was a dramatic increase in population, and socio-political organization became much more centralized. Although we can document these changes, we are not sure what caused them, nor can we fully explain their subsequent cultural decline after about A.D. 1400. The Indian groups encountered and described by the de Soto entrada of 1541, as well as by subsequent explorers, were certainly the descendants of the temple mound builders, but they had a much simpler way of life.

If the emergence and decline of the temple mound way of life is still poorly understood, we do nonetheless have a good general understanding of what life was like in the Mississippi Valley at the peak of the period.

The label that archeologists have attached to these late prehistoric temple mound builders is "Middle Mississippi" because of their location along that portion of the Mississippi River. The use of the term "Mississippi" in identifying these Indians is appropriate in another way, since the river virtually shaped their way of life. These Middle Mississippians were farmers, and it was in the fertile and well-drained sandy soils of the river-deposited levees that they planted their crops. The natural fertility of these soils was periodically renewed by floodwaters, and the small fields, scattered along the low ridges, yielded good harvests of corn, beans, and squash (carbonized remains of each have been recovered from their settlements). Each of these fields or garden plots would have been cleared of trees and brush, planted with crops for a number of years, and then abandoned when weeds and brush reinvaded the clearings. With primitive tools it was far easier to clear a new field than to hoe the weeds from an established one. Once abandoned, a field plot would not have been cleared again until the forest vegetation had reclaimed the land. You might say that these Indian groups were continually "borrowing" small parcels of land from the forest for a few years before returning them to the natural successional process.

While the rich levee-ridge soils provided excellent locations for fields, the channel-remnant oxbow lakes that paralleled these ridges provided a bounty of another kind. The abundant and varied fish populations that occupied these narrow, sinuous lakes provided an inexhaustible and easily accessible source of meat protein to balance the carbohydrates obtained from crops. Each spring the flood waters carried nutrients to the levee-ridge fields and replenished the oxbow lakes with fish from the main channel (fish scales recovered from the settlements indicate that fish were harvested primarily during the spring and summer months). During the spring and fall these oxbow lakes were also visited by huge numbers of migratory waterfowl.

Judging from the great abundance of their bones in Middle Mississippi settlements, fish and waterfowl together accounted for over half of the meat consumed by these groups annually. During the late fall and through the winter months, Mississippian hunters shifted their attention to three important prey species—the white-tailed deer, turkey, and raccoon (sometimes referred to as the terrestrial trinity). Deer jaws found at settlement sites indicate that the white-tailed deer was by far the most important source of meat protein in their diet. It was also during the months of autumn that hickory nuts and acorns were collected, processed, and stored, to be eaten through the winter months. Clearly, these prehistoric Indians were not eking out a precarious hand-to-mouth existence in a hostile landscape. Far from it. They existed in a naturally abundant environment and utilized a variety of its energy sources in a manner that did not endanger or drastically modify it. This is the essence of successful long-term adaptation.

These Indian groups had also attained a sophisticated "chiefdom" level of socio-political organization. Such chiefdoms are characterized by the existence of a family or kin-grouping enjoying elite social and political status. At the top of the hierarchy was the chief, who, along with a

Left, carved on a neck ornament, or gorget, a temple mound athlete prepares to hurl his "chunky" stone. The game was played by later Creeks, Cherokees as well. Stone ax, above, denoted high status of its bearer.

small group of closely related kinsmen, made many of the important decisions that faced the society. The elite kingroup, the family of the chief, was set apart from the rest of the population in a number of important respects. The vast majority of the people that comprised a Middle Mississippi chiefdom (they are thought to have ranged in population from less than 500 to sometimes well over 1,000 individuals) were scattered over the landscape in small villages and in a large number of single-family farmsteads. In contrast, members of the chiefly elite lived in a ceremonial center which formed the socio-political and religious focus of each chiefdom. These ceremonial centers varied considerably in size from chiefdom to chiefdom, but shared certain characteristics. They were invariably fortified, functioning as a refuge for outlying settlements in times of hostility with neighboring chiefdoms. The fortification system consisted of a perimeter ditch and palisade wall, often with bastions. Inside the fortifications, a central plaza area was the location of public ceremonies and games. Bordering the plaza were ceremonial structures and the houses of the elite kinsmen, often situated on rectangular flat-topped earthen mounds. These residential mounds can usually be easily distinguished from the larger mound that supported the "temple" or meeting house of the chiefdom. All of these earthen mounds, consisting of thousands of individual basketloads of dirt, were, like the fortification systems, constructed through communal labor projects, under the direction of the chiefly elite. Lower status families also lived at these ceremonial centers, but because they were not very closely related to the chief, they occupied smaller houses away from the central plaza and its mounds.

In addition to being set apart from the general populace in terms of their elevated residences adjacent to the central plaza of the ceremonial center, the elite kinsmen could also be easily identified by their clothing and by the "markers of office" they wore or carried. These status markers were often made of non-local or "exotic" raw materials, primarily copper from Lake Superior and conch shells from the Gulf of Mexico. These high-status objects, along with more mundane items such as chert hoes and ceramic vessels, were exchanged along long-distance trade networks which are as yet poorly understood.

High-status items were also decorated with symbolic designs that the general populace was restricted from using. Common symbolic subjects were raptorial birds—often the peregrine falcon.

The most interesting and informative of the objects are those that show humans, clearly of the elite group, garbed in ceremonial regalia. These "falcon dancers" are often depicted in an elaborately stylized falcon costume adorned with a variety of high status objects (copper ear spools and hair ornaments, masks, feather cloaks, conch-shell gorgets and beads), and carrying symbols of power comparable to a field marshal's baton, such as copper and flint axes and knives. Although the exact symbolic meaning of these objects (and the total costume) is not known, it is clear that these high-status "dancers" filled an important ceremonial and socio-political role within the society.

Until about 10 years ago archeologists were primarily interested in studying the way of life of the elite of the Middle Mississippi chiefdoms, with excavation focusing on the mounds of the ceremonial centers. It is only recently that some archeologists have begun studying the smaller villages and single family farmsteads to reconstruct the way of life of the general populace.

The most successful of these archeological projects was carried out by the University of Michigan from 1968 to 1974 under the direction of James B. Griffin and James E. Price, and focused on the Powers Chiefdom, located in southeastern Missouri at the western edge of the Mississippi Valley.

Hoes of Mill Creek chert, left, from southern Illinois, were highly prized, widely traded by far-flung temple mound culture. Also typical of mound civilization was clay "elbow" pipe, above, used for smoking.

The ceremonial center of the Powers Chiefdom was first described and excavated by Col. P. W. Norris of the Mound Exploration Division of the Smithsonian Institution in the early 1880s. Norris drew an accurate map of the 12-acre site which was located on the property of William Powers. The Norris map shows a fortification ditch and three small mounds bordering the central plaza on the west side (probably high-status residential mounds) with the larger temple mound located on the north side of the plaza. This ceremonial center, called "Powers Fort," is situated on a sandy levee ridge less than a mile from the Ozark uplands which mark the western border of the Mississippi Valley. Powers Fort was thus ideally suited for access to and perhaps control of a major trade route which followed the edge of the Ozarks as far south as Little Rock, Arkansas, before turning southwest toward Texas.

Several low levee ridges to the east of Powers Fort supported at least seven smaller fortified villages, distributed in a semicircular pattern around the ceremonial center. Two of these villages were excavated by University of Michigan crews, providing a detailed picture of the internal organization of such settlements.

The Turner site was the smaller of the two excavated villages, having a total of 44 rectangular houses in orderly rows around a central courtyard. Each of these houses was probably occupied by a nuclear family—a husband, wife, and their children. The central courtyard of the Turner site also served as a cemetery, and over 100 individuals were buried there, each with varying amounts of pottery vessels and other goods. None of these burials contained high-status items, indicating that none of the inhabitants of the Turner site were very closely related to the chiefly elite who lived at Powers Fort, three miles to the northwest.

Located only 200 yards to the east of the Turner site, the Snodgrass site was over twice as large, having a total of 90 structures arranged in uniform rows. The Snodgrass site was also more complex than the Turner site; a white clay wall served to separate a central courtyard and 38 fairly large structures from the 52 smaller houses located outside the wall. These smaller structures may have been occupied only when the inhabitants of numerous outlying farmsteads sought shelter from enemies.

Although it is now thought that a significant percentage of the general populace of Middle Mississippi chiefdoms lived in scattered single-family farmsteads, very few have ever been excavated. It was for this reason that I selected the Gypsy Joint site, one of the small Powers Chiefdom farmsteads, for excavation in 1974. I hoped that such a small settlement would yield valuable information about the everyday life of an average non-elite nuclear family within the Powers Chiefdom, and it did.

After carefully removing the eight-inch layer of soil that had been disturbed by the farmer's plow, we found evidence of two houses surrounded by a series of shallow pits. The smaller of the two houses we uncovered was undoubtedly a "winter house," used primarily for sleeping and keeping warm during the coldest weeks of the year. The other, larger house structure discovered at the Gypsy Joint site served as the center of daily life at the farm, with broken pottery vessels and tools recovered from inside the house testifying to the wide variety of activities that were carried out within its walls. Just outside the north corner of this larger "summer house" we recovered the burned remains of the wooden mortar that had been used in the grinding of corn kernels. About 20 feet east of the summer house we located a large number of burned corn kernels, marking the probable location of the corn crib. Squash and beans were probably also grown in garden plots, but we can not be sure since no remains of these were recovered during our excavation of the site. A wooden mortar fragment we recovered was good evidence that adult females lived at this small settlement, since the preparation of wild and domestic plant foods was typically a woman's task in all of the historical Indian tribes of the eastern United States.

Additional abundant evidence of the presence of women consisted of thousands of acorns and hickory nut shell fragments within one of the shallow pits to the east of the summer house. Clear evidence of traditionally male activities was also found—the hunting and butchering of wild animals (white-tailed deer, raccoon, rabbit, squirrel, and beaver), and the manufacture of stone tools (arrow points, knives, scrapers). The varied remains of plants and animals found at this small settlement also allowed us to determine that it was quite probably inhabited on a year-round basis. Although we can not be sure, the size of the two house structures suggests that from five to seven individuals of both sexes, undoubtedly comprising a family grouping, shared each other's lives in this place at around A.D. 1300.

We learned many things about the way of life of this small family as a result of our excavation of the Gypsy Joint site—how they manufactured and used a variety of tools, the different kinds of domestic and wild species of plants and animals that contributed to their diet, how the plants were processed for cooking, and how the animals were butchered. But our research also uncovered a number of questions that may never be answered. The farmstead was occupied for only a few years before being burned and abandoned. Why was it abandoned so soon? Did the decreasing fertility of field plots force the move? Did the inhabitants deliberately burn their houses on abandoning the farmstead, or were they burned by a raiding party from a neighboring chiefdom? Why didn't we find any burials at the farmstead? Perhaps no family member died during the short occupation, or perhaps they were carried to Powers Fort for burial with their kinsmen.

And of course we can never know the dreams and desires of this long dead family—their hopes for their children and their everyday concerns about what the future would bring. These feelings are lost forever.

Artist John Douglass visited Missouri sites to recreate scenes at Gypsy Joint, right, and Powers Fort center, page 149. Homesteaders at Gypsy Joint hunted, raised crops on Mississippi lowlands, retired to center (in distance) in times of danger. Carson red-on-buff pot, left, was probably used by elite.

Designs on the Land

By Paul D. Spreiregen

Whether you fly over the American land or drive across it in an automobile or just look at it on a map, you can't help noticing one obvious feature: Myriad distinctive geometric patterns outline, divide, and subdivide our countryside, towns, and cities. These patterns belie one of our sturdiest myths—that the designs we see across the land happened without planning or forethought.

Far from mere happenstance, the patterns reveal deliberate intentions, for land planning has been an integral aspect of American history from the earliest colonies to the present. San Antonio, for example, still stands out today as clear evidence of Spanish regional planning. Established in 1718 as a military encampment at the edge of the fault scarp where the coastal plain meets the uplands, San Antonio became the largest settlement in Texas, guardian of the farms and missions that stretched along the river running southeast of the Gulf of Mexico. In such diverse places as San Juan, Puerto Rico; St. Augustine, Florida; Santa Fe, New Mexico; and San Diego, California, one sees similar remnants of that classic, square-block *quadra* and *presidio* pattern that the Spanish had inherited from their Moorish and Roman ancestors.

Certainly the French colonists, too, were heirs to a considerable legacy of planned development. Their techniques were perfected by Sébastien Le Prestre de Vauban, Louis XIV's great military engineer and town planner. Wood and stone instead of adobe, the French colonial towns were planned as fortified entrepôts for a far-flung fur trade. Characteristically they were located on major rivers (see illustration, page 31), and the farms nearby were laid out in long rectangular strips—the narrow end bordering the river, the sides stretching away at a right angle. This was a distinct contrast to the Spanish pattern and, from the air, the contrast is still perceptible today in such places as Detroit and New Orleans.

Because the English lacked traditional military or imperial planning techniques, and because they operated in diverse landscapes, their town plans look completely different from the French and Spanish. For the very reason that political and military domination of their regions of settlement was ordinarily assured, their towns were laid out, rather, as places for social activities, commerce, and (later) manufacturing. The English colonists did, however, plan aggressively for the takeover of vast hinterlands, as is reflected in the boundary lines of several of the original colonies which stretched westward more or less indefinitely.

Clearly, then, the attitudes, indeed the cultures, of distinct groups of settlers have been important factors in town planning. The first English migrants to Massachusetts, for example, were sophisticated in the realm of civil institutions though not in urban planning. With a kind of urban theocracy in mind, they founded a college very quickly

after their arrival and centralized governing mechanisms. In contrast, the English settlers of Virginia were rural people whose plantations encouraged open fields, fine houses, and strikingly different, though no less sophisticated, governmental institutions.

The most appealing of the English settlements may be the villages of New England, largely designed on-site and built with an advanced comprehension of wooden construction technology. Yet more ambitious plans flowered elsewhere. In Williamsburg, Virginia, a long flat area was laid out with differentiating axes—a baroque town design—the intention of which was to feature principal buildings, specifically the Governor's Palace and the Capitol and the ensemble of structures for the College of William and Mary.

The plans for Philadelphia, Pennsylvania, and Savannah, Georgia, reveal grander intentions. Philadelphia's was truly regional, a plan for developing a town and its envi-

Architect of a nation, Jefferson designed own living space, Monticello, opposite, and proposed 14 new states. Philadelphia grid of 1682.

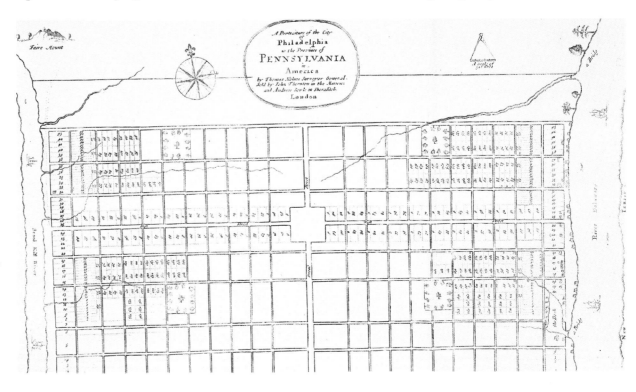

157

rons simultaneously. Savannah's was that too, but with a definite social objective as well—to reestablish former debtors and criminals in circumstances which would foster economic cooperation and thereby permit them to attain respectability. There is no colonial plan in America whose physical pattern so clearly expresses the social and economic intention behind it.

These varied beginnings suggest that planning, for regions as well as for towns, was part and parcel of the nation's settlement. Further, visible patterns on a landscape, urban or rural, are like a key to the values and aspirations of given groups of inhabitants. To a knowing eye, colonizing patterns are still as readable as texts. But they were just the start, the early layers.

The bases for subsequent layers—which ultimately added up to a comprehensive design for developing the entire United States—were formulated between the mid-1780s and the first decade of the 19th century. Then planners were concerned with settling the West, establishing governmental institutions there, and linking it physically to previously settled parts of the continent.

Imagine the issues confronting the members of the Continental Congress after the Revolution. While trying to cope with a depressed economy, they were faced at the same time with such questions as how to make use of western lands and pay the debts incurred during the recent war. Specifically at issue was the vast territory, newly won from the British, between the Ohio and Mississippi rivers. As often happens in planning, a single issue presses for resolution; so it was at this moment.

No less than seven states had claimed territory beyond the Appalachians. States without claims naturally pressed for the creation of a common domain, and Maryland refused to sign the Articles of Confederation unless this was done. Following Virginia's cession of its sweeping claim to all land beyond the Ohio, most other states followed

suit; it then fell to the national government to devise procedures for surveying, selling, and governing this territory.

Distinct and contrasting systems for establishing land claims had previously been adopted in the South and in New England. In the South, a would-be settler traditionally located a plot and filed his claim in terms of its natural boundaries. In New England authorities established a process which entailed setting aside townsites, surveying rectilinear boundaries, and systematically parceling out plots of equal size.

It was this gridiron system that was adopted for the Northwest in the Ordinance of 1785. Though the basic idea was ancient, the scale of application was unprecedented. Eventu-

To entice settlers, land agents sent imaginative bird's-eye views of towns. Below, Black Earth, Wisconsin, in 1867.

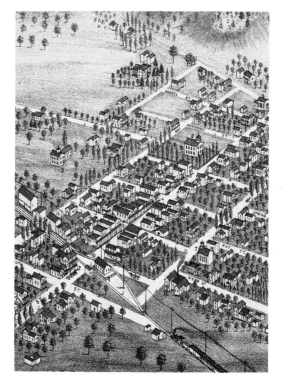

ally the pattern was to cover the nation, except for occasional interruption by a lake, a mountain range, or a waterless desert. The gridiron system divided the land into a pattern of six-mile squares called townships. Each township was subdivided into 36 smaller squares, one mile on a side and 640 acres in area.

The pattern was initially established on the banks of the Ohio, about 30 miles west of Pittsburgh, and covered some 2,300 square miles allotted by Congress to a veterans' group for services rendered. But usually land was auctioned to the highest bidder, section by section, at a minimum price of $640. The law, aimed at providing revenue for the national government, favored jobbers and speculators (of whom there were many in Congress). Frontier farmers could not raise $640, nor could they tend a whole section even if they could buy it. After 1800, however, various measures were taken to liberalize land distribution policies. The result was the Great Migration and the appearance of an endless panorama of checkerboard farmsteads stretching across the vast region that was to become the nation's heartland.

For administration, the Ordinance of 1787 established a Northwest Territory with a governor appointed by Congress. When population of a specific part of the territory reached 5,000, that area was eligible to elect a representative assembly; when it reached 60,000, it was eligible for admission to the Union on the same footing as the original states. The Ordinance of 1785 assured an orderly disposition of the land; the administrative plan of 1787 assured the orderly growth of the nation.

As the nation expanded westward, the need for developing an adequate transportation network became increasingly evident. After the turn of the 19th century the nation's leaders were much in mind of the historical experience of Rome as a colonizer of Europe and the role of roads in that experience—as well as the more recent public road and canal programs of France. In 1803 President Jefferson approached Napoleon about purchasing the Isle of Orleans—that corner of Louisiana east of the Mississippi River. Control of the area by the United States was essential to assure the flow of waterborne commerce the full length of the Mississippi, a matter crucial to the settlement and growth of the whole Mississippi Valley, and the Ohio too. To the astonishment of the American negotiators, France offered to sell the *entire* western watershed of the Mississippi River. Jefferson could not refuse. The result was the Louisiana Purchase, an agrarian "empire for liberty" that more than doubled the size of the nation.

A few years later, Jefferson's Secretary of the Treasury, Albert Gallatin, drafted a plan for a national transportation system running north and south (following both the Atlantic Coast and the Mississippi) as well as east and west across the Appalachians. With the Union thus knit together, Jefferson told Congress, "new channels of communication will be opened between the states; the lines of separation will disappear, their interests will be identified, and their union cemented by new and indissoluble ties." Yet Congress did not act—there was a serious question about constitutionality—except to call on Gallatin to submit a comprehensive report on roads and canals. Though few aspects of Gallatin's admirable plan were developed until many years later, it presaged our nation's present land and water transportation network. Again, the physical pattern we can see is best understood in relation to the intentions behind it.

A significant accomplishment in American town planning at the moment of nationhood should also be noted—the design of our national capital by the French military engineer and artist, Pierre Charles L'Enfant. Pursuant to a commission by George Washington, L'Enfant drafted, in less than a year, the basic plan for Washington, D.C. This

plan set a standard of farsightedness and even civic grandeur that the nation still strives to realize. It was based on concepts similar to those employed at Williamsburg, but on a much greater scale and conceived with considerably more imagination. Urban development was to be concentrated around high points connected by broad radial avenues. Overlaid was a gridiron in the form of a rectilinear block system. And, just as Williamsburg had its central axis, so Washington would have its grand Mall.

L'Enfant planned for a city of about 800,000 (not far from the capital's present total), quite a visionary leap when the population of the whole country was but a few million. He planned a city well fitted to its

natural setting, and one which could grow in an orderly way. Its actual development fell short of L'Enfant's vision, though recently his ideals have been revived and staunchly pursued.

As a model for other cities, the plan of Washington, D.C., was relatively unimportant. Yet, symbolically it expressed a high level of aspiration, a capital worthy of a classic republic. It was and is a visible assertion of a multifaceted democracy in what was once a new land—and what is still a searching land. As its sophistication expresses a loftiness of purpose, so its incompleteness (and the continuing efforts at refinement) expresses an intention to fulfill the ideals of the Revolution.

Township grid, below, with public, private land holdings in northwestern Ohio, was approved by President Jackson in 1836.

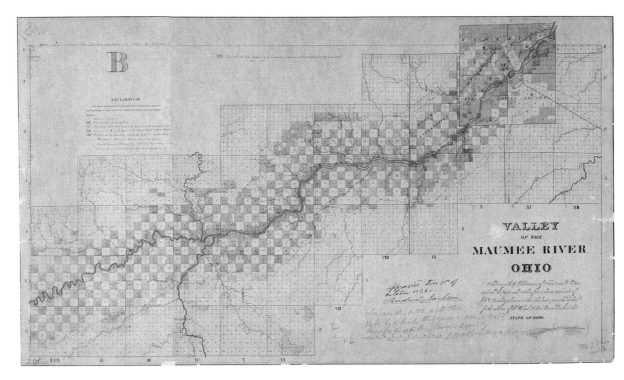

New Amsterdam of 1660, above, reflects design concept which mushroomed into today's towering, Central-Park-surrounding borough of Manhattan. Fortified wall of New Amsterdam formed uptown end of city, became Wall Street. By early 1800s rectangular block pattern appeared on town plan.

Looking at the larger land design system introduced at nationhood, we see, in less than a quarter-century, the establishment of the conception and groundwork for a comprehensive process of national development. Deceptive in its simplicity, it was awesome in its results. It is because the original intention was realized—a land designed to accommodate a mobile people—that there was and is still so much more to do.

Even with a practical system for development, there were formidable obstacles to rapid western settlement. The hardship of pioneering was one, as were sheer distance and the loss of contact with traditional manifestations of civilization. In the early 19th century the federal government tried to spur improved transportation by ceding corridors of land to road and canal companies, a practice later continued with railroads.

Settlement was encouraged by a series of modifications to the laws pertaining to distribution of the public domain. The minimum amount one could buy was reduced, while, at the same time, the advent of the McCormick reaper vastly multiplied the amount of land a single farmer could harvest. The gold rush of 1849 acted as a magical lure to the Far West, and the Homestead Act, enacted during the Civil War along with legislation on behalf of a transcontinental railroad, enabled citizens to claim 160 acres of surveyed public domain after they had occupied it for five years.

These and other factors underlying western settlement were complemented by the evolution of American industry from its early 19th-century origins in the textile mills of New England. Eastern manufacturing and western settlement both gained momentum as a result of railroad development. By 1840 a 2,800-mile rail net operated in the East; by 1880 a national system of 70,000 miles united the country. After the Civil War, railroads surpassed even steam-powered river boats in the carriage of passengers and freight.

Railroads did for the trans-Mississippi West what steamboats had done for the East. By the third quarter of the 19th century the hierarchic pattern of major and secondary termini had begun to emerge. Chicago's development, for example, had been spurred by a federal land grant for the Illinois Central Railroad, which linked Chicago and New Orleans. Subsequent grants, mostly for lines crossing the western half of the continent, totaled well over 100 million acres and boomed the fortunes of such western towns as Omaha and Kansas City. Thus, the federal government's intention of unifying the land manifested itself in the overall development of the West, and in the growth of cities where the railroad roundhouse was the vital center of commerce.

The pattern of these urban and regional developments remained the grid, a pattern so ubiquitous in American land development that it deserves examination. Although the grid may be sensitively applied to the landscape, it is also prone to inappropriate use or misuse. In a town or regional plan, a grid can be relieved by natural open spaces, stream parks, or hills (Jefferson himself had suggested an application with alternate squares treated as parks). Not only can this enhance a town's beauty, it might limit the spread of disease or fire. Nineteenth-century American town planning, in fact, includes numerous examples of grids incorporating broad expanses of open parkland. Louisville, Kentucky, is a splendid case in point. But grids were often applied without any pause or relief. Moreover, the grid tended to foster land speculation, which more than once contributed to financial crises of national impact.

So it is that the grid has come to symbolize the exploitative excesses of the 19th century, the careless and often irresponsible use of the land. What we must remember is that, while there was a strong component of agrarian idealism in our national plan, just as strong—ultimately far stronger—were the forces pushing for urbanization and industrialization. As that reality became evident, new planning concepts were formulated by visionaries intent upon preserving human values and aesthetic ideals.

One such concept was the establishment of natural reserves in urban settings. In 1851 the distinguished landscape designer, Andrew Jackson Downing, drafted a plan for the Mall in Washington, and supervised creation of a park around the Smithsonian "Castle." A few years later, the equally distinguished Frederick Law Olmsted began draining and regrading for Central Park in midtown Manhattan. After the Civil War, Olmsted undertook to transform the marshes of Boston's Back Bay into parkland, an assignment that eventually grew into a plan for a city-wide park system.

As for the larger natural landscape, Yosemite Valley was designated a state park in 1864, and the first national parks were established in the 19th century. In the same year that Yosemite was initially accorded some degree of protection, a remarkable book appeared—*Man and Nature: Or Physical Geography as Modified by Human Action,* by George Perkins Marsh. If Marsh did not introduce the concept of ecology, he did formulate the most persuasive early warning that man's power to transform the environment must be tempered with a commensurate respect for the natural relationship between living organisms and their environments.

Another innovative notion that began to gain currency in the late 19th century was the "new town." Of course, every American town was "new" at its moment of origin, but none had been planned from scratch in every detail, as was Olmsted's masterpiece, the Chicago suburb of Riverside. Other planners followed with similar developments such as Roland Park in Baltimore and Forest Hills, Long Island. Such communities provided a seldom-realized ideal for the American residential suburb. Conceptually they represented an attempt by the affluent

to shut themselves off from the ills of the burgeoning city. But they also mirrored an age-old quest for attainment of a harmonious relationship with nature and neighbors.

Another, quite different type of "new town" was the company town. Although antecedents went all the way back to the mill town of Lowell, Massachusetts, ultimately the most common sort were those built in conjunction with large-scale western mining operations. The classic example, however, was Pullman, built near Chicago for employees of the great railroad car works. The ideal was to meet every basic need of every resident; the reality was a form of paternalism that today seems fraught with perils to the human spirit.

Indeed, when casting a retrospective look at the entire historic process of planning our land—a process whose origins have been sketched here and which will be examined further in subsequent chapters—one becomes aware of numerous disparities between ideals and realities. These are manifested in ugly discontinuities that reflect such ills as poverty and pollution. But it is no less true that we have accomplished a great deal, though perhaps too often with a rough hand when a fine touch would have been preferable.

For example, the fact that our metropolitan explosion has so swiftly obliterated beloved farms and fields does not mean that human intentions—good intentions, even—have not been lacking in this process. Though sometimes hard to discern, the metropolis surely does have form, and it is a deliberate form that can serve genuine needs and enhance fundamental ideals.

In all their complexity, past and present patterns are tangible evidence that planners have recapitulated our cultural condition in the shaping of the land. The establishment of these overlapping patterns is a never-ending process and surely one of the most revealing processes in the continuing saga of our interaction with our land.

The Ground Breakers

By Joe Goodwin

Don't you remember Sweet Betsy from Pike,
Who crossed the big mountains with her lover Ike?
With two yoke of oxen, and a big yellow dog,
A tall Shanghai rooster, and one spotted hog.

Don't hardly see oxen anymore. Yet those massive beasts pulled the wagons with the pioneers across the land where we live today. And on the land for one or two nights a year, around our vacation campfires, we still voice the delightfully irreverent trail songs of the pioneers.
Singing Too-Ra-Lee-Ooo-Ra-Lee-Aye

The words and music still shine bright. And children still snicker at the stanza that tells how Betsy got tight and "showed her bare arse to the whole wagon train."

Somehow, though, our robust pioneer forebears seem to have settled another country entirely, one separated from us not by seas but by the fast-widening abyss of time. To cross the gulf, to grasp the real import of the past, many of us travel, visit museums, work with historical and genealogical organizations, and otherwise study the country's saga.

On pilgrimage to the now almost legendary past, we often become aware of the dual nature of the pioneers: They were the forest cutters, but they were also the twig benders. Our management of soil and forest, a restless propensity to exploit the land to make a quick killing, a feeling that the land belongs to us right now rather than to nature and to the future, all started to grow way back then.

That's not to say that the pioneers ruined the land, then passed the buck in our direction. To America's eternal benefit they often initiated plenty of things both gentle and enlightened. Take one small example: "I was flipping flapjacks over the open fire," an aging pioneer of the Old West told his grandchildren. "We were camping at the homestead site since we hadn't built the cabin yet. And when I glanced out beyond the fire I saw three tough-looking Indians studying me most intently.

"I was scared, of course. But not knowing what else to do, I just kept on flipping more flapjacks until the batter gave out.

"And then I called for your grandmother to come from the tent. We invited the Indians to breakfast, and from then on our folks and theirs became loyal friends."

In the early 1800s there was no way to encourage the good deeds or the good folks. There was certainly no screening agency set up on the jumping-off place to keep bad people from entering the territories. The sovereign rule was "Wagons ho!" Claim all the land from sea to shining sea.

Up until about 1840, traders, trappers, and missionaries predominated on the western trails. The tide began to turn, and during 1845 at Fort Laramie in what is now southeastern Wyoming, traders counted 3,000 homesteaders outward bound on the Oregon Trail. Five years later the annual number of settlers passing this point perhaps tripled, with 5,000 wagons counted at Laramie in 1850.

The prairie schooner business boomed, especially around Independence, Missouri—the City of the Trails—where the Oregon and California Trails and the Santa Fe Trail began. Heavy Conestoga wagons sufficed for crossing the Appalachians, but a lighter, even more rugged rig was required for the great West.

Spanish and French influence ebbed as the new immigrants swarmed into the West. English speakers of the United States and Canada pretty much had the field all to themselves. And that's one reason why our daring duo from the song could push largely unopposed into the world's center cut of agricultural lands, the Great Plains.

Only, as Robert Frost put it, "America is hard to see." For many, the lure of gold was blinding, and Sweet Betsy, Ike, and that great surge of '49ers just kept on rolling to the Mother Lode in the Great Golden State of California.

Another wave of settlement, including many Scandinavian and German farmers, swung north across the Plains. Remembering their evergreen-forested homelands, they sought out the Great North Woods—places like Minnesota and Wisconsin—believing that soil able to produce a forest was the only kind that could grow grain. Either less choosy or more daring, later emigrants—the meek—inherited the plains.

Magnificent irony! While the '49ers froze in the mountains of California, lost their shirts, or worked or drank themselves to death, humble farmers warmed to prairie life. In places like Nebraska or Oklahoma they cooked their grub over straw and cattle-chip fires, and learned to coax amazing yields of hard red winter wheat from the rich prairie subsoil. They earned their nicknames, sodbusters, from the tiresome work of breaking through the virgin layer of tough, matted turf over the dirt. Some of this sod they sliced into spongy blocks—stacked and chinked, it made the walls of their cozy dwellings, called soddies.

Once they knew how to handle the land, life became wholesome and often secure. One key to growing prosperity was a wheat that fitted the land. While the climate of the Plains was often extolled as gentle and temperate, settlers soon came to know better. Dryness and deep cold met their match in the freeze-resistant wheat brought by Ukrainian farmers from their old homeland.

Native-born Betsy and Ike quickly discovered that many of their wagon mates hailed from abroad. A very plain little verse, presumably first sung by a foreigner, goes a very long way toward pinpointing the most reliable sources of good luck and good fortune in pioneer U.S.A.

When I first came to this land
I was not a wealthy man
But the land was sweet and good
I did what I could.

Lucrative pioneering depended, naturally, on just such a willingness to work, coupled with generous measures of rich soil, true grit, and axle grease. Many people, however, believed that dumb luck brought the really big payoffs. Thus even such evident scamps as Betsy and Ike stood a real chance of making a killing out West—not that many did.

Perhaps that enduring belief provides one reason why so many Americans, and foreign visitors, travel so far and spend so much at the casinos of Reno and Vegas. In some small way the modern-day pilgrimage may help to create, or recreate a sense of the big frontier gamble, the splendid hazard of the pioneers, and their magnificent optimism that great wealth lay just beyond the sunset horizon.

Such gentle self-deception may have been justified back then. Stern realities lay behind pioneerdom's golden vision, and to dwell on the dangers might turn a brave man into a coward. The slogan of the Society of California sums up the uncertainties of the 180-day trek from the Mississippi to the Pacific: *The cowards never started and the weak ones died by the way.*

Rickety Mormon Handcarts carried 500 pounds of supplies and infinite provisions of faith. Those who struggled with the small vehicles certainly needed both. The trek west from Illinois and Nebraska proved arduous enough for wealthier Mormons who voyaged by prairie schooner.

With 64 good wagons and teams, Brigham Young's advance party of more than 140 people crossed nearly 1,000 miles in 111 days to reach the valley of the Great Salt Lake. Families with carts sometimes toiled for six months to traverse the Great Plains and the Continental Divide.

Despite the hardships, though, Mormons found it far easier and more prudent to pick up and leave the East than to stay. Joseph Smith, American-born Prophet of The Church of Jesus Christ of Latter-day Saints, had been assassinated by a mob in 1844. Ill feeling toward his followers had burgeoned into hatred in Illinois and Missouri.

Several factors had fostered violence, including plural marriage, the close social structure of the faithful, and their remarkable degree of industry and thrift. And had the Mormons held an introspective faith with few worldly motivations, their neighbors might have thought them a bit peculiar and left them alone. But to this day Mormons are activists and collectivists who focus economic power to achieve worldly goals toward spiritual ends.

For instance, Joseph Smith admonished his people to acquire peacefully large tracts of land in and near thriving Independence, Missouri. He taught that some very ancient and very holy sites lay thereabouts. And it was the sworn duty of the Church to build a temple and raise a holy city, a New Jerusalem, in the hallowed precincts of Missouri.

In view of the violence, Brigham Young's particular group of Mormons decided to push on, the time not being ripe to build up their following in the East.

From the arrival of Brigham Young at the Great Salt Lake in 1847, to the coming of the railroad in 1869, nearly 70,000 Mormons trekked west. The brethren who made it the hard way jeeringly referred to train-borne latecomers as the "Pullman pioneers."

Religion aside, by 1900 the Utah Mormons had amassed a remarkable store of pioneering experience. Church leaders kept successful homesteaders on the move. These experts were sent out time and again to plant crops, build houses and schools, and then turn over the working communities and

I was born on the prairie and the milk of its wheat, the red of its clover, the eyes of its women, gave me a song and a slogan.

–Carl Sandburg

Sharing unknown dangers, Mormons fled from religious persecution in Missouri and Illinois. Brigham Young's tiny advance party reached the site of Salt Lake City in 1847, and over the years thousands of Latter-day Saints followed. Left, in their zeal, Saints with no money for wagons pull handcarts to Utah, where an arid promised land with Biblical overtones awaits. Bonneville Salt Flats at dawn, center. Snow-fed streams provide water for rich valley soil. Vigorous work and neighborly cooperation soon create lands of plenty.

farms to green newcomers who needed a boost. The active pioneering venture reached into neighboring territories and into Canada. And even today, Mormons assert, a certain amount of pioneering still goes on.

Remarkable similarities between Utah geography and that of the Holy Land further convinced Mormons that theirs was indeed a land of destiny for a chosen people. For instance, a sweet-water river pours out of a lake at Provo and carries its water to the Great Salt Lake, much as fresh water from the Sea of Galilee travels down to the briny Dead Sea by way of River Jordan.

Like Biblical Palestine, much of Utah is desert. Experiences gained by living near dry wilderness opened up new insights into the Bible. Settlers in Israel today consult Old Testament writings to gain practical knowledge of their dry country, themselves, and the people who settled there before them. The Book of Mormon describes a people wandering in desert America long ago.

High mountains in Utah give Mormon farmers an important economic advantage over Israeli settlers. Snows in the high ranges provide abundant meltwater to settlements planted near canyon openings.

Mormons still believe that a great new settlement will one day rise at the site of Independence, Missouri. Yet their pioneer experiences lead Mormons to believe that in the Mountain West, too, God's Country is being found.

Where Have All the Pioneers Gone? Why, through genetic processes they have been transformed and transmuted into us. Where have all the pioneer lands gone? Why, we've dammed them up, planed them down, ditched them, divided, and bridged them. We've bulldozed and filled, plowed and planted, and allowed them to erode.

During the accumulating decades we've changed the land greatly. And humankind has emerged into a geologic force in its own right. But that isn't all, for as we've changed our surroundings we've changed ourselves.

All in all, our pioneering's about done, except perhaps in Alaska and on the moon, and in these places in a qualified way only. Yet upon very close examination of the American scene, we can say—once more in a qualified way—that the pioneers never died. Look!

Up near Sand Mountain in Alabama you'll meet a few who fight valiantly for their solitude.

"Dag-nabbit," one such tough mountain man exclaimed with sadness in his voice, "the county's just put gravel on my little dirt road. Guess it's time to pull up stakes again and

move on, and just after I'd dug the new well out back and my wife kilt all the snakes around the place."

One-room schoolhouses, a dead giveaway for those who would seek the pioneer spirit, still appear in such places as South Carolina, Tennessee, Georgia, and Arkansas. But educators have opined lately that what appears to be a primitive arrangement is not, after all, a bad way to educate children. So we may see a resurgence in years to come.

After school, where can we find childhood's pioneers of the local stream, cave, or barrow pit? Have Huck Finn and Tom Sawyer gone? Why, many of them are apt to be caught lounging before the TV, as glassy-eyed as the tube.

Black people arrived unwillingly. Dixie's slave economy put them to pioneering for Ol' Massah's benefit. Sharecropping laws after the Civil War kept most of those of African descent tied to the southern land. A few fortunate blacks made their way west after 1865, becoming cowboys, soldiers, and settlers. Some of these still unheralded pioneers settled in established communities and in the numerous mining boom towns. Others homesteaded and founded successful towns of their own. For many of these people, the West indeed proved to be a land of opportunity—as it had for those of so many other ethnic backgrounds.

Particularly during and after World War II, blacks from the South and East have joined the new westward migration. While many have found welcome and new opportunities in the West, others have arrived only to find that the prejudices of older parts of the nation have also migrated.

As for the Indians, their tribes increase, they continue to affect the land, and vice versa (see pages 278–283).

The farmer still feeds us all. But he's up to date, cultivating from the cab of a supertractor, and each year sinking just a little deeper into debt as the price of gasoline, tractor repair, feed, interest on loans, and grocery-store food all rise.

Soaring land prices, complexities of agribusiness, and the demanding regimen of farm life still drive young people from the soil into the suburbs. But many proudly and nostalgically cherish their country origins, while others, new pioneers young and old, give up the city life for a chance at rural hardscrabble farming.

Out in the Rockies, men set aside their weekends for recreational mining—what an apparent contradiction in terms. They go out in the rough country looking for the Lost Dutchman or some other equally chimerical vein of good luck. What magnificent optimism!

Recreational vehicles travel where the trusty prairie

Photographers record such details of frontier life as a Utah school in 1899—its students assembled. Mother and child in Kansas bring in sun-dried dung, buffalo chips, handy fuel on the treeless prairie. Kids often imagine how life must have been in pioneer days, as in a great regional favorite of Midwesterners, the cartoon "Injun Summer" at far left. Another sketch, "From Iowa and Proud of It" captures the spirit of the heartland today—the breadbasket of the world.

in pioneering peasant families from Mexico and Old Spain.

This latter group helped establish a Spanish presence in the Southwest, perhaps as a basis for further territorial claims. In addition, conquistador Don Juan de Oñate, arriving to settle New Mexico in 1598, needed the support of local people for his expeditions in search of precious metal.

Hispanic pioneers accompanied burro- and mule-pack trains. Humble people walked or rode in two-wheeled *carretas*. Political leaders and the military often arrived on horseback. After 1770, occasional ships helped supply the Alta California mission settlements.

Eventually cut off from regular trade with Mexico, the Hispanic settlers of New Mexico produced by hand almost all their tools, furnishings, and objects of devotion. Local wood, leather, wool, fibers, clay and adobe mud, and stone sufficed for material, along with a little metal obtained through trade with Mexico, and with the United States after 1825. Copper was mined locally.

Their old ware, now prized by collectors and museums in many lands, includes textiles and leather apparel, religious pictures and statuary of carved and painted wood, trunks for storage, benches and tables.

The settlers introduced fruit trees, much admired by the Indians, and raised grapes for food and fermentation. Vintners produced not only wine, but after 1800 a distilled grape brandy widely known as Taos Lightning.

Anglo salesmen arrived from the States, and the railroad came. Descendants of the original settlers often abandoned their arts and crafts and local industries; supplied with cheap tinware and gimcracks, they lost their everyday dependence on traditional skills. As times changed, many members of the Hispanic population began to lose faith in themselves and their ways. But today the tide has turned.

Artistic, social, and economic accomplishments of Hispanic people in the United States earn wide admiration. Demographers note that the Latin community may be the fastest growing segment of the population. Through interests and attachments to areas outside the States, Hispanic people here help ally the nation to important movements throughout the Western Hemisphere.

Far more importantly, Latin people of the United States have long managed to live with verve and pride on the land though lacking an abundance of material goods. In view of today's shortages, inflation, and the large numbers of older Americans moving to the sun country of Florida and the Southwest, the Hispanic example there of vital living with less can be a truly priceless key to the future.

schooner once rolled. Campgrounds still fill up with gasoline-powered pavilions. Mercifully, a great many Americans can leave town to recreate in the country, if only on holiday. The hills and the valleys, land unadorned, still have the power to teach, inspire, and strengthen people.

In the age of atoms and oil, a specter rises that all our hard-won institutions and our machines may run out of fuel or burn up in a war. If so, could we be pioneers again? Could we be as determined, courageous, and as self-sacrificing as our pioneer ancestors?

I have a disease of the heart that can only be cured with gold.
—Hernán Cortés, Conquistador

Like a stubbornly unrepentant child, Cortés freely admitted his basic motivation. He crushed the Aztecs to take their gold. Not that the brutal Aztecs didn't have it coming to them. Yet Mother Church and Father Spain saw little wrong with the murder, plunder, and rape just so long as heathen souls were saved in the process and part of the swag reached Europe. From the double heat of conquest and inquisition Hispanic America was forged—though tempered by examples, and sometime inspiring ones, of genuine faith, courage, self-sacrifice, and concern for the public weal.

Possibly because there was so little loose gold up north, in lands now part of the southwestern United States, Spain's rule there was comparatively benign, yet marked by some atrocities. The foreign overlords were content to half enslave the Indians, extract conversions from them, and to bring

Vineyards and mission churches survive, poignant souvenirs of an era when Spanish adventurers turned from plundering in Old Mexico to planting in New Mexico, California, and Florida. Right, restoration plan for Mission San Jose y Miguel de Aguayo in San Antonio, Texas; the compound's buildings include barracks, Indian quarters, convents, a granary and mill, and craft shops. Below: Mission San Xavier del Bac gleams near Tucson, Arizona. The welcoming edifice is known as the White Dove of the Desert.

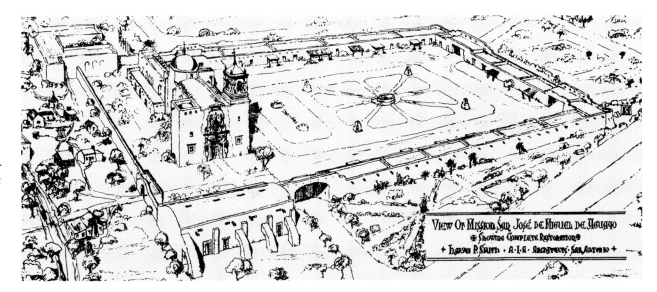

VIEW OF MISSION SAN JOSÉ DE MIGUEL DEL AGUAYO
SHOWING COMPLETE RESTORATION
HARVEY P. SMITH · A·I·A · ARCHITECT · SAN ANTONIO ·

The dean of aerial cameramen, William Garnett is photographed at the controls of his brightly polished Cessna 170B by his son. At right, Garnett finds rich color and sensuous forms in the Dunnigan Hills of California.

Photographs by William Garnett

A View From Above

By Edwards Park

It was a reunion for the three of us: Bill Garnett, myself, and the Cessna 170B. Once before I had helped Bill slide open the telescoping doors of Hangar Number 5 at Napa Airport and roll the old silver plane out into the California sunlight. And here we were, doing it again, partly because Bill says I bring him luck.

Garnett is the dean of aerial photographers. All the others in the world who see meaning and beauty and maybe a story in the land's face as they look down upon it owe something to Bill, if only because he is apt to have done it first. He's been shooting pictures from the air since he was first exposed to the wondrous, shifting views from above in the navigator's seat of an Army transport on

a cadged ride home to California for Christmas in 1945. He is a genius at seeing abstract art in patterns of landscape—where other viewers, gazing down, perhaps, from a 737, see only, say, the outskirts of Omaha. He teaches photography at Berkeley and, by example, his instruction spreads far beyond the University of California. You can't look at his work without wondering how you've managed to stay so blind.

The Cessna is Bill's little mistress. She was built in the '50s, a four-seat monoplane with an old-fashioned rounded rudder and conventional landing gear—she's a "tail-dragger," though you'd never want to say that to her face.

She's also bright silver. Her graceful wings

and slender flanks have been buffed to a mirror finish with hours of muscle-wrenching work by her lover and anyone else he can dupe into helping. In the sunlight she dazzles; when she flares out over a runway she's unmistakable. At perhaps a score of airports in California the controller is apt to add a small "Hello, Mr. Garnett" to the formalities of taxiing instructions for this gleaming little visitor.

Bill is a superb pilot. I had flown with him previously and watched him at work with his cameras. I had heard him wax enthusiastic over some formation on the land that made a picture in his eyes, and fume at some desecration committed in the name of the almighty dollar.

I had driven out to his hillside home in Napa Valley earlier this morning. From his picture window you look out on his grapes, a couple of acres of them, carefully tended.

That window also illuminates mural-size enlargements of some famous Garnett photographs—one of rivulets running together to form a stream. It comes across as a wide-spreading oriental tree with trunk, boughs, limbs, branches, tiny twigs, all softened by their eroded banks so that they seem to be rich with foliage. There are others. I especially remember the sand dune, caught from above in such a light that it becomes alive and voluptuous, the hip and thigh of a nude. I remembered that Bill plans his photographic flights around what the light will be doing at such-and-such a place and time of day. Sand dunes need low light, but I was with him once at midday as he circled endlessly above some lava beds that came into bloom, so to speak, only under a high sun.

The Garnett darkroom, where many wonders are wrought, adjoins the house. When I called in, I caught him just emerging from some dark alchemy, stepping out to sniff the air and, inevitably, to study the sky. "The fog's gone," he said. "Let's go fly. You can cope with a little crosswind, can't you?"

"Of course," I said, secure in the knowledge that Bill is insanely jealous of his little silver mistress and would quickly put a stop to any hanky panky she tried with me. And so here we were at the airport, climbing aboard in reunion.

There was quite a bit of crosswind, enough to stir a Garnett anecdote as we slowly taxied toward the active runway. "She weathervanes badly on the ground in a wind like this," Bill began. "All tail-draggers do. Here, you take her. Feel that? Ooops! Watch it! Reminds me of a time I was flying out of Page, Arizona. Near Navajo Mountain.

"There was a summer storm coming up over the desert with rolling clouds. I *had* to go get them. I asked the airport manager— one guy did everything there—if he'd read off ground wind velocities on his radio every few minutes so I'd know when I ought to head back to the barn. Well, he thought I was kind of odd, I guess—Look out! Here comes another gust!—But he did it while I flew near the clouds and got my pictures. He called in 15 miles per hour, then 20 and 25, and he said, 'I think you'd better come in.'

"So I did. But once I got on the ground I couldn't hold her straight. I had to call the manager out onto the runway to walk beside me, holding a wing. By the time we got her tied down, the wind was up to 40 knots or so. Great pictures, though."

I got us down to the end of the runway and handed over to him. His voice slid into microphone jargon, getting takeoff clear-

Earth-hide turns out to be the sun-crinkled rind of Arizona's Painted Desert. Overleaf: As if space travelers had imposed a human image on the land, a Washington wheat field reveals its sinuous torso.

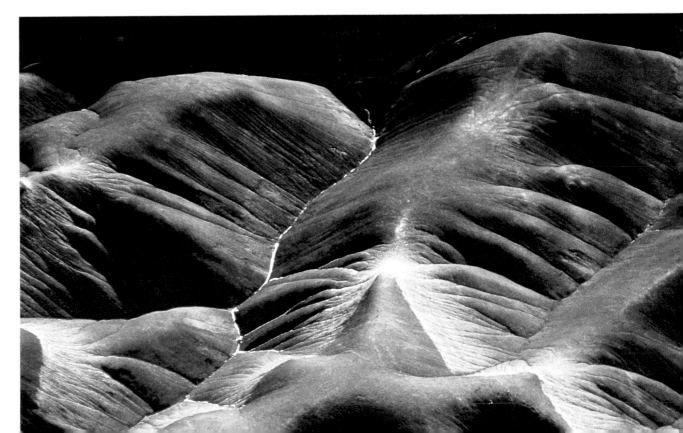

ance. In a moment we were off the ground and he turned her over to me again. "Wherever you want to go," he said in that half-shout that pilots use.

"River?" I half-shouted back.

"Fine."

I had noticed, flying previously with Bill, that he tends always to take a look at certain areas or specific spots where good photographs can be made. Near Napa, there's a pool of discolored water, salt-edged. There's also a city dump that glints with various cast-off metallic things—washing machines, refrigerators, fenders, filing cabinets—who knows? There's a parking lot filled with cars newly unloaded from freighters—acres of shiny rectangles in their fresh Japanese paint jobs, all neatly aligned. In the Sacramento River there's a clot of mothballed naval vessels. Bill has probably shot all these and various other spots many times, but always the light is a little different, the angle of the aerial camera ever changing.

So he checks up on them, like a mountain man following his trap line.

I slid over the river at about 2,000 feet and cut some rather sloppy figure eights above the clustered ships, drab and lifeless, yet visually interesting because of their symmetry. Bill didn't pay much attention to them. He was preoccupied by my handling of his mistress and when, with a wrench (for she is a beautiful creature to play with), I turned her controls back to him, he was obviously relieved.

The first time I flew with him, I hardly touched the Cessna. The idea was to see how he does his job alone, so I simply sat in the right-hand seat and watched, waiting for him to zero in on some abstraction that would appear unmistakably on the Earth's face. I soon realized, of course, that the compositions he sees are not distinguishable to everyone.

We had flown north, up the Great Valley, to where Mount Shasta rose magisterially. Any fool could see that Shasta, in early light, was magnificently photogenic. And sure enough, Bill opened his window, banked around the summit, and clicked away. But it was the lava beds in southern Oregon that enchanted him. To me they were a bleak, dark desert of molten rock that sent endless thermals bubbling upward to bounce the Cessna sickeningly as we circled. Bill's technique is to roll into a steep left bank, trim the plane for slow flight with the nose high, open his window, push his inevitable straw hat back on his head, and fire away with two cameras while holding his turn with his rudder and his right elbow. Around and around. Click, click, click. He was seeing subtle lines and shadings of tone in that dreary landscape and he was framing his visions with his view finder. He seemed very pleased with what he got.

The only modification Garnett has made to his plane is to remove his side-window restrainer, which allows an opening of only a few inches. Without that little arm, the window flies wide open to the wind and stays there, held by the slipstream. He told me that in the early '50s when he was starting his career, he flew a Cessna 140 with a hole cut in the floor between the tracks of the right-hand seat. He'd remove the seat before taking off, then just lean over and shoot through the hole. This technique with the wide-open window is better. At least he can see where he's going.

Garnett has no trade secrets, but he does have habits and superstitions. He always uses a Pentax camera—two of them, actually—and he always wears his broad-brimmed straw hat which appears to be a refugee from a West Indian isle. He also likes having me along because I bring him luck. On this reunion flight I brought him a picture opportunity, though he was minus cameras. We had landed for lunch at a "fly-in" restaurant that's well-known in the San Francisco-Sacramento area. Taking off and climbing out again, we came up behind another Cessna, this one towing a gleaming white sailplane. With a glance at each other we went winging after the pair.

Bill likes photographing other planes, but usually as part of a landscape. I was with him when he circled above a rice field in the Valley as a crop duster worked it over. Bill made a broad orbit at 1,000 feet while the yellow "ag" plane swept low over the green, water-glinting field, a stream of spray feathering out behind it.

This time he climbs, rising above the towed sailplane and when it releases, over a ridge—one of the long line of hills that mark the western edge of the Valley—we are in position, above and slightly west of it. The sailplane pilot hugs the highest ridge, soaring on the west wind which is deflected upward as it strikes the hills. He is very low over that rounded height, whispering along, nose down, as if sniffing the stunted trees for the whiff of a rising current that will lift those long, tapered wings.

Bill has throttled back to hold position.

We are half-soaring ourselves, and we wag our wings at our friend and he wags back.

Bill likes to ride an updraft when he can. When I flew with him before, he would stay on the windward side of the Sierras, cut back to about half the normal rpms and let the great surge of air that is flung aloft by those peaks lock him in. "I like to save fuel," he told me. "And it makes it easier to talk."

We climbed a good part of Mount Whitney that time by soaring up the slope, but we needed full power to clear its 14,500-foot summit, for the air is thinning out up there. I remember how, on the southeastern side of it, we spiraled down into the oven heat of Owens Lake, below sea level. There was a salt pan there with a scum of ruby-colored water in it, and Bill couldn't let it alone. Up went the window, back went the crazy hat, over went the Cessna into its slow, nose-high bank, and down thrust a Pentax to compose and frame a new Garnett abstraction. Well, hardly "new." He'd shot that salt pan dozens of times. But this time the light was perhaps a little different, the water level had changed, he was higher or lower above it. It was one of the Garnett sites, one of the visual traps that he must always investigate.

The sailplane is sheer luck—a nice sight, fun to shoot if he had a camera. But as we leave and slide back down to Napa, I reflect that it has always been the land itself—not the things on or above it—that catches Garnett's eye. Not that he chases after pockets of wilderness. What man does to the land is often more interesting to Bill.

Plow contours, for example, make wonderful patterns on the land, and Garnett knows where to find them. And every jet traveler glancing down from 37,000 feet over the West, may sometimes see those perfectly round green circles that stare upward from brown, dry-farming areas. They seem to have been scribed by a compass—and so they were. Rotating irrigation nozzles marked out these circles and painted them green with growth. Bill Garnett sees these,

also, and is as fascinated by them as anyone.

"The other pictures are all there on the land, too," he once said as we were talking in his darkroom. "All you have to do is keep your eyes open."

I knew he was right, but I also felt that only the sun-soaked western landscape could provide such richness as he finds. And leaving him this last time, back at Napa (he let me land, and I did remarkably well), I had a niggling worm of envy for his California flying with its infinite variety, ample room, and—in the Valley at least—good visibility. I reluctantly said goodby "until next time," thinking not only of my friend and his Cessna, but of the experience itself, the delight of seeing from the air.

And then, back in the hazy, crowded East, I found a free day and went to the local airport, on Chesapeake Bay, to take up a rental plane, another Cessna, but newer and less glamorous. I got off the ground and straightened myself out with my usual ineptitude, and then, as I relaxed, I saw below me a small stream fed by tiny creeks and runs, and the whole system began to look like a strange little tree. . . . And now, below my left wheel lay a freshly plowed field, its furrows following the soft contours of the land in curving parallels that formed pleasing figures. . . . And then we passed over a black, marshy pond stippled with white dots as gulls rested upon it. . . .

And I found myself beginning to see.

The gentle geometry of a Wisconsin farm has been carved out of a secluded wooded valley, opposite. Below, windrowed hay in California awaits the hay baler—from above it could be confused with a computer drawing.

The
Suburban
Dream

By E. Ogden Tanner

For a good many decades, a favorite pastime of upwardly mobile Americans has been curling up on the living room sofa with a second cup of coffee and the Sunday real-estate ads. There, in the curious, glowing shorthand of Realtorese, beckon hundreds upon thousands of variations on the American Dream. Newlyweds can ponder the virtues of a Starter Ranch versus a Storybook Cape Cod; growing families can aspire to a Charming Center Hall Colonial, an Executive Ranch, or even a Custom Colonial Ranch. Older couples whose children have left the nest can opt for a Luxury Adult Condominium or a Leisure Village Townhouse, complete with Private Swim Club, Racquets Complex, and Someone Else To Mow The Grass.

Whatever the spellbound prospects decide on (and can afford), each decision adds another small stone to the vast, sprawling edifice of U.S. home ownership—an edifice that has made homebuilding and automobiles the nation's largest industries, real estate its biggest licensed profession, and Suburbia, the home turf of all three, the most far-reaching phenomenon to be visited upon the American land.

The exodus from cities to suburbs in the United States has in fact been the greatest mass migration in history, dwarfing even America's own earlier migration westward and the subsequent abandonment of farms for bright city lights. The census of 1970 revealed the startling fact that for the first time in the annals of the United States, or any other nation, more people were living in the areas just outside cities than in the cities themselves or in the rural regions beyond. Today the number of suburbanites is approaching 100 million and the trend shows few signs of abating; an estimated 1.5 million acres of raw land are being gobbled up every year.

The impact of this peculiarly American pattern of settlement, of course, has been enormous, affecting the natural landscape, transportation, commerce, living habits, attitudes, and just about every other thread of the fabric of American life. Suburbia has enriched the idiom with concepts that never existed before: indoor-outdoor living, back yard barbecues and swimming pools, power mowers, snow blowers, and garage sales; station wagons, Welcome Wagons, Little Leaguers, PTAs; freeways, shopping centers, drive-in churches, Big Macs, and Holiday Inns. Along the way the suburbs have taken their share of lumps from social critics who have blamed them for everything from pollution to rising divorce rates and a lot of other things they have found repellent in the American Way. Neither the critics nor anyone else, however, planners and government administrators included, have been able to do much to stop the phenomenon, nor even to guide its growth more than superficially on a national scale. From all indications, moreover, it is the denizens of Suburbia who will determine the shape of the future, for they hold the balance of economic and political clout.

> Boston holds nothing for you except heavy taxes and political misrule. When you marry, pick out a suburb to build your house in, join the Country Club, and make your life center about your club, your home and your children.

When a wealthy Bostonian gave this advice to his son in the late 19th century, the state of mind of many Americans was already becoming clear. The nation had been founded on the rocks of individual freedom and the pursuit of happiness—and a strong, abiding hunger for land. From the beginning the American Dream was an agrarian one: Thomas Jefferson

In idyllic 1856 scene, opposite, country homes outside Lawrence, Massachusetts, promised utopia for gardening, strolling. Above, densely populated Oakland, now part of greater San Francisco metropolitan area.

had envisioned a nation of independent, prosperous farmer-freeholders and had viewed cities as "pestilential to the morals, the health and the liberties of man." Spurred on by such notions, Americans moved ever westward, settling, moving, settling again, until the frontier finally disappeared. During the 19th century the twin tides of industrialization and immigration began to transform the nation's growing cities into the very antithesis of the Jeffersonian ideal: crowded, smoky, dirty places, increasingly vulnerable—like the European cities Americans had so eagerly left behind—to the crimes of the desperate, the rule of corruption, and the outbreak of disease. The deep-rooted American distrust of cities seemed justified indeed.

The rich, naturally, were the first to get away. They escaped to what were to become the Gold Coasts of Long Island's North Shore and similar enclaves outside Boston, Philadelphia, and Chicago, where they could play gentleman farmer-sportsman. There they were far enough removed to avoid rubbing elbows with the newer immigrants (especially in summer, when it was hot and some folks were lucky to get one bath a week), yet close enough to keep their eyes on their downtown fortunes and the city's cultural lures. But the masses were not far behind. As early as the 1820s, paddle-steamer ferries plied New York harbor, helping less affluent commuters to colonize bedroom communities in Brooklyn, Hoboken, and Staten Island; by the 1850s horse-drawn streetcars carried clerks and artisans from Boston's Hub to new outlying rowhouses. Soon the gentleman farmers, with some distaste, were looking down from their English country manors upon a growing ethnic grid.

The tempo of suburbanization stepped up smartly late in the century with the advent of electrified trolleys, street railways, and the first commuter trains. Traction tycoons, real estate speculators, and publicists hawked irresistible "back-to-nature" deals in new communities that ranged from sedately landscaped Arcadias to Coney Island honky-tonks. The era of the streetcar suburb merged into that of the railroad suburb; growth was still fairly concentrated since most homes had to be within reasonable walking distance of the station, around which clustered a small but thriving "down-

town" of services and shops. Some of the tonier suburbs like White Plains, Scarsdale, Montclair, and those along Philadelphia's Main Line—which had been given Welsh names like Radnor and Bala Cynwyd by railroad real estate agents to lend them Old World charm—organized civic associations and tried valiantly, if not always successfully, to save their shade trees and stem the tide of workers, rooming houses, billboards, overhead wires, and general uglification that lapped menacingly at their heels.

Though suburban settlers had been creeping outward from the city for nearly a century, the first real explosion came in the Roaring Twenties, when widespread ownership of America's new toy, the automobile, cut the suburbs from their bondage to the transit lines and started to splatter them all over the map. Real estate speculation began in earnest; land became Suburbia's basic commodity and prices went in one direction—up. By the late 1920s Americans were taking out more than five billion dollars in mortgage loans a year and snapping up Chevies and Model A Fords as fast as they came off the assembly line. Wealthier suburbanites drove Cadillac Phaetons and Packard Runabouts and played the increasingly popular game of golf; buoyed by the prosperity of the Coolidge era, even $4,000-a-year salesmen, in historian Frederick Lewis Allen's words, dreamed of buying "a fine house and all the good things of the earth."

The era also saw the birth of something far less visible but equally important in determining the future's shape: the Standard State Zoning Enabling Act of 1924, which would encourage the formation of no less than 65,000 separate governmental entities across the nation, each jealously guarding its powers of restrictive zoning to keep its suburban virtue spotless and exclude from the community the kind of people it did not like.

Town and Country must be married, and out of this joyous union will spring a new hope, a new life, a new civilization.

Ever since 1898, when an English court reporter, Ebenezer Howard, wrote these words in his book *Garden Cities for Tomorrow,* planners and reformers had been seeking ways to reconcile the realities of a burgeoning urban population with the romance of the rural ideal. In America, Clarence Stein, Henry Wright, and a handful of other visionaries attempted to demonstrate concepts of rational suburban planning. Featuring attached housing in superblocks around common greenswards, with separate circulation for pedestrians and automobiles, such planned communities as Radburn, New Jersey, went virtually unnoticed in the real-estate-building binge of the '20s. The subdividers were too busy putting up what most buyers seemed to want: the dream of a one-family, detached house on its own sacred plot of land.

Then came the Crash and the Depression; Suburbia, like everything else, staggered to a halt and hung on, trying to survive. Government briefly came riding to the rescue in the person of the Resettlement Administration's Rexford Guy Tugwell, who talked of building 3,000 new suburban "garden cities" to house families trying to escape the urban slums as well as those being driven off the farms. Tugwell's superiors cut the number to 25 and Congress slashed those to three: Greenbelt, Maryland, outside Washington; Greendale, near Milwaukee; and Greenhills, outside Cincinnati. Without industry or a mix of housing for various income levels they turned into suburban bedroom neighborhoods primarily for middle-income commuters, a little greener and better laid out than most of their counterparts, to be sure, but not quite the pioneering, self-contained communities the planners had in mind. The vision of the garden city sank out of sight. The suburbs seemed destined to continue as an escape from the city for those who could afford it—and a heady game for speculators and developers, who had found they could extract undreamed-of dollars out of bloating land values and the insatiable desire of Americans for a home of their own.

Little boxes on the hillside,
Little boxes made of ticky tacky,
Little boxes on the hillside,
Little boxes all the same.
            Song by Malvina Reynolds

In the late 1940s and early 1950s, the lid clamped on the demand for housing by the Depression and World War II blew off with a spectacular bang. What emerged was a genie that the august editors of *Fortune* magazine studied somberly and christened The Exploding Metropolis. Others saw it simply as the wildest housebuilding, housebuying spree in the history of man. The fresh surge in Suburbia was made possible by several new factors: the ex-GI with a marriage certificate in one hand and a government-insured mortgage in the other; a vast new peacetime army of roadbuilders, carpenters, masons, plumbers, and electricians; smart merchant builders like Abraham Levitt and his sons, who applied wartime assembly-line techniques to the mass production of low-cost, one-family houses. And, of course, the

Precariously perched on terraced hillside, new homes in San Fernando Valley defy mudslides, make maximum use of available space. Opposite, construction in the Valley, a former ranching area, boomed after Korean War.

automobile, now more widely in demand than ever, and now abetted by other liberating influences like four-lane highways, telephones, and the humble but vital septic tank.

The critics looked aghast as the potato fields of Long Island and the orange groves and hillsides of Los Angeles sprouted new crops of look-alike boxes with carports, "picture" windows that faced the street, shiny mechanized kitchens that opened onto breakfast "nooks" and dining "ells," and identical foundation shrubs that stood guard duty over identical patches of crabgrassy lawn. The new suburbanites who bought the boxes, glad enough to have their piece of the Dream, went about their lives enthusiastically. They produced babies (by the thousands), hired babysitters, commuted, mowed lawns, washed cars, discovered the joys of gardening and home repair, ate Girl Scout cookies, held cocktail parties and back yard barbecues, formed carpools and Little League baseball teams, paid school taxes, bought dishwashers, outdoor furniture, encyclopedias and Tupperware, and worried about what to do with all the bills.

As the housing boom continued into the late '50s and early '60s the critics—most of them confirmed intellectuals and defiant city dwellers—recovered their wits sufficiently to launch an orgy of social investigation into this newest bastardization of The American Vision: what they called the "slurbs."

While some of the accusations were undoubtedly true, more careful studies revealed that a lot of them were highly overblown. Whatever their shortcomings, John and Mary Drone, as one novelist uncharitably named his suburban protagonists, by and large were individuals caught in the stream of events like everyone else. It was just that they were fed up with, and increasingly frightened by, city living. They had moved out in search of a little fresh air, a few trees, a decent school for the children, and a house of their own they could fix up as they pleased without some landlord telling them what they could and could not do everytime he collected the rent. (Years later, results of their newfound pride in home ownership could be seen in places like Levittown, Long Island, where the "little boxes" had grown up into distinctively different places in which to live, thanks to landscaping, remodeling, and many gallons of paint.)

Need for emergency services drives up Suburbia's taxes, below. Opposite: older storybook home in famous Beverly Hills boasts fanciful architecture typical of the '20s, and mature plantings, great for climbing and swings.

The principal reason we have 500 new companies in Elk Grove Village is that it is close to where the boss lives.

Chicago real estate broker

The new suburbs, like the older ones, were being colonized primarily by white, middle-income, would-be-homeowners who had left behind them a city core that was becoming increasingly black. But they were not the only ones. Manufacturers had practical reasons to move out of cramped, creaky lofts and onto level land. There they could build sprawling one-story factories better suited to their production lines and find ready access to highways for their trucks, increasingly in competition with trains and barges.

Retail and service industries, too, had been following their customers out to Suburbia; the small-town grocer soon found himself in competition with the chain supermarket, which linked arms with the branch department store, the discount house, and an army of smaller specialists catering to suburban whims to form bigger and bigger shopping centers. The biggest and most daring began to usurp the role of older downtowns, offering landscaped, fountained malls, and celebrating their new status with civic trappings from art shows to concerts by the high school band. These great commercial circuses, eighth wonders of the Western world, were perpetually surrounded by the chariots of their paying public—shiny, multicolored seas of thousands of parked cars. Finally, corporations, colleges, government agencies, and just about every other American institution caught the supermarket fever and got into the exploding act.

Many vexing problems were created by the corporate, institutional, and manufacturing campuses: nerve-frazzling rural traffic jams every morning and evening that made the old train-commute look like a lark in retrospect; skyrocketing home prices and a related shortage of lower-echelon personnel who couldn't afford to live in the boss's community or even in the somewhat less pretentious one next door; a creeping loss of contacts and sales as it became more and more of a drag for executives to leave their suburban idylls for the nitty-gritty of the marketplace. Nor were the suburban towns, which had competed so hard to lure the corporations and their tax dollars to Happy Acres, particularly enchanted with the way things were turning out. More than one found that with all the new buildings and traffic, and the need they generated for still more roads and other services, the rural charm that had attracted everyone in the first place had become severely compromised, if not destroyed.

The task is to produce community—community in which a man, his wife and children are important, come first ahead of buildings, streets, and automobiles. This is the only legitimate purpose for our 'cities or our civilization: to grow better people.

James Rouse, developer of Columbia, Md.

Suburbia, in all its manifestations, has certainly brought a version of the good life to many Americans, but at the same time the real cracks in the picture window are becoming increasingly plain to see. The raw material and profit generator of Suburbia is land; its manufacturing process is a thousand separate, self-oriented actions on housing, schools, stores, sewers, roads; its end product is massive, inefficient sprawl. Development dots single houses in the middle of single lots, wasting land and raising road and utility costs (and leaving a lot of people with a lot of unusable outdoor space and a lot of grass to mow); then it leapfrogs out to devour still more and cheaper land. Forests are cut to make building easier, valleys filled, streams buried in culverts, meadows paved over for parking lots. Distances lengthen from home to work, to shops, recreation, places of worship, making people ever more dependent on one or more family cars. Inflated by rising land and labor costs, the price of housing soars out of the reach of many, especially the young, the old, and the poor. The already recurrent specter of an energy crisis—a dollar or more a gallon for heating oil, signs at service stations reading "No Gas"—threatens to pull the whole loosely woven fabric apart at the seams. As the scale of Suburbia grows, moreover, it becomes centerless, blurred, repetitive, dull. (As Gertrude Stein is reputed to have said of California cities like Oakland, "When you get there, there is no there, there.") And as the city creeps out after them, suburbanites begin to experience the discomforts of the very urban problems they sought to escape: congestion, pollution, crime—not to mention occasionally savage battles for a parking place. Older pieces of the fabric begin to wear out: housing, sewers, roads. Those who can afford to, begin to think of moving on before land values really start to slide. The suburb is on its way to becoming a slum.

Is this dismal scenario the fate of the American Dream? Have we, as some of our more pessimistic seers insist, become a throwaway society right down to the communities we live in, destined forever to use up, cast aside, move on?

Some forces at work suggest the doomsayers may yet be wrong. One is the growing concern about environment and conservation, which seems to have more staying power than

the eco-fad some regard it to be, coupled with the realization that land is not so much a commodity to be bought and sold as a finite resource that is all too easily lost. At the same time, pure economics are starting to dictate a more frugal use of land. Influenced by smaller, harder-to-find building sites and a changing market—including a rising proportion of older people, singles, and childless couples—developers are building more multifamily housing than single-family housing for the first time, despite the last-ditch efforts of some suburbs to cling to the rural one-family dream.

Aiding the trend to concentration is increasing use of the so-called cluster idea which groups individual dwellings, often attached in the form of "townhouses," on one or more portions of a given tract of land and leaves the rest, including attractive features like woods and streams, as common ground. One study showed that clustering, compared with conventional subdivision, reduced space consumed by housing as much as 75 percent, yielding that much more room for recreation and untouched patches of nature that bring sorely needed visual contrast and vitality back to the urban-rural scene. Clustered dwellings, the report noted, could also reduce building costs as much as 50 percent by joining outside walls together and cutting down on the total amount of

streets, sewers, and other utilities required, and could lower both energy consumption and air pollution another 50 percent by making heating and cooling more efficient and by reducing people's near-total dependence on automobiles.

The notion of clustering is hardly new; it is, after all, what people have used in one form or another since cities began. In the United States it can be traced back through the concept of Radburn and other early planned communities to the basic idea of the New England village green, where houses faced a commons shared by villagers for pasturing livestock and training militia, and later for Sunday strolling, Fourth of July picnics, and concerts by the town band. The new versions of the village green would undoubtedly surprise our forefathers; communities packaged around themes of leisure, recreation, or "carefree" retirement are focused on almost any major attraction—golf courses, tennis clubs, community swimming pools, ski areas, nature preserves, or lakes.

By far the most ambitious efforts aimed at creating a new kind of Suburbia, however, have been a score or more of large planned communities that have attempted to combine both clustering and open-space concepts with a wide range of housing and communal facilities in balanced, self-contained towns. The very scale and complexity of these, combined with the high cost of land and the relentless burdens of long-term financing, have brought some to disaster despite federal help in the form of loan guarantees. Perhaps the most successful (though even it has not yet paid off its huge investment) is Columbia, Maryland, a remarkable experiment in private-enterprise town building conducted by Baltimore banker and developer James Rouse.

Columbia—named after a small farm community it supplanted, and billed by its salesmen as "The Next America"—is Rouse's personal answer to what he sees as not only the inefficiency but the inhumanity of unplanned sprawl.

Within 15 years of its creation, Columbia has grown to a city-in-the-country boasting 50,000 residents—with an eventual population of 100,000. Housing of all types and income levels by different architects and builders—single-family homes, attached townhouses, rental and condominium apartments—is clustered on broad, curving streets and quiet cul-de-sacs. A typical neighborhood of 800 to 1,200 families centers around its own elementary school of about 500 pupils—who can reach it easily by a network of walking-bicycle paths instead of conventional school buses—and on a multipurpose meeting hall, a communal swimming pool, and a small convenience store. Several neighborhoods form a village that has its own larger shopping center, a middle or high school, and some major recreation facility like a tennis club, ice rink, or boating lake. Seven villages, separated by fingers of open space, are served in turn by a central downtown consisting of a lakefront civic center, office buildings, two cinemas, a hotel, and a big skylighted, air-conditioned mall containing more than 100 shops and eateries ranged between two major department stores. Nearby is a wooded area with a children's zoo and a large pavilion where the Washington Symphony and other groups hold concerts under the stars; not far away are a new county hospital, an arts center, and three community colleges. Rounding out the town on the outskirts are industrial parks housing close to 200 manufacturing and distribution firms, highlighted by Rouse's prize: a 1,100-acre General Electric appliance center. Some 20,000 people, including one quarter of the heads of households who live in Columbia, work in the 800-odd businesses and institutions in town.

In Columbia and other planned communities, and in older, once-rural towns that have been either wise or lucky enough to control their growth, people have found some measure of stability in a shifting and sometimes confusing society, and to enjoy that elusive feeling planners like to call a sense of "place." But even if dozens or hundreds of such communities could be replicated—and such a prospect seems unlikely—not everyone could afford, or want, to live in them, nor could they account for more than a fraction of Suburbia's projected growth. Most Americans, in the nomadic fashion that has become a national trademark, continue to move around according to the more immediate dictates of employment opportunities, budgets, lifestyles, or just whim. The statistics are fascinating and endless. Item: Only one in five of the chief wage earners in suburban households around New York City still commutes into the city itself; the rest work in the suburbs. Item: Well over a million Americans now travel 50 miles or more each day, each way, to work, and some considerably more. Item: In Florida, California, and elsewhere there exist whole communities with thousands of residents living in fully furnished, wheelless trailers. Though in some cases they are retired couples soaking up the sun on a modest pension, in many others they are hardworking folk who drive 100 miles a day back and forth to their jobs because they can't get any closer at a price they can afford.

Perhaps the most interesting trend, however, has to do with quite a different frontier. As the rings of rising property values radiate outward from urban bull's eyes, land prices in run-down central areas become increasingly attractive. Just when lower-income groups and minorities are finally getting their turn to move out toward the good life, more well-heeled suburbanites, disillusioned with the idea of living in an aging Scarsdale split-level, are beginning to pass them going the other way—looking for a brownstone in Soho they can pick up at a bargain and remodel into a pad more convenient to the central job market, the action, the trendy restaurants, art galleries, discos, stores. In this process of inner-city "gentrification," as some urbanologists quaintly call it, the sons and daughters of suburban squires (and some of the squires too) are creating still newer kinds of suburbs within the city itself. As they do, they raise property values, speeding the exit of still more city dwellers with longer tenure but less cash—out to the older suburbs to find housing *they* can afford.

And so the American Homesteader marches on, clutching his bank balance and credit cards in one hand, and, with the other, reaching for the stars.

Its circular pattern reflecting its name, Sun City, Arizona, far opposite, offers handy shopping, recreation for retirees. Clustered dwellings at Reston, Virginia, share community space, fewer leaf-raking chores.

The Unprecedented City

By Peirce F. Lewis

1930s postcard extolls for Depression-ridden folks back home the "glamour" of Manhattan's Great White Way, Chrysler Building, foreground, and other towering symbols of the leading U.S. urban triumph.

In the last two hundred years America has converted itself from a nation of farmers to a nation of city dwellers. The rate of urban growth has been so rapid and so dramatic that many Americans have overlooked a fact which is no less remarkable. We have lately been building a city with a new form—a city whose very geography is unprecedented in world history.

More accurately, this new city is not a city at all, but rather a compound metropolis, made of two distinctly different parts, with one clustered around the center, the other part strewn around the margins. (The terms "inner city" and "suburbia" are the closest we get to describing the two areas but, as we shall see, neither term is really correct.) The two parts look different because they are different, for each is a creature of a different time and a different technology. No American city makes much sense unless those two kinds of origins are clearly understood and sharply distinguished.

The older central part of the new compound city dates from the heyday of railroads and before—when Americans depended on public transportation (or their own feet) to get them from place to place. The new marginal part is a creature of the automobile—or, more precisely, the introduction of a new, cheap, democratized automobile, when Americans suddenly and delightedly discovered that they could go almost anywhere they chose, almost any time they chose. The boundary line in most American cities is a sharp one historically, for the automobile got into Everyman's hands around the time of World War I—give or take 10 years. The geographic boundary line is just as sharp, for it marks the difference between two urban worlds. The boundary is clearly visible on most city street maps, for in most American cities the two urban worlds are simply glued together.

It is not an easy thing to manage, this new "compound city"; horror stories in the newspapers make that very clear. What many planners and most urban critics fail to realize, however, is that this new and unprecedented city offers an unprecedented variety of opportunities for its residents—opportunities which neither the purely old nor purely new cities are capable of offering. The unprecedented compound city is often a terrible headache, but it is simultaneously a magnificent opportunity if one understands how it works, or fails to work. And to understand that, one needs to turn the clock back to see how each of the two parts came to be.

The pre-automotive city focused on a single nuclear center. Originally, it was simply a matter of commercial logic, for the center was where the roads and later railroads came together, and it was there—close to transportation terminals—that commerce flourished most vigorously. But logic often gave way to pride, and most such cities marked their "downtown" foci with magnificent squares, often endowed with grandiloquent names, and martial statuary. Thus, Detroit had its Campus Martius and Grand Circus Park, and New Orleans its Jackson Square and Lafayette Square in memory of the city's most honored heroes. Wherever possible, main roads headed directly for the center, so that cities like St. Louis and Chicago and Cleveland and Detroit all had street maps that looked like spiderwebs. So, too, the railroads focused there, and just as the road junction was cause for celebration, urban railroad terminals were more than simply functional buildings. They looked instead like gates to the city, or temples to the city's gods.

Above all, this old city was compact and often crowded—especially near the center, where tradesmen vied with each other to get as close to the action as they could. Competition for land often led to a continuing process of urban renewal, and if an old building was seen to have outlived its usefulness, it was promptly torn down and replaced with something better—with the word "better" usually defined in terms of commercial utility. Near the center, where competition for land was especially fierce, activities literally crowded on top of one another, like spectators at a parade, where parents hoist their children on their shoulders to let them see the action. The natural result of such crowding was the building of skyscrapers, which provided markets for Mr. Otis's safe new elevators, and enormously increased the density of downtown activity. The newcomer to any American city could immediately spot the downtown area merely by looking for a cluster of high buildings. Cities were proud of their skylines because the size and height of buildings were a crude measure of downtown prosperity and everybody knew it.

Downtown was a fine place to do business, obviously, but the noise and congestion made it a terrible place to live, and besides, nobody could afford to pay residential rents in crowded commercial areas. Poor people tended to cluster near the downtown area, often in close proximity to warehouses and factories which were put close to the center for similar reasons. Affluent people, however, commuted to the outskirts, making use of an increasingly efficient system of streetcars and suburban railways that fed into the city's center, and some of the city's grandest houses came to be lined up along great boulevards that led out from downtown.

Since all these 19th-century cities grew outward from the nuclear center that nourished them, their outer limits were usually sharp and crisp. One traveled from city land to farm-land, from an urban world to a rural world, with no transition between. And, since proximity to the center was highly valued, it was rare to find unused land left "open" inside the city. By mid-19th century, it became obvious that the iron hand of the marketplace would produce a city that consisted of nothing but a sea of buildings and pavement. So it was that certain foresighted city governments began to buy hunks of peripheral countryside to be made into parks, in anticipation of the day when the city would grow out around them.

It is easy to forget this chapter in American urban history and dismiss it as irrelevant to our contemporary urban problems. That would be a serious mistake, if only because most American cities remain at least partly nucleated, and some older cities are largely so. Equally, it is easy to bring judgment on that densely packed old nuclear city, and there is no difficulty finding partisans to praise or damn it. But in our rush to judgment, Americans commonly forget that the old

Contemporary painter Richard Estes finds a certain unhuman beauty in the clutter and crunch of downtown Manhattan. Using photos as a starting point, he dynamically filters and polishes the city's reality.

Strategic location in nation's heartland made Chicago grow like Topsy, a polyglot of rail-yards, slaughterhouses, mills. Steel mills still crowd mouth of Calumet River, forging one-fifth of United States' production.

It was all prices to them: they never looked at it: why should they look at the land?

−Archibald MacLeish

nuclear city was a genuine working machine, the rational consequence of 19th-century rules of transportation technology which decreed that centrality was the ultimate urban good. When the automobile came along we threw away the old rulebook, but we could hardly throw away the old cities.

Meantime, however, as the 20th century rolled on, there were other things to worry about, for we had started building something entirely different in the way of cities, and had begun gluing it to the edges of the old cities—first gingerly in bits, then in patches, and finally, enthusiastically, in great massive chunks.

The new urban morphology is familiar to anyone who lives in America today—or, indeed, anywhere else in the world where automobiles are common, land is plentiful, and land-use controls are weak. Despite its familiarity, it is useful to describe that morphology, simply to remind ourselves how radically it differs from the old nucleated form.

To begin with, the new city looks so wildly different that one finds it hard to believe that it really performs the same basic economic functions as the old. But it is true: People live in the new city, they work there, and they do their business there. The difference lies in the way those functions are arranged, and it is a mighty difference.

Instead of gathering things close to a center, the new city arranges its people and buildings in loose, separated clusters, rather like galaxies floating in space. Merchants in this galactic city no longer crowd tightly around a city square, but instead are located in widely spaced shopping centers, some of which are so big that their size can be appreciated only from the window of an airplane. Industry no longer operates from grimy multistoried factories with smoke-belching chimneys; instead, the new factories are clean-cut, low-slung horizontal buildings, set down amidst manicured lawns, with sweeping driveways and signs so small that it is sometimes difficult to decide just what product is being assembled or manufactured. (Just as the factories look anonymous, the names do too. Typically, a place that used to be named The Middletown Mattress Company will now be called Sleepwell Industries, or perhaps even more ambiguously, Technology, Inc.) But it is the residential sections of the new city that contrast most strikingly with older patterns. The old grid-pattern streets are gone, and so are the small lots with two- and three-storied houses; instead, we find mile upon mile of low, spread-out houses (ranchers, they are called, or Cape Cod ramblers), on big lots along winding streets.

It was the automobile that created this new city, of course—the vehicle that could go anywhere, just as long as there was gasoline to fuel it, and roads to drive it on. So too, the backbone of the new city is the high-speed, limited-access freeway, and the city's common element is its vast horizontal extent. Compactness, previously a virtue in the old nucleated town, became a positive liability, since compactness meant traffic jams—anathema to any red-blooded driver. People went where cars could go, and that meant parking lots, mile upon mile of parking lots in shopping centers and around the new low-rise factories. Even houses were equipped with parking lots, two- and three-car garages or carports, with enormous driveways that often doubled as basketball courts or playgrounds for children on tricycles.

The new galactic city form provoked a storm of outraged criticism, especially in the decade after World War II when it first began to appear on a large scale. The protests came (and still come) in two forms—both results of misunderstanding. The first misunderstanding is to treat the new galactic city as some kind of temporary aberration in the evolution of American urban form. In fact, it is no aberration. The galactic city is the standard form of American cities, and it has been so ever since the automobile got into the hands of the masses. The evidence for this statement is plain enough: There have been no new nucleated cities built in the United

States since the Model T began rolling off Henry Ford's assembly lines in 1908. Nor have we been adding nucleated tissue to existing nucleated cities. In fact, we have been building galactic cities, and nothing else. Nor does the size of the city make much difference. Just as the nucleated part of Chicago is not growing, neither is Des Moines, nor even Gopher Prairie. The growth of the smallest towns—if they are growing at all—occurs by the accretion of galactic clusters, in exactly the same manner as the large cities.

The second misunderstanding—really a serious mistake—was to use the word "suburbia" to denote the new galactic urban form. A suburb, after all, is a kind of satellite, a town that depends on a larger town for its existence. But it is a plain fact that the galactic city does not depend on the nucleated city for much of anything. In the years since World War II, it has become a largely independent entity.

Despite the fact that the galactic city had taken over most (if not all) of the functions of the old nucleated city, it was hard for most Americans to face up to the fact. Part of the reason was inertia; after all, we had grown comfortable with nucleated cities, we knew what to expect of them, and indeed, we measured our lives by them. One could properly think of oneself as 50 miles from Philadelphia, for example, and that meant you were 50 miles from the tower of City Hall. But how could you measure distances to or from a mass of urban tissue that seemed to ooze formlessly over a dozen counties of Pennsylvania and New Jersey and Delaware?

It was all very frustrating. Meantime most urban critics continued to call the galactic city a "suburb," which was inaccurate—or to denounce it, which served little purpose—or sometimes they tried to ignore it, which was impossible. In their agitation, the critics had overlooked one simply ineluctable fact: that by the latter half of the 20th century *every single growing American city, without exception,* was taking

Planning goes awry as San Jose, California, freeway interchange stands like an unfinished sculpture. "How can you know what to try with traffic until you know how the city itself works . . . ?" asks urbanologist Jane Jacobs.

You will drive on an expressway . . . testament to the sad illusion that there can be a solution to the unbridled automobile.

–Ian L. McHarg

187

on a new galactic form. Behind our backs, it had become the standard form of American city.

But nobody, however mistaken in other ways, could ignore the fact that the old nucleated cities were in sickly condition. Downtown stores by the drove were going bankrupt or moving to outlying shopping centers. Old factories were left to stand empty. Huge numbers of people, mainly white, departed the compact city for new homes in the galactic suburbs. The old city was being abandoned like a piece of worn-out debris, to be claimed by anyone who could afford nothing better, mainly poor and increasingly disenchanted blacks. Obviously something had to be done, and beginning in the 1950s, all kinds of government agencies rallied around to administer restorative medicine to the area that Americans were beginning to call "the inner city."

Two kinds of medication were prescribed. The first was to build high-speed limited-access highways to "improve the city's circulation." Some of the highways were designed to link the outskirts to the center, in the reasonable belief that they would help people to get downtown more easily. Others were built to bypass the old cities—the Washington and Baltimore Beltways and Boston's Route 128—so that through-traffic could avoid downtown completely and thus reduce

traffic congestion. A second kind of medication was to demolish large areas in and around downtown. That process, once called "slum clearance" but newly renamed "urban renewal," worked on the belief that old buildings were obsolete and thus interfered with economic progress. If such buildings were removed from valuable downtown land, shiny new buildings would soon spring up on the empty land, and that, in turn, would attract people downtown once more.

It was emergency medication, and nobody really waited long enough to discover whether or not it would work. It is unfortunate that they did not wait, for both turned out to be disastrous mistakes. By the time American city dwellers realized the magnitude of the mistakes, the combination of freeway building and urban renewal had done grave damage to most American cities—and in some cases, irreversible injury. The reason that both programs failed to work was simple and deadly: With the arrival of the automobile, centrality had lost its magic, and the nucleated city had lost its reason for being. It was as if the magnet had suddenly reversed polarity.

Thus, the new highways had exactly the opposite effect that they were supposed to have. City dwellers used the new freeways, not to go downtown, but to gain easy access to industrial parks at the edge of town, and the result was a new phenomenon called "reverse commuting," in which residents of the nucleated city commuted *to* the suburbs, not from them. And city dwellers in droves began to do their shopping at big new suburban shopping centers like Victor Gruen's Northland on the fringe of Detroit. As more and more residential houses became available on the outskirts, it became obvious that one didn't have to live in the nucleated city at all—and, in fact, the ordinary white American could simply forget that it existed. Many did.

Widespread urban renewal exacerbated the trouble. When the wrecking balls and bulldozers had finished their work, huge areas stood devastated and depopulated, while city officials stood back to wait for new buildings to arise from the ruins. In many cities, they are still waiting. Very few people, it turned out, wanted to invest money in areas that looked as if they had been heavily and systematically bombed. Grady Clay, the journalist and landscape architect, has called such areas urban "sinks"—places where cities dump their physical and human debris, and then forget about them. The riots and looting of the 1960s did a good deal of property damage on the fringes of these areas, but afterwards it was hard to tell which areas had been destroyed by rioters—and which by the decision of urban reformers.

So it was that America entered the last quarter of the 20th century with an unprecedented compound city—part nucleated, part galactic—with unprecedented problems, but with unprecedented opportunities also. One cannot talk about those problems, however, nor the opportunities either, unless one first recognizes that the compound city comes in three or four subspecies, and each differs from the others in important and challenging ways.

One type is represented by cities like Detroit and Columbus, cities where urban renewal (combined with neglect) had practically eviscerated the old nucleated city, while meantime the galactic fringe flourished. Many of these cities were located in the nation's midsection, west of the Appalachians and east of the Rockies—not the country's oldest cities, but not the newest ones either. It is hard to know why urban renewal's effects were so particularly cruel in the nucleated parts of Detroit: Perhaps it was the city's steadfast dedication to "progress"—perhaps the widespread feeling that a "dynamic" city like Detroit really didn't need history and thus could dispense with its oldest buildings. When, finally, Henry Ford II came along and built the futuristic cylindrical towers of the Renaissance Center at the foot of Woodward Avenue, the national press touted it loudly as a last-ditch effort to "help Detroit come back." To many observers, including this writer, the project was indeed last-ditch—about 30 years too late. The huge silver cylinders of Ren-Cen looked like objects from outer space, set down in the wasteland of a nuclear holocaust. But with or without the Renaissance Center, a map of Detroit looks like a doughnut—big and puffy around the edges—hollow in the middle. Maps of Columbus and Syracuse and Saginaw and St. Louis exhibit many of the same properties, for the center-cities have lamentably been carved out and thrown away.

A second kind of compound city, entirely different from Detroit, is represented by Los Angeles, which did most of its growing during the age of the automobile, and whose urban tissue is therefore mostly galactic. In Los Angeles the basic transportation system was designed with the clear understanding that centrality was an obsolete idea. Thus, instead of laying out freeways in the conventional Eastern manner, like a spiderweb, Los Angeles' system came out as a kind of fishnet, which eventually made all locations in the huge Los Angeles basin almost equally accessible. There was no need to glue the galactic city onto the fringe of downtown, since there was very little downtown to begin with. Most Angelenos have lived in a galactic city all their lives, and know nothing else.

Los Angeles, of course, is not the only post-automotive galactic city in the United States. Indeed, the Southwest and South are full of them, and in some—like Phoenix and San Jose—downtown is even smaller and less relevant than in Los Angeles. In such cities, a resident quickly comes to terms with a galactic form, or he goes elsewhere.

But the modal kind of American city is neither totally eviscerated, like Detroit, nor totally galactic, like Phoenix. A substantial number of America's older cities contain both substantial nucleated sections and galactic sections, and are coping with the combination with varying degrees of success.

The best examples are old eastern cities like Boston and Philadelphia and Baltimore, with large nucleated sections that grew up during the 18th and 19th centuries. And, when those cities continued to grow into the 20th century, they also collected a sizable ring of galactic tissue. (Such compound cities are rare in the South or West, simply because most southern and western cities were too small before the time of the automobile to have developed much in the way of nuclei. The exceptions like New Orleans and Seattle and San Francisco are spectacular, and much beloved.) Some of the eastern cities, Philadelphia, for example, were seriously mauled by interstate highway building and urban renewal, but still managed to preserve a recognizable chunk of their pre-automotive nuclei. Unlike Detroit, they were not disemboweled.

The modern urban-industrial complex is based on a series of radical disconnections between body and soul . . . community and earth.

–Wendell Berry

Those old nuclei have been proving valuable lately, serving as magnets to increasing numbers of people who want to live in an antique environment, close to what they call "urban amenities" (a code-phrase which means they don't like shopping centers). Many of these newcomers to the nucleated city have gotten into the expensive business of "inner city preservation," in districts like Beacon Hill in Boston, Society Hill in Philadelphia, Georgetown and Alexandria near Washington, D.C., and the Garden District of New Orleans. Such historic districts have received a good deal of publicity lately, partly because the districts are spectacularly handsome, and partly because their buoyant good health contrasts so vividly with the run-down atmosphere of most nucleated cities.

As usual in such matters, the silver lining has a cloud attached. What the popularizers of inner city preservation commonly overlook is that districts like Society Hill account for an extremely small part of the inner city of Philadelphia. The bulk of nuclear Philadelphia remains black, poor, and isolated from the national mainstream—and it maintains no functional connection with Society Hill at all.

Despite all the obvious problems, there is increasing evidence that centrality may be regaining some of its old psychological magic—and some strange and encouraging things are afoot in a few corners of urban America. In a few big cities, conspicuously Denver, Atlanta, Houston, and Minneapolis/St. Paul, the old decrepit downtowns have begun to act like Chicago's Loop or Midtown Manhattan and are sprouting clusters of big and expensive new skyscrapers. These buildings are so bold and conspicuous that some optimists have begun to talk about a national urban renaissance. That prediction seems plausible until one notices that such skyscraper-building is mainly confined to a handful of big regional economic centers—Atlanta for the "New South"— Denver for most of the Great Plains and intermontane West—Houston for the Gulf Coast—and the Twin Cities for the upper Midwest. Not surprisingly, the towers of Denver turn out to be headquarters for banks and insurance companies and communications industries for the western region. Not surprisingly either, company executives tend to go home at night—which means, in Denver, someplace out in the galactic fringe. The urban renaissance, therefore, if it is that, is not something that one can expect on a nationwide basis; there is a limited number of cities, after all, that can serve as regional capitals.

Is there a solution to our urban problems? We would like to think so, of course, but experience teaches us to be skepti-

Fields and trees teach me nothing, but the people in a city do.

−Socrates

Long Island shoppers and commuters stream past New York's LaGuardia Airport. More than seven million have jobs and summer playgrounds at city's periphery, avail themselves of downtown pleasures when desired.

cal. Indeed, some of our "solutions" have done more damage than they have good, and one is forced to conclude that our cities would now be better off if we had in the past spent more time thinking and less time acting. For it is clear that much of American urban thinking is ridden with stereotypes, fixed ideas which have acted as blinders, preventing us from thinking clearly about the new unprecedented city that we have been building.

Consider some of the fixed ideas, and where they have gone wrong.

Fixed Idea Number One: That there is a solution to our urban woes, if we only look hard enough. That belief is dangerously wrong on several counts. First of all, it suggests that all American cities are basically alike, and that is plainly untrue. For another thing, it reinforces our idea that all American cities are fundamentally in bad shape. Some parts of some cities are indeed in bad shape, but there is tremendous variety and vitality in the American urban fabric; large parts of most American cities are very much alive and well.

Fixed Idea Number Two: That "urban sprawl" is some kind of nasty aberration which can somehow be corrected. It is not. To repeat, the galactic city (a more accurate term than sprawl) is the standard form of newly built American cities ever since the arrival of the automobile.

Fixed Idea Number Three: That the nuclear downtown can and should be revived, so that it will serve once more as the core of the city. Well, maybe it should be revived, but the fact is, it will never again serve its 19th-century role as the place where everybody goes to do their shopping. Transportation and population are far too decentralized for that to happen, and the alternatives to downtown are much too accessible and attractive.

Fixed Idea Number Four: That we can cure the ills of our galactic cities by building fast new railroad lines, which will whisk people in and out of the city, and thus do away with automobiles. Even the most confirmed railroad buff must recognize that the fixed-line urban railroads (like the New York subways, or Philadelphia's Main Line) rely on dense concentrations of people who live close to transit stations. Maybe something like Washington's Metro will work (after a fashion, as long as it serves a dense focal concentration of people and buildings), but the galactic city, by its very nature, is much too widespread to be well served by one or two fixed-line railroads.

Fixed Idea Number Five: That we can ameliorate urban problems by encouraging people to escape the city and return to the small towns of their youth. In reality, the idea is romantic nonsense. Most small towns are utterly unprepared to receive large numbers of urban refugees, much less provide them with the kinds of amenities they are accustomed to. Furthermore, if a small town receives many urban immigrants, the town obviously won't be small for long.

Fixed Idea Number Six: That we can be color-blind in approaching our urban problems. We cannot. America's most crippling urban troubles derive from the fact that our nucleated and galactic cities really embrace two separate systems—one largely black, the other largely white. It is not overstating the case to say that most urban blacks are caught in a geographic trap; that trap is especially cruel for teenagers, about half of whom are permanently unemployed and who grow into adulthood without knowing the disciplines and satisfactions of productive work. The process is circular, of course, and breaking that vicious circle is overwhelmingly *the* most important challenge facing urban America today.

Fixed Idea Number Seven: That our old cities are hopeless, and we should therefore start afresh to build new cities. That idea is just plain silly: American cities represent a gargantuan capital investment, and no responsible person seriously advocates abandoning it. But above all, it ignores the fact that much of our urban tissue is in very healthy condition indeed; if we are wise, we will try to identify those healthy places and keep them sound.

We need to stop thinking of our cities as homogeneous blobs. As we have seen repeatedly, the nucleated and galactic sections of our cities look different because they *are* different. We need to judge the strengths and weaknesses of each, and do it independently.

Our nucleated cities, to begin with, need to be treated like the antiques that they are. Even though they have been badly damaged, they are worth special attention, for they are scarce and irreplaceable commodities.

As we have seen, there is little prospect that the old nucleated cities can be converted into the downtowns they once were, and that fact has disappointed many people. There is no need for disappointment, however. While downtown Los Angeles is no longer the center of town, it is an extremely attractive *part* of town, serving a useful dual function. It is a working neighborhood shopping center for a sizeable local population, and handsome *fin de siècle* structures like the Bradbury Building are increasingly sought after by professionals who are seeking office space with style. Similar things are happening in old Boston, along the fringes of Society Hill in Philadelphia, and in Washington's Georgetown.

One feels almost Scrooge-like to complain about such

A city that outdistances man's walking powers is a trap for man.

–Arnold Toynbee

places. Nevertheless, one has a strong feeling of *déjà vu* after one has walked through several of them—in Boston and Philadelphia and Georgetown and San Francisco—and seen the same Magic Pan crepes, the same scented candles, the same Yugoslav and Philippine baskets and spice racks, and the same overpriced antiques in trendy little gift shoppes—while Gray Line buses groan slowly up the narrow streets, dodging flower carts. This is not downtown in any meaningful sense. Meantime, however, such places are pleasant and harmless even though they do not tax the imagination. And above all, they are fending off the wrecking ball in a very effective way.

Just as we have rediscovered the glories of the old nucleated city, it is time to begin exploring the galactic city—urban America's great unheralded as well as unprecedented wonder. Despite the sneers of planners, architects, and people who write songs about ticky-tacky boxes on hillsides, it is a

Georgetown, restored oldest part of nation's capital, glows in autumn sun. Residents invested money rather than tear down. Pittsburgh's "Golden Triangle," opposite, gained smoke-free skies from pollution control.

A city's very wholeness in bringing together people with communities of interest is one of its greatest assets, possibly the greatest.

−Jane Jacobs

plain fact that the American galactic city dweller, in his single-family house and two-car garage on his curvilinear street, occupies one of the most satisfactory living environments on the face of the Earth. At the elementary physical level, most of those streets are safe and clean and healthy—which is a good deal more than one can say for most of the world's residential areas. To be sure, we hear complaints that "suburban living is dull," but a close look gives the lie to that claim. If one takes the time to walk by and look at the average yard in Fairfax County, Virginia, or San Mateo County, California, or Macomb County, Michigan, one can see how very unaverage those yards really are. It is quite unnecessary to admire our neighbor's back yard tastes, but it is important that we understand how much he loves his back yard, and how much intelligence and imagination and hard work he has lavished on it. Small wonder that so many middle-class galactic city dwellers in the United States are politically conservative creatures. Most of those people know a good thing when they see it.

There is no denying that parts of the galactic city really are boring. Most shopping malls are carefully policed to exclude eccentric people and behavior, and the results are numbingly predictable. One thing is missing, and that is spontaneity—the essential ingredient of an exciting or even an interesting city. That is why our old downtowns are often good places even when they are seedy, and why so many residential back yards are good places too.

The most serious threat to the galactic city, of course, is the rising cost of motor fuel. The galactic city, after all, grew up because auto travel was virtually free; that will never be true again. Thus, it is entirely possible that America is ending a great period in city building—that just as the automobile put an end to the nucleated city, the high cost of gasoline is making the galactic city obsolete.

But obsolete or not, our cities are a mixed bag—partly wonderful, partly terrible, and a good deal that falls somewhere in between. It serves little purpose to deny these qualities, for neither Pollyanna nor Cassandra will serve our urban needs very well. What we need to do is to *understand* our cities better.

The suburban back yard has something to teach us along this line. It is a satisfactory place because it is the bit of geography we know best—the place we have cared for with greatest attention and greatest affection. Above all, it is the place for which we are ultimately responsible. Americans could do much worse than to apply this homely back yard lesson to their unprecedented cities.

Forces

His hat's gone with the hot wind and his crops and cattle, too, if nature holds back moisture much longer. For the Texas farmer can no more break free of drought than a fossil fly can escape its tomb of amber.

Authors in this gallery of the book deal with North America's interplay of topographics and atmospherics. The forces shape our lives and living space. Mountains catch clouds and milk them of their rain. Lands beyond the peaks grow dry, lying in rain shadow. Plains heat up almost enough to pop growing corn. Winds and rains and rivers sculpt the hills and valleys.

Let us put aside for a moment the blizzards, hurricanes, flood-making rains, and Earth's worst tornadoes. The seasonal and seasonable alternation of atmospheric humors does, on the whole, help create a very productive land. Rains return to break droughts. Even the Middle West's dryness, as compared to the Atlantic Seaboard's seemingly blessed moisture and greenery, fosters the production of sound grain.

Now, returning to the titanic forces; all those storms, floodwaters, freezes, and hot blasts must come from somewhere. One view of the Olympian fury in our skies reveals a near stand-off on a planetary scale. Arctic cold parries with the heat of the tropics over this middle ground, this "temperate" battleground we call home.

Even with wild Alaska thrown in, the edge must be given—as far as atmospheric

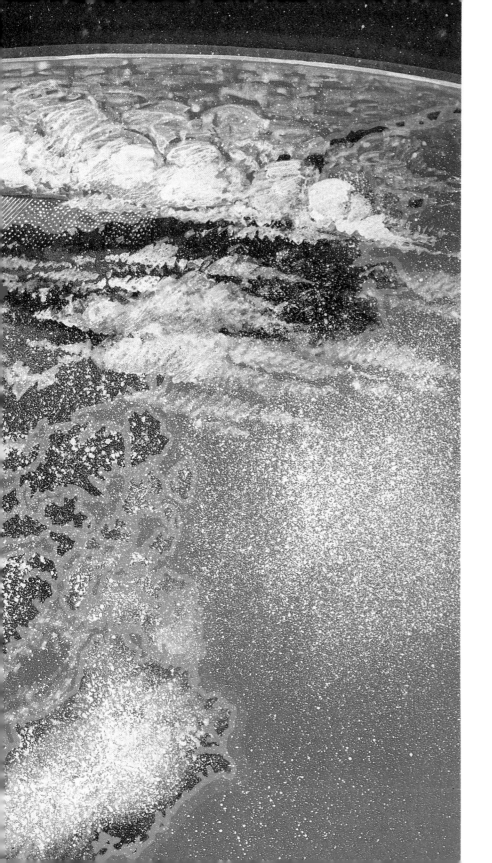

power is concerned—to the golden-green Spanish tropics at the southern fringes of Anglo settlement. At the other extreme, Polynesian Hawaii is perfect, albeit fiery and prone to quakes and tidal waves.

Because of the great, flat hinterland, the interior of the continent suffers quite high summer temperatures and low winter ones. So does Siberia, a similar piece of real estate. But Kansas City lies 1,000 miles closer to the Equator than does Krasnoyarsk. So, now secure in the knowledge that the land is truly temperate in spite of appearances—though a bit on the warm side—we can serenely view some of the extremes: longest dry spell, 767 days at Baghdad, California; biggest one-minute rain, 1.23 inches at Unionville, Maryland; highest temperature of 134 degrees F at Death Valley; greatest snowfall in one storm of 189 inches at Mt. Shasta Snowbowl, California; −70 degrees F at Rogers Pass, Montana, the U.S. lowest temperature excluding Alaska; greatest 24-hour temperature drop, 100 degrees F at Browning, Montana; world's highest surface wind of 231 miles per hour on Mt. Washington, New Hampshire; world's greatest two-minute temperature rise of 49 degrees at Spearfish, South Dakota; and the world's largest officially recorded hailstone of 1.67 pounds from Coffeyville, Kansas.

Heat energy born of the tropics tangles with polar cold over the land to create the myriad effects of hurricane, tornado, blizzard, and flood detailed in articles that follow. Strongly influenced by Earth's rotation, weather over the United States generally sweeps in from the Pacific to encounter the Rockies, or spirals northward and eastward from the direction of the Gulf of Mexico.

My Favorite Hurricane

By Edwards Park

When it comes to New England weather, Mark Twain said it all. "It is utterly disproportioned to the size of that little country," he pointed out in an 1876 speech. "She can't hold a tenth part of her weather. You can see cracks all about where she has strained herself trying to do it."

There have been times, though, when the weather has mobilized its forces and ripped New England wide open. These times are the hurricanes.

You tend to think of these great tropical storms as products of the Caribbean or thereabouts and not of much concern to flinty old New England. Spawned usually in late summer and early fall, hurricanes are a constant threat to Florida and the Gulf coast where they have, over the years, caused death and damage beyond all assessment. More commonly, they wander aimlessly for a few days like spinning tops, then set a course along a low pressure trough and churn off roughly northeastward to raise Cain in the shipping lanes. But sometimes . . .

A hurricane is a gigantic, vastly powerful whirling tropical storm with very low barometric pressure (around 28 inches of mercury, or even less), with heavy rain and wind of 70 miles per hour and over. The wind rotates, counterclockwise, around a center or "eye." The whole mass may be two or three hundred miles in diameter and it moves forward along its course at, usually, 20 or 30 miles per hour.

It stands to reason that anything on the eastern side of this moving, whirling mass is in a lot of trouble because the rotating wind is augmented by the forward motion. West of the eye the wind is not as fierce. So when a hurricane follows that well-worn path curving northeastward from the Caribbean, its center skirts the North American coast just offshore of New England, and that region is struck by strong gales and may suffer damage from high tides and thundering surf. But the really devastating part of the storm is way out to sea, east of the eye.

Sometimes, however, a hurricane moves north or even northwest and plunges *inland* along the coast. And then anything to the east of its center is in for it. And since New England juts out so far eastward, it has caught a few of these errant hurricanes, bigger and stronger than ever by the time they reach that coast.

Take 1954, a vintage year for hurricanes. On August 31, "Carol" smashed across Long Island, into Connecticut and up through Massachusetts and New Hampshire. It killed 50 people and devastated some of the most heavily populated areas of the country. Eleven days later, "Edna" sliced through Cape Cod. And a month later "Hazel," having hit New York state, struck Vermont with those winds on the eastern side of the eye. What with all three storms, New England suffered losses of more than half a billion dollars.

My wife and two small boys were spending a few weeks in Marblehead, Massachusetts, that summer while I commuted between there and my job on the *Boston Globe*. "Carol" came upon us with considerable warning, and I called my editor and suggested that I stay home because Marblehead might see some action. He agreed.

We saw action all right. The wind rocked our small rented cottage so frighteningly that we moved in with a neighbor. And then, itching for a better chance to see what was going on, we ventured toward the har-

bor, clinging to each other and to telephone poles to keep from being blown away.

In the shelter of a line of houses we drew breath. The harbor lay just on the other side of them. But as I contemplated the best way to get closer, I saw something white and ghostly flying above the rooftops, appearing, vanishing, reappearing in the murky, rain-slashed sky. Suddenly I knew what I was seeing—sheets of spume torn from the tops of giant waves. I could see this flying *above* the roofs of those houses. No wonder the rain that drenched my face had a salty taste! I hastily changed my mind about getting any closer.

"Carol" knocked down the steeple of Boston's Old North Church, where two lanterns, hung on the night of April 18, 1775, had warned Paul Revere that the British troops were setting out on the foray that started the Revolution. A couple of amateur photographers were smart enough to shoot some fuzzy but highly historic pictures of the old steeple falling, and our paper managed to buy them. I remember talking on the phone with one of the photographers who was pleased with our rather modest bid. I suppose none of us realized then how famous those photographs would be.

Then I was assigned to help out on a special "Carol" supplement for the *Globe*. We worked hard on it, compiling statistics and photographs of the devastation, but, ludicrously, by the time we hit the streets with it, "Edna" had roared by and rendered us out of date. It was quite a year, '54.

But to me, all New England storms pale before the onslaught of September 21, 1938. I was living in New Hampshire, about to return to college, and I went through it—an event that altered the face of New England, that changed procedures at the Weather Bureau, and that has given me something to talk about for years.

This hurricane arrived with no warning and no name. The Weather Bureau lacked the means to track it and did not expect it to

Hurricane Belle, 1976, followed a path like that of the hurricane of 1938. Opposite are hemispheric weather conditions as Belle builds up steam near the Florida coast. In enlargement, below, Belle is seen competing with a storm to the northwest. Bottom, two days later, Belle approaches Long Island, closely following the track of the '38 hurricane.

hit land. After all, it had been half a century since such a storm had come ashore in that region. So though New Englanders had read newspaper accounts of a hurricane churning around in southern waters, they considered it more interesting to follow the fortunes of the Boston Red Sox.

But the storm began moving northward along the coast at about 60 miles per hour—an incredible forward speed. When it slammed into the underbelly of New England, its eastern side packed winds that were measured, just outside Boston, at a steady 121 miles per hour with one gust reaching a fantastic 186! It cost us more than 600 lives and 300 million of those 1938 dollars and it earned a champion's title: the Great New England Hurricane. Just that. No woman's name (later to be deemed sexist). Just the Great New England Hurricane, or as my father's friend Slocum called it, "That God Damn Storm."

The G.N.E.H. (or, if you prefer, T.G.D.S.) damaged our town badly and left us all with vivid impressions. But each of us remembers it the way one does an auto accident or a battle, with a clear and dramatic picture of one's own experience but little idea of the whole scene. I was astonished to learn, several days later, how the storm had thundered ashore along the southern New England coast, with 30-foot waves smashing buildings and grounding large vessels along the main streets of seaports. I was sobered by the many deaths that I had not known had occurred.

One reason for our restricted views of the disaster was the loss of communication. Indeed, those of us living outside our town had lost touch with the rest of the world *before* the hurricane struck, for we had suffered a couple of days of heavy rain that gouged craters in the gravel roads and sent telephone poles sagging into the mud. By September 21, we were without electricity and could not drive to the village.

Slocum, who lived on a wooded hillside

Boston's North Church steeple topples as Hurricane Carol comes to town. Arriving before the days when hurricanes were named, the storm of '38 hurtled up the Connecticut valley, taking more than 600 lives.

about three miles from town, was, like most countrymen, philosophical about the rain and its hardships. But when the wind came it was a personal affront, and he expressed his outrage so vividly—and vehemently—that after World War II, I got hold of a wire recorder and ran it while he told his own story of his own unprintable storm.

A word about Slocum, whom I occasionally quote in other writings without the bother of an introduction. He lived alone in a splendid little house dating from 1790, which he hung onto despite the tempting offers of vacationists, or "summer complaints" as he called them. He hired himself out at everything from haying in July to advising a New York summer resident how many hams she could expect to get from a 350-pound hog.

Just a word, too, about Slocum's speech, for when I transcribe him I don't think I can attempt to capture it. He talked New Hampshire Yankee: no vestige of an "r" except to

lead off a word; the exaggeration of diphthongs ("daown taown"); a partly long "a" in "calf" or "laugh." The "oh" sound in words like "road" became almost an "uh" sound: "rud." But "God," as in his full name for the hurricane, was stretched out almost to "Gawd."

And that brings me to a word of warning. Slocum was a decent and rather Christian sort of man, but he salted his speech with oddly innocent profanities and vulgarities. I shall try to weed these out, but may at least indicate some colorful usages. I've cut his discursiveness about local people. If it's all right with you, I shan't bother to use quotes around the transcription.

I never seen such a sky as that morning. The rain was still comin down the way it had for two days, but by the jesur, you'd a thought it was sea water, it was that green in the sky. I'd got my truck down the road to the blacktop the day before, but that morning my hill was washed out. There was an

eight-foot ditch right down the middle of the gravel, with about a lake's worth of water boilin down it.

My food had run short, so I knew I'd have to walk down town to stock up. But oh my God when I looked at that sky I got a mite dubious. Still, around noon I put on my slicker and set out.

I'd thought there was a little let-up to the rain, but when I got into it, it come through the slicker like green corn through the hired man. I went down my hill, and just above the wash-out there was a gap in the stone wall, and ef you'd lived as long as me you'd know that's the loggin road through the Marvin place—all that white pine they've brung along since the War [Slocum meant World War I, of course]. The rain was easier in the trees. I knew I could get through to the blacktop over toward West Village if I followed that loggin road.

I made pretty good time, but when I come out of the trees, they'd started wheelin and singin with a fresh breeze. You might say it was . . . [here Slocum used a phrase that sounded like "hermin up" or maybe "harmin up." I believe there used to be an expression like that in Maine] . . . for to blow. I remember my Daddy sayin "First the rain and then the wind, sailors take your topsails in," and I thought, by the jesur we're in for it now, but at least it ain't snow.

I got into the village across the only bridge that wasn't under water. I hadn't realized the river had come up so high. They didn't have any more 'lectricity than I did back on the hill. The butcher's was lit with kerosene lamps. They needed the light. The sky was dark green now.

I remember Phil Charles, the butcher, sayin he guessed that this was that damn hurricane he'd read about in the Boston papers. "I thought it was down around Carolina or Florida or one of them places," he said, "but I guess those storms are kind of crafty."

Well, sir, I filled my sack with things I

needed, and was just payin up when the steam whistle in the fire house went off with a signal for a fire right in town. Phil and I went to the door, and by the Godfrey there was smoke and flames comin out the roof of the old feed store by the river. We found out later they had a short circuit and it touched off some grain bags. The building was just enough flooded to short those old wires.

I went down after the engine, with all the volunteers. We tried to get a hose to the building, but the flood had gone right around it and the water nicked the volunteers off their feet, one by one, when they tried to run the hose out. And by then the roof took hold and the sparks blew into town with all that wind behind them, and it ended up we lost a lot of stores.

I didn't stay for that last, because the whole day was starting to churn me up. The wind was comin in like somethin ye could touch, and the rain was just flat, hitting like buckshot. And down town, the river was a brown flood, eight feet deep on South Street, and one whole end of Main Street was bright with flames, and no one could do anything about it.

I picked up my sack and crossed back over that same bridge, and the water was over the top of it now, and one of the constable's deputies told me to get off it, and I told him to go straight to hell—I was headin home, and I didn't hold with bein kept back.

I went humpin up the blacktop for three quarters of a mile to the loggin road and then I turned into the pines, thinkin I'd get out of the wind. But this time it was all through there, too. The sky now was just black, but mostly that was from flyin twigs and leaves and branches and bark and finally some full-size boughs, filling the air overhead. And I hadn't got more than a few rods into the woods than the pines started comin down around me.

They didn't fall just one at a time, but maybe three acres to once. White pine's got shallow roots, you know, and all of that

damn rain loosened the soil so the roots pulled right out and the whole tree would go over, sort of tired, and that would open the way for others to go, so they did—they went almost to once, just like a bunch of dominoes. It was a sad thing.

It waren't too damn healthy for me, either, I'll tell you. I'd see a couple comin down ahead of me and I'd hold back and then climb over them. And I'd hear somethin swishin behind me, and I'd hurry ahead and. . .
[At this point the wire broke. It was fine wire that passed through the recording element at four feet per second, so when it broke—which was not unusual—it made you feel as though you were in a roomful of spaghetti. You were supposed to find the two ends, tie them together and weld the knot with a lighted cigarette. But this time I had trouble with the weld, and I had to re-break and tie it again several times, so I lost a few words.]
. . . added about a mile to the trip because of the dodgin. It's a good thing I'm a tough old bugger or I wouldn't a made it home.

The wind made it easy. It was comin out of the southeast, so strong you could lean back against it. By the jesur that was a wind. You could a sliced it for dinner. But anyway, when I finally come out of Marvin's woods, what was left of them, the wind was behind me, and it pushed me up my hill quicker than . . . [here follows a brief and pungent vulgarity, remarkably effective]. And then I saw Haskell's silo, down the road from my place, busted wide open and flappin in the wind like a wet sheet. And the roof of Haskell's horse barn was half gone, and there was a sort of mist, like smoke, comin out of it, and I realized that was about two hundred years of dust and old oats and mouse dung and bits of straw blowing away in the hurricane. Haskell told me later his horse barn had never gotten so damn clean.

I just can't tell you what I felt when I saw

my house still standin. The hardwoods around it had saved it. They'd lost some boughs—dead boughs—but they stood and broke the wind. And so my house stood. They say it went through a bad wind storm in 1878, and another in 1821, and another in 1815 when it was only 25 years old. It's a good house, tough as I am.

But when I got inside, I went up to the loft to change my clothes, and by the Godfrey I couldn't keep a candle lit. The wind found enough places to come through so it kept snuffin it out. Now I'd reshingled only a couple of years before, and I knew that roof was on tighter than . . . [here follows a somewhat complex and highly descriptive vulgarity, typical of Slocum] . . .but that wind got through it, and I could feel the floor shift, and I went down below.

That's about all. The wind died off in the night, and I slept as though I'd been pole-axed. I woke once because way down in the village the fire whistle started to blow again—one long blast that just went on and on until you knew something was busted. Finally someone shut it off. The folks down town said that was almost the worst part of the whole time—that damn whistle goin off for nothin after it was all over.

Next morning was a still day, and sunny. There was a little bit of haze as though the dust was settling. I couldn't make out what was wrong with the look of the land, and then I saw it: We'd had some good foliage up until then, the maples turning right on time. Now it was all gone. The hardwoods were all gray. All their leaves had been blown off.

As for the white pines, they were mostly done for. Whole stands were down, thousands of acres in all, they tell me. And the only thing we could do with em was log em. Everyone who wanted a job loggin got one, hiring out to a landowner to clean up white pine. I know I did it—and it put me a little ahead of the game for once. But there weren't enough of us local fellers, so the owners brought in loggers from Quebec and

Maine and finally even from places out there in the West—Oregon and Michigan and places like that.

The phone companies, too . . . they needed more men to fix the lines, and they brought fellers in from Texas. Hell, they were harder to understand than the Frenchies from Canada. All winter them damn foreigners would get drunk Saturday nights down at Maloney's Bar and Grill, and it would always end up in a fight until one night a Canuck threw his axe at a Texan and it split open Maloney's airtight stove, which was red hot, it bein February, and the whole shebang burned down. Not much loss, some folks said. But I don't know. I still kind of miss it.

Canucks is always bad in a fight, not caring where they throw their axes. But the Finns they got into town later, they was worse. They threw their axes at each other, and they kept it up afterwards when they was back in the woods. All next fall, hunters would find Finn loggers with double-bitted axes wedged in their skulls.

You know, we only had the one constable before That God Damn Storm. But the next winter we had to get two more full time and two volunteers. The whole town changed.

But there was some vartue to be had from it, you know. The storm took all my pine, on the eastern side of my hill. And after the Canucks and Finns and Michiganers and State O'Mainers and I got it cleaned up and sold off, I had the beginnings of a medder there. It gave me a view of East Mountain for the first time since Daddy farmed there.

The growth's comin back now, but I guess I'll keep that view. A person ought to have a mountain.

Winter storms may be less severe than hurricanes, yet wreak havoc on New England coasts. Historic Minot's Ledge lighthouse, near Boston, is pummeled by giant waves.

Mechanics
of the
Atmosphere

By Robert C. Cowen

The sounds coming through our bedroom windows were ominous. We recognized the "crack-crash" punctuating the almost tangible silence as the noise of snapping, falling limbs. Two decades of New England woodland living had accustomed my wife and me to the winter ice storms and clinging wet snows that "trim" the pine trees. But this was early May in Massachusetts—a time of lilacs and apple blossoms. And the cannonade was the most intense we had known. It made sleep impossible. In the morning, news reports confirmed what we could see around us; an untimely eight-inch snowfall (May 9-10, 1977) had done as much damage to trees as a hurricane might do. Oaks and hickories, maples and birches—whose bare branches shrug off winter snows—were now in leaf. The weight of the snow uprooted whole trees or snapped them off at mid-trunk. The storm was a sobering finale to the savage winter of 1976-77, which brought the first snow in living memory to Miami, Florida,

the coldest season since the 18th century to many central and eastern states, unseasonal warmth to Alaska, and record-breaking drought to the western United States.

Later that year, on the night of July 19–20, there was a recurrence of the famed 1889 Johnstown, Pennsylvania, flood. There followed a winter that, in its fashion, was as severe as its predecessor. The western drought broke so vehemently that Californians had to cope with floods. By February 1978, snow covered 74 percent of North America—a record for the 12 years that satellites have monitored snow cover. And in late January and early February, a storm pattern developed that gave the Midwest some of its worst weather on record. It included a rare type of snowstorm that immobilized the Northeast for nearly a week, making much of the region an officially declared disaster area.

Such a run of extreme weather might seem to vindicate those prophets of climatic doom who say that the weather is

deteriorating and slipping toward a new ice age. But a check of the records gives a different perspective. The winters of 1918, 1940, and 1963 were almost as severe as the extremes of the 1970s. The Johnstown flood was a repeat of a natural event that had occurred not only in 1889 but again in 1936. Even that May snowstorm had its antecedents. The challenge of variable weather is very much part of living on the American land. If that challenge seems more severe now than in the past, it is because, as in many other parts of the world, too many people are trying to live beyond the carrying capacity of the land. They are losing the ability to cope with what should be expectable extremes of weather.

In a world where grain reserves scarcely make up for bad harvests, you don't have to invoke a return of the Ice Age to appreciate that humankind is increasingly vulnerable to the normal swings of the weather. This is the real climatic threat. The World Meteorological Organization (WMO) sums it up

Expecting harsh winters, New England youngsters delight in outdoor skating. Lovely but dangerous ice storms damage ornamental shrubs, bring down power lines. Rare but violent rains erode an Arizona plateau, below.

by noting that any genuine climatic change "is likely to be gradual and would be almost imperceptible." However, the WMO adds, "The natural shorter-term variability of climate is becoming of increasing importance as the result of growing pressures on natural resources. It is this variability which has been highlighted by the disastrous droughts and weather extremes in many parts of the world. . . ."

One reason the weather takes us by surprise may lie in a distorted sense of what is "normal." Weather for several decades preceding the mid-1960s was reasonably benign in many areas. This led to a false sense of security in, for example, semi-arid lands. These lands—such as the Soviet Union's "new" agricultural region or Africa's Sahel—are quick to suffer when the weather turns nasty.

In fact, the widely publicized "abnormal" droughts of the Sahel find a parallel in the United States' Great Plains wheat lands where the drought of the mid-1970s was also considered abnormal. Yet tree ring studies show recurring drought to be characteristic of the Great Plains region. There is a clear 20- to 22-year drought cycle going back to 1700, the limit of the study.

Climatologist Helmut Landsberg of the University of Maryland has this perspective in mind when he says he would like to get rid of the word "normal" as far as weather is concerned. "Normal" implies an ideal state (such as normal blood pressure), a departure from which is pathological. Such a concept simply does not apply to weather which varies historically from year to year.

This is not to imply there is no such thing as *climatic* change. For two million years, ice ages have been a recurring feature of our planet. There have been eight glaciations in the past 700,000 years. These relatively cold periods are separated by warmer interglacial spans of 10,000 or so years. The present interglacial period began about 11,000 years ago.

Solar research at Kitt Peak National Observatory may shed light on sun's effect on weather and climate. Complex, founded in 1960 on Papago Indian land near Tucson, Arizona, includes world's largest solar telescope.

If you kill a spider, it will rain.

—Old saying

Even it has had climatic ups and downs. One of the more notable swings was the "Little Ice Age," a relatively cold period lasting from about 1400 through the early 18th century. Tree ring research at the University of Arizona suggests that during an especially cold period, 1619–1655, 70 percent of the Northern Hemisphere winters may have had air circulation patterns and associated temperatures like the winters of 1976–77 and 1977–78.

More recently, climatologists have been intrigued by a Northern Hemisphere warming trend of about 0.1 degree Celsius per decade that persisted from 1885 through 1944. It then turned into a cooling trend of about the same magnitude that continued through 1974. At this writing it is hard to say what the trend is doing, aside from encouraging some of the climatic doomsayers. In 1976, a widely quoted CIA forecast predicted adverse weather for the next four decades, or perhaps for several centuries, and widespread crop failures.

But this kind of prediction is dismissed by most meteorologists, who believe that the mechanisms of weather and climate are too poorly understood to permit reliable climatic forecasts. If prediction is impossible, one alternative is an opinion poll of experts to see if a consensus emerges. The National Defense University reported the results of such a poll in 1978. It amounted to a collective guess that weather through the last quarter of this century will most likely continue to resemble that of the previous 30 years.

Most meteorologists are reluctant to forecast climatic change because they know that the atmospheric system has an inherent capacity to counteract variations. Thus world climate tends to be relatively stable for thousands of years even though it is always fluctuating slightly. Think of the atmosphere as a vast heat-driven, self-tuning engine for redistributing solar energy around the planet. While 29 percent of the sunshine is reflected back into space, and about 19 percent is absorbed by the air, the bulk of it, 52 percent, is absorbed by the land and the sea. To balance this income and keep the planet from heating up, Earth returns an equal amount of energy to space in the form of infrared (heat) radiation. But while income and outgo balance for the planet as a whole, there is usually an imbalance in any given latitude zone. It is this imbalance that drives the weather.

In general and averaged over a year, Earth has a net energy income in lower latitudes, within 38 degrees of the Equator, and a net energy loss toward the poles. The contrast is greatest in winter. If there were no swirling storms of circulating ocean currents—that is, if there were no weather—the tropics in the winter hemisphere would heat up unbearably while the polar regions, darkened by perpetual night, would cool to near absolute zero (273 degrees below zero Celsius or about 460 degrees below zero Fahrenheit). Such extremes don't develop because constantly interacting weather systems and ocean currents spread tropical energy to maintain a more-or-less-livable climate throughout the world.

The tropics are a key factor in this global climate-maintaining circulation for they are the "fire box" that powers the weather machine. In 1735, British physicist George Hadley developed a concept which meteorologists still find handy in thinking about the role of the tropics. He envisioned air flowing at low levels from the subtropics toward the Equator in both hemispheres. When these air currents (the trade winds) converged, warmed and moistened by the underlying sea, they would flow upward, generating systems of convective clouds and rain. This would pump energy to higher levels where air flowing out toward the poles would carry it north and south. By such an overturning, the tropics would feed energy into the general atmospheric circulation.

This so-called Hadley circulation is oversimplified. Meteorologists now know that much energy is carried by swirling eddies such as the great mid-latitude storm systems. Nevertheless, they still consider Hadley's concept to be a useful model for imagining the workings of the atmosphere. It applies most aptly to the Intertropical Convergence Zone (ITCZ) where the trade winds meet. Here air does rise in organized convective systems as Hadley suggested, showing up as bands of clouds in satellite photos. But how these cloud systems pump energy out of the tropics, if they help to do so directly at all, remains unclear.

The role of hurricanes is equally puzzling. These violent storms, a prominent feature of North American weather especially along the eastern and Gulf coasts, have been considered important transporters of energy and moisture. Yet William M. Gray of Colorado State University points out that annually their contribution to world rainfall and energy budgets is only about 2 percent. On the other hand their contribution during the hurricane season looks more impressive. Year after year, about 80 tropical disturbances called cyclones appear; half to two thirds of them become hurricanes. Most occur in late summer and fall when rain over land is otherwise relatively scanty. During this period, Dr. Gray estimates, they may account for 4 to 5 percent of the world's precipitation. Fall tropical cyclones and hurricanes also inject substantial energy into the motion of Northern Hemisphere winds at a time when that circulation is building up for winter. It's as though these tropical storms were part of

Fire and hail; snow and vapour; stormy wind fulfilling his word . . . .

—Book of Psalms

a mechanism by which the atmosphere taps the energy of the tropics when there is a special need.

Exactly how all of this fits together to drive the atmospheric weather machine, no one knows. Nevertheless, meteorologists are convinced that the overall working of that machine is remarkably consistent. Drought in one area is likely to be compensated by excess precipitation in another. Why then are there significant climatic changes at all? Why are there ice ages? Why are there interglacials lasting about 10,000 years? Why are there fluctuations like the Little Ice Age within them? The short answer is that no one really knows. The longer answer highlights clues to possible mechanisms. Various factors are implicated—factors such as variations in the sun's energy output, changes in Earth's orbit, and shifting of continents, to name a few.

To begin with, the geological record suggests that the planet has been largely ice-free for much of its development. The present ice-age epoch is only a few million years old. There is no general agreement as to what creates an ice age. However, the position of continents could be crucial. Chester Beaty of the University of Lethbridge in Alberta, Canada, who champions this theory, maintains that the presence of large land masses in sufficiently high latitudes to catch and hold a lot of snow is enough to create ice-age conditions. At present, major land masses are located in high latitudes and the Earth, for whatever reason, seems locked in an ice-age cycle. That being the case, other factors must be at work causing the periodic warm periods called interglacials.

Three of the most certain of these factors are changes in the shape of the Earth's orbit and in the wobble and tilt of its axis. The ellipticity of the orbit varies with a period of about 96,000 years. The tilt of the Earth's axis also changes, causing the Earth to nod up and down relative to the sun over a cycle of some 40,000 years. Finally, the pull of sun and moon makes the Earth wobble like a spinning top and swings the North Pole around every 21,000 years. James D. Hays of Columbia University, John Imbrie of Brown University, and Nicholas J. Shackleton of Cambridge University (England) have found that the chemical makeup of deep-sea sediments and the relative abundancies of tiny temperature-sensitive animals in them reflect climatic fluctuations that correspond to the astronomical cycles.

The influence of possible small changes in the energy output of the sun itself and of the cooling effect of volcanic dust is less clear, although it may help account for the Little Ice Age. During that particularly cold period from 1645 to 1715, sunspot activity virtually ceased, perhaps implying a slight drop in solar energy flow. Also, there was much volcanic activity which filled the high atmosphere with fine dust, blocking some of the sunlight during parts of the Little Ice Age period. Whether or not these were immediate causes of that cooling episode, the climate did recover. Dr. Beaty points out that it may be no coincidence that the Earth, which in its orbit is closest to the sun during the northern winter, now receives much more winter sunshine in the Northern Hemisphere than during the last glaciation, which peaked 18,000 years ago. This enhanced warming may have been enough to counteract any short-term cooling that might otherwise have triggered a new glaciation. "Little Ice Ages may develop, as happened a few hundred years ago," Beaty suggests, "but big ones can't."

But what of humanity's impact on this climatic system? The main concern here is the possible warming effect of carbon dioxide released by increasing use of fossil fuels. Carbon dioxide is a heat-trapping gas, absorbing infrared radiation from the land and sea, radiation that otherwise would go out into space, and redirecting some of it back toward the surface. As carbon dioxide accumulates in the atmosphere, it could begin to warm the planet. It is hard to estimate how much of a threat this may be. The carbon dioxide build-up depends on such poorly known factors as the future rate of use of fossil fuels and the fate of the carbon dioxide released. Not all of the gas that goes into the air stays there. Scientists are not sure where it is going (they think some is probably dissolved in the sea) or how much of the increasing carbon dioxide burden of the atmosphere ultimately will be removed. Projections suggest that, without conscious effort to curtail fossil fuel use, the carbon dioxide effect could warm the planet several degrees over the next couple of centuries.

No one knows whether this would be good or bad. One danger would be possible melting of some of the Antarctic ice cap which would flood many coastal areas and low-lying cities. On the other hand, a mild warming might help hold back the next ice age. These questions now are the subject of intense international research. Meanwhile, and without taking it too seriously, John Imbrie has made his own ice age forecast. He thinks the astronomical influences account for most of the variance in climate. He predicts that their joint effect will be to continue a 6,000-year overall cooling and drying trend. Other influences, including any carbon dioxide effect, may superimpose fluctuations and even bring some warming. But the sluggish long-term cooling will eventually win out. So here's his forecast: "A warming trend tomorrow (i.e., the next millennium), chance of ice age in 3,000 years."

That may be an intriguing tidbit for dinner table conversation. But Imbrie himself points out that such a vague and distant projection is of little use to anyone today. It is the weather of this century with which Americans have to be concerned, and the interaction of the American land with the global weather machine offers more than enough challenge for forecasters.

Returning to patterns of atmospheric circulation, air flowing out of the tropics at higher altitudes sinks back toward the surface in the subtropics over a vaguely defined latitude band centered, on the average, about 30 degrees north and south of the Equator. This subsiding air tends to produce regions of fair weather with little precipitation, and there are located many of the world's great deserts, including those of the United States Southwest.

Mountains also help keep some of America's semi-arid lands dry. The subtropical fair-weather zones are more or less transitional regions between the belts where the easterly trade winds blow and temperate latitudes where average winds are westerly. The spines of America's western mountain ranges thrust upward into this westerly flow. Air masses moving in from the Pacific are lifted and cooled as they expand under the lower pressure of higher altitudes. Their moisture condenses and drops out, creating mountain snow packs that subsequently feed rivers and underground aquifers farther east. The now-dry air becomes drier still as it descends the eastern slopes, warming by compression under the higher pressure of lower altitudes, just as air in a bicycle pump warms when compressed. Sometimes this down-slope effect can be extreme, producing hot, dry, violent "chinook" winds. An Indian word, chinook means "snow eater," which aptly describes the winds' effect. Southern California suffers from a similar wind, the Santa Ana, when air flowing over the Coast Ranges and Sierra Nevada mountains subsides into the Great Basin, then turns southwestward to flow down mountain passes to the coastal plains. A hot, dry, fiercely blowing Santa Ana can fan chaparral fires, making them almost impossible to put out.

While the western mountains leave land to the east in a rain shadow, they help channel both warm, moist air from the Gulf of Mexico and cold air masses from the north. The interaction of such air masses provides energy to fuel thunderstorms, tornadoes, and winter storms. In many parts of the country, topographic features such as mountains or the sharp contrast between continent and ocean perturb the boundaries between such air masses (fronts), causing disturbances that can grow into storm systems. This makes regions east of the Rockies, around the Ozarks, and off the Carolina coast favored nurseries for storms.

General weather patterns are also influenced by factors farther afield. Working with four years of satellite data, Jay S. Winston and Arthur F. Krueger of the National Oceanic and Atmospheric Administration have found distinctive tropical weather patterns that foreshadowed the severe winters of 1976-77 and 1977-78. As this two-year period approached, cloudiness expanded to alter the distribution of energy income in the tropics, while on the average, upper air temperatures rose a degree or two. This warming represented an increase in atmospheric energy, some of which could be exported to the winter circulation at higher latitudes. Meanwhile Jerome Namias of Scripps Institution of Oceanography has studied the relation of North Pacific sea-surface temperatures and associated air flows to North American weather. He too found anomalies that foreshadowed the

Like crashing surf, clouds engulf the San Juan Mountains in southwest Colorado. Moisture-filled winds from the Pacific rise as they near the range. Clouds dump rain, snow on the western side; eastern slopes stay dry.

harsh 1976–77 winter several months in advance. These ocean conditions were linked to air circulation off the western United States that diverted rain-giving storms from California, brought winter warmth to Alaska, and contributed to the continental circulation that sent unusual cold and heavy snows to eastern states, especially areas such as Buffalo, New York, located near the Great Lakes.

Though often ornery, American weather nevertheless represents a relatively benign climate. Enough of the land is arable to more than feed the people, and most of it is habitable. As the land is used ever more intensely, the challenge is to learn to work with this weather rather than against it.

Tornadoes offer a good case in point. In the 1940s, there was something like one death per reported tornado, as an average figure. By the late 1970s, in spite of population increases, that death rate had fallen nine-fold thanks to a long-term program of forecasting, warning, and public preparedness. With the help of radar and satellites, tornado conditions can be detected and warnings issued. Preparedness programs at the local level help people respond intelligently and seek shelter in time.

These measures save lives. But what about property? Studies by the Institute for Disaster Research at Texas Tech University show that much can be done to make public buildings and homes tornado-resistant. Tornado experts and the public are beginning to work together to cope intelligently with a natural weather hazard. Meteorologists wish this were true of other such hazards as well. The American Meteorological Society (AMS) has warned that heedless development along the Gulf Coast and Eastern Seaboard has put millions of people at the mercy of hurricane storm surges. In a hurricane, low-lying, often hard-to-evacuate regions would be rapidly swept by water. The situation is even worse with flash floods, now called by the AMS the number one weather hazard in the United States. Continually expanding development of flood-prone areas, including mountain canyons, has greatly worsened the danger.

Dealing with this hazard calls for many measures—improved forecasts and warning systems, public preparedness so that warning results in effective evacuation, and better land use planning. But the greatest change has to take place in the minds of the people involved. An attitude of "it can't happen here" or "won't happen again" underlies the problem. The real tragedy of the modern Johnstown flood is that, in a town whose name is synonymous with flood danger, people have gone on living in a flood-prone gorge. "I couldn't understand why the good Lord picked on me," one man told a United Press International reporter, "But we're going to stay, by God, we're going to stay. We are the valley people. My roots are damn, damn deep." But another native observed, "They call it the 'spirit of Johnstown,' but, heck, that's a bunch of baloney. It's not a spirit. It's pure ornery stubbornness."

Nevertheless, this is the spirit with which generations of Americans have faced extreme weather. By and large, it has enabled them to muddle through. Yet it is a dangerous strategy for the future. Robert D. Miewald of the University of Nebraska has pointed out that extreme weather should be considered a "social event," meaning an event whose impact depends on how well people can cope with it. Taking the western drought as an example, he asks, "Do we regard drought as just an unpleasant event in an otherwise happy world? If we just regard drought as so many 'bad years' to be endured, that may be its worst impact of all." Impose a little rationing, sink more wells into over-used aquifers, appeal for emergency aid—such measures can still tide over a region such as California or the Great Plains. Meanwhile, the real problem intensifies: too many people trying to live in ways that are beyond the carrying capacity of the land. This kind of approach, Dr. Miewald warned, could ultimately make the problem of drought unsolvable.

Thus it is that American weather is raising broad new questions about the use of the American land. How much and what kind of development can the desert and semi-arid regions support? How should land use be controlled in regions exposed to natural flooding and to hurricane storm surges? How can densely populated regions subject to extreme winters better organize energy supply, communications, and other essential services? If such issues are squarely faced and wisely answered, this can continue to be a bountiful and livable land.

The oldest voice in the world is the wind . . . in truth it is one of our masters . . . .

–Donald Culross Peattie

A roaring whirlwind of dirt and debris, tornado bears down on fields near Fargo, North Dakota. Warm, moist winds from Gulf meet cool, dry winds from Canada, bringing yearly destruction to Midwest, southeastern states.

Poisoning the Earth

By Gary Soucie

No matter where you turn these days, pollution meets the eye. Not just physically and literally, as in the case of the chemical bludgeoning of the eye by the tear-inducing components of our contemporary urban atmosphere. No, I mean figuratively. Climb an imaginary Olympus and survey the scene. At every point of the compass, pollution: Kepone in Chesapeake Bay and the James River; DDT in the Tennessee River at Triana, Alabama; dioxins in Michigan's Saginaw and Tittabawassee Rivers; radioisotopes in the Susquehanna downstream of Middletown, Pennsylvania; mercury, cadmium, and other toxic heavy metals in Corpus Christi Bay; nitrogen supersaturation below the dozens of dams in the Columbia River system; toxaphene in Georgia's estuarine bays and marshes; fecal coliform bacteria in Nebraska's Platte River; sulfites, mercury, arsenic, and other pulp mill, smelter, and refinery wastes in Commencement Bay, Washington; throughout the West, what the Environ-

Though vapors from an Indiana oil refinery stain the sunset, nearby industries create much of the general pall. Airborne poisons crack the surface of a tire, opposite top. Auto graveyard smoulders in desert West.

mental Protection Agency almost euphemistically calls "non-point-source pollution," sediments, chlorides and other dissolved salts of minerals and metals, nutrients, sulfates, organic and inorganic chemicals, pesticides, and other contaminants washed into lakes and streams from farms, feedlots, pastures, and fertilized and "bug-proofed" fields, or carried there by the irrigation ditches that threaten to turn into deserts that which they are intended to vitalize. And that's just a partial catalogue of stream and lake pollution problems recently in the news.

In the summer of 1978, environmental pollution seemed to take a threatening new turn and to take on a whole new urgency with the discovery of the Love Canal chemical dump site in Niagara Falls, New York, where decades earlier the Hooker Chemical Company had dumped still unknown quantities of more than 200 different chemicals and chemical wastes, some of them extremely toxic. By 1978, some of those chemicals had begun seeping into the basements of the homes that had been built on and around the canal site; others had begun belching up to the surface in the vicinity of back yards and school playgrounds. Hundreds of families had to be evacuated and official, public, and press attention turned to other abandoned chemical dumps, including several more in Niagara Falls, some of them larger and potentially even more dangerous than the notorious Love Canal. That fall the Environmental Protection Agency published a list of 32,254 other potentially hazardous dump sites in the country, of which 638 were known to contain a "significant quantity" of hazardous materials and posed "imminent health hazards." Within a few weeks, acting on a tip, a federal investigator checked on a rural valley near Louisville, Kentucky, and discovered more than 100,000 barrels of chemicals and chemical wastes, discarded like so many empty cans and bags of garbage along some roadside or in some casual woodland dump. The "Valley of the Drums," as the dump has come to be known, wasn't on EPA's list, not even the list of suspect sites.

News like this makes you stop and wonder what the world is coming to—whether we are making any progress at all. For that matter, progress isn't an easy thing to measure, and hardly anyone could give you a decent definition of it, not even by example. Many of the material things that often are touted as evidence of progress, particularly in advertisements and TV commercials (New! Improved! Bigger! Better!), I would consign to the category Mark Twain once called "all the modern inconveniences."

While the actors in the beer commercials are toasting "the

Protecting the environment must now become part of the cost of doing business.

—Walter J. Hickel

good life," those in a certain wine company's are always remembering fondly and drinking to "the good old days." That's another of those elusive but popular images from our social mythology. I doubt whether a pollster would find much consensus as to just when those "good old days" occurred. According to the "good life" beer drinkers, they must be happening right now, which at least gives the wine drinkers something to look forward to. Or maybe it is just part of what some have called the "survival syndrome"; as Byron put it, "The 'good old times'—all times, when old, are good."

I recall hearing Les Pengelly, a wildlife biologist at the University of Montana, holding forth on the subject one April evening a few years ago at one of the Borah Foundation symposiums held annually at the University of Idaho. "People are always running around talking about 'the good life,'" Pengelly said, "but I'm not sure I know what they mean. If this is 'the good life' we are leading, I'm getting

pretty tired of it. I don't know about you, but I'm ready for something better than 'the good life.'" Judging by the applause, so were a lot of the students and professors and townsfolk and lentil and split-pea farmers in the audience.

One man's progress is another's poison, but it can be more confusing than that. On opening day of fishing season, I went out armed with a fiber-glass rod of uncanny strength and light weight and with a reel filled with the new, almost incredibly abrasion-resistant monofilament polymer the Du Pont Company calls Fluorescent Stren. Rod and line I would have to count among what Du Pont's advertising copywriters used to call "Better things for better living through chemistry." Yet if I had headed for the Housatonic River, hitherto a logical opening-day locus for the stalker of rainbow, brown, and brook trout, I would have been confronted by another legacy of modern chemistry. Posted on the bankside trees along the Housatonic these days are signs that read: "Eating fish from this area is not recommended. The Commissioner of the State Health Department has determined that fish in these waters contain concentrations of chemicals which may be harmful to humans. He recommends that fish from these waters not be used as food. Sportsmen are requested to release all fish unharmed."

Contrary to the cautious words used by Connecticut's health commissioner, there isn't any maybe about the health hazard of those chemicals: They are polychlorinated biphenyls (PCBs), carcinogens so potent that their use and manufacture in the United States were banned as of July 1, 1979. Too late to save the Housatonic, alas, but a step in the right direction. (In matters involving pollution, sometimes progress must be measured in very tiny steps.) PCBs formerly were widely and routinely used in this country as insulators in the manufacture of electrical equipment, and most of the Housatonic's PCBs came from a General Electric Company transformer and capacitor plant upriver at Pittsfield, Massachusetts. Two similar plants in New York state are responsible for poisoning the Hudson River with PCBs.

Besides being concentrated in the tissues of the fish and other creatures that live in the Housatonic and Hudson and other similarly contaminated waters (such as the Great Lakes), the PCBs also saturate the very muds and sediments of the bottoms—a source of food-chain contamination for years to come. Dredging the bottoms would be physically impractical and economically ruinous, and the disposal of all those millions of cubic yards of poisoned soils would raise other pollution and environmental questions.

The poor old Hudson has more than its fair share of trou-

Though sparked by an "act of God"—stroke of lightning—a refinery fire at Beaumont, Texas, spawns a hellish cloud of pollution. Metal refinery fumes, like those rising in Utah, opposite, can damage lung tissue.

bles. A recent report by the Environmental Defense Fund and the New York Public Interest Research Group found that the Hudson is, in the words of the President's Council on Environmental Quality (CEQ), "contaminated with a complex spectrum of toxic substances such as PCBs, benzene, xylene, cyclohexane, tetrahydrofuran, toluene, and chloroform, all of which pose a health threat to the 150,000 people upstate who drink river water." Appalling as that list is, it fails to mention the "old fashioned" pollutants that have been known for years to plague the Hudson: DDT and other pesticides, fertilizers, and animal wastes washed out of fields and farms, the leachates of municipal and industrial dumps in the valley, spilled oil, hot water from power plants along the river, and raw and improperly treated sewage.

Manhattan Island, as sure a symbol of modernity and progress as exists anywhere, dumps some quarter-billion gallons of raw, untreated sewage into the Hudson and East Rivers daily. Manhattan hasn't got a single sewage treatment plant, the sort of statistic that usually relegates societies to a backward category. Can Manhattan Island truly stand for progress? Maybe it can. This, from CEQ's annual report in 1978, on the levels of carbon monoxide in metropolitan skies: "CO levels in Manhattan, although still the worst in the United States, are improving."

CEQ's "report card" on our environment shows mixed marks: Most city levels of photochemical oxidants and carbon monoxide are improving, but no trend of improvement shows for nitrogen dioxide. Ninety-five percent of the 1,162 sources of air pollution subject to hazardous pollutant standards were found to be in compliance with the standards for asbestos, beryllium, mercury, and vinyl chloride; however, "benzene, which is implicated in causing leukemia, is still found at hazardous levels in consumer products" like furniture stripping products. On and on the report goes, for 599 pages—a step forward here, a slip backward there.

The National Wildlife Federation, which has been publishing annual Environmental Quality Indexes as long as CEQ has been issuing official annual reports, recently published a 10-year analysis of the EQIs, and the results are worth noting. The actual numbers used in the EQI are somewhat arbitrary (and absolutely meaningless when not accompanied by explanations), but I have listed them so you can see how much or little we've come or gone.

Air Quality: A tiny bit better (from an EQI of 35 in 1969 to one of 36 in 1978), but of the nation's 105 largest cities, only Honolulu has truly clean air.

Water Quality: Worse (EQI 33, down from 40). After the expenditure of $19 billion in federal construction grants to build sewage treatment plants, two thirds of our cities are still dumping only partially treated sewage into waterways.

Wildlife: Slipping badly (down to an EQI of 43, having started 10 years earlier at 55), thanks mainly to habitat losses. In 1969 the federal government had 89 animal species on its endangered species list; by 1978 the number had climbed to 192 species.

Forests: Staying about the same (at a respectable EQI 75), but timbering and recreational use of forest resources have increased three-fold since 1953. Also, the demand for wood, paper, and other forest products continues to grow, but tree growth is leveling off.

Soil: Worse (EQI slipped from 80 to 70), principally the result of unabated soil erosion and increased urban development of arable rural land (50 billion tons and 17 million acres, respectively, over the past decade).

Minerals: Worse (from 50 in 1969 to 37 in 1978). With 6 percent (one seventeenth) of the world's population, the United States uses one third of the energy and one fourth of the other minerals produced in the world. And we throw away, after only a single use, 70 percent of the metals we use, even though it takes 20 times as much energy to mine and process virgin ores as to recycle scrap.

Living Space: Worse (an EQI drop from 60 to 46), because we simply are running out of room for our increasing numbers and our expansive and expanding lifestyles. Only nine states have comprehensive land-use plans, and national land-use planning legislation has failed twice to make it through the congressional wickets. You know what Will Rogers said about land: "They aren't making it anymore."

Direct application of chemicals, above, may sap soil vitality, as can intensive tillage which opens land to wind, water erosion. Atomic power plant looms, opposite. Safety procedures help limit escape of radioactivity.

With five of the seven categories trending downward, and one each running steady and trending ever so slightly upward, it is safe to say that overall we still have a declining Environmental Quality Index. There aren't many silver linings or sunny rays of hope among the massed thunderclouds, but the environmental forecast isn't entirely bleak.

Some of the recent bad news—the discovery of the hazardous chemical waste dumps at Love Canal and 32,000-odd other places and of the radioactive radium mining dumps in Colorado, the PCBs in the Hudson and Housatonic rivers, the doubling of the species on the endangered list, the nearly catastrophic accident at the Three Mile Island nuclear power plant—things like these don't represent new problems, just new discoveries of old ones. In matters environmental, what you don't know really can kill you; environmental ignorance is not bliss. When the nation, circa Earth Day 1970, more or less discovered and adopted the environment as a battered foundling in need of rehabilitation and tender loving care, it was like sending a suffering person to the emergency room for treatment. The doctors go to work to stanch the bleeding immediately, but they also begin making a more complete diagnosis. In the case of our battered American Earth, the course of treatment has begun, but the results of the lab tests

are just coming back. The diagnosis isn't yet complete, but it looks as if the environment is in worse shape than we *thought* it was. That doesn't mean it actually is getting worse. The patient is under observation and the outlook is guarded, as anonymous hospital spokesmen are always telling the press in newsworthy medical cases.

Still, don't look for an early or even a complete recovery. It is going to take plenty of expensive, time-consuming therapy to get the old American environment back on her feet and functioning normally. She might always walk with a limp and need crutches, but if we clean up our act sufficiently, she will survive.

In times of trouble it is tempting to point fingers, and to look for someone to blame. Too often it is an exercise in futility, not only because it wastes time, but also because the layers of blame are almost as happy bearding a scapegoat as getting at the real roots of a problem. In the environmental crisis at hand, it might not be a bad idea to take a backward glance and look for causes, not so much for apportioning blame or responsibility, but so that we might learn something from our mistakes and better understand how to correct them. As George Santayana said, "Those who cannot learn from the past are condemned to repeat it."

While technology—both capitalist and communist— might very well turn out to be the instrument of environmental injury, the "smoking gun" of the inquiry, it is merely the weapon, not the felonious perpetrator. The gun is, after all, in our hands. Are we, then, suicidal maniacs? Is modern society some sort of bedlam for the criminally insane? No, the situation is more like that described by Julian Huxley more than three decades ago: "At the moment, humanity is rather like an irresponsible and mischievous child who has been presented with a set of machine tools, a box of matches, and a supply of dynamite." Admiral Hyman Rickover, who certainly is no stranger to or refugee from advanced technology of the most lethal sort, almost put his finger on the real problem when he wrote: "It troubles me that we are so easily pressured by purveyors of technology into permitting so-called 'progress' to alter our lives without attempting to control it—as if technology were an irrepressible force of nature to which we must meekly submit." The real engine of social submission, the ersatz force of nature that steamrollers our will, is that so-called progress.

Progress is a fine and desirable thing, perhaps subordinate only to survival as a social goal. But that is true progress I am talking about, not the phony notion of progress that we have. True progress is difficult to measure and to assess because we haven't got a very good definition of it. Like "the good life" and "the good old days," progress is a concept that is as intoxicating and as evanescent as the heady vapors of distilled liquors. Never mind what the dictionaries say about progress, it is what people think that matters here. And when it comes to progress, people seldom think, they react reflexively, like a leg whose knee has been tapped. The march of progress sometimes resembles the mindless, potentially self-destructive, zombie-like stalk of the sleepwalker.

Like most Americans, maybe all Americans, I grew up taking progress—like clean air to breathe and clean water to drink—for granted. We didn't learn the words in public school, but we were well indoctrinated with convictions like Browning's that "Progress is the law of life," or Spencer's that "It is part of nature," and assumed that it had always been so. I was wrong on all counts. I can still remember my astonishment at learning—as an undergraduate at the University of North Carolina, in Professor Alfred G. Engstrom's course, French 81: French Literature Before 1800—that progress is, as ideas go, a fairly new one. The Idea of Progress as we know it, progress as a social program, was born during the late 17th century (some say with the publication in 1687 of Newton's *Principia*) and was nourished into full flower during the 18th, a period in history known as the Age of Reason or simply the Enlightenment.

It was a bold and audacious period, the Enlightenment, certainly the most intellectually exciting time since the Renaissance. An understanding of Enlightenment thought is important to an understanding of the environmental crisis in America because it was during the Enlightenment that the United States was born and that the Industrial Revolution was launched. Franklin, Jefferson, Madison, John Adams, Thomas Paine, Noah Webster, Benjamin Rush, Manasseh Cutler, John Logan, and dozens of others of our founding fathers were men of Enlightenment as surely as were Voltaire and Diderot in France, Goethe, Lessing, and von Haller in Germany, Priestley, Bentham, and Hume in England, Linnaeus in Sweden, Genovesi and Beccaria in the Italian States.

The period preceding the Enlightenment in Europe had been traditionalist, orthodox, artistic, even formalistic, national, psychological, religious—devoted to stability. The Enlightenment was free-thinking, skeptical, practical and scientific, cosmopolitan, metaphysical, secular, even anti-Catholic—devoted to and delighted in change. Both periods had a strong conception of order in the universe; the preceding period believed in an order imposed by the will and laws of God, the Enlightenment in a natural order imposed by

physical nature and the environment. However secular the Enlightenment might have been, it wasn't lacking in faith.

A belief in progress would seem to imply a concern for the future, but it doesn't. If progress is inevitable, then the future will take care of itself. As Jefferson wrote to Madison, "The earth belongs always to the living generation." Rather shortsighted, that, and not all that dissimilar to the sentiment expressed by the cartoon character who said he was tired of worrying about future generations: "What have they done for us, anyway?" Jeffersonian or jocular, that sort of thinking has sown poisoned seeds across the social firmament, and we now are reaping the bitter and melancholy fruits. Blind faith—in progress or anything else—demands a surrender of will and therefore a surrender of self-control. If progress is inevitable and natural, we needn't work at achieving it. Simply by "doing what comes naturally," progress must follow. Since the Industrial Revolution and

all during the continuing rapid advancement of science, what comes most naturally to modern society seems to be mechanized, large-scale environmental modification and manipulation. Bertrand Russell noted in 1956 that those man-induced changes have "something of the inexorable inevitability of natural forces," and he wondered whether we would survive the consequences of our "halfway cleverness."

Science and reason ought to be just two complementary facets of the same intellectual and social gemstone, but Alfred North Whitehead pointed out, as early as 1925, in *Science and the Modern World,* that science "has remained predominantly an anti-rational movement, based upon a naive faith." The secular *philosophes* of the Enlightenment ridiculed the blind faith and trust in divine providence of their devout precursors, but their faith in natural progress was as blind, as naive, as divorced from rational analysis. Society has been adrift ever since. As Whitehead ominously warned more than half a century ago, "It may be that civilization will never recover from the bad climate which enveloped the introduction of machinery."

Recent developments and discoveries on the environmental pollution front would seem to bear him out. On the other hand, maybe all the bad news is really good news in disguise—a sheep in wolf's clothing as it were. Nothing instructs so well as experience, and as the proverb says, experience is a hard teacher. The Three Mile Island nuclear power plant scare in the spring of 1979 probably had more effect on the pro-nuclear optimists than on the anti-nuclear or neutral pessimists. The pessimists could smugly say, "I told you so," but the optimists had to reexamine their basic attitudes about nuclear energy. (As for the nuclear optimists whose faith wasn't shaken, we can fairly, if not safely, ignore them as fools who do not profit by their mistakes.) PCBs have been totally prohibited. The signs are not altogether bleak.

Pittsburgh used to be a perfect model of air pollution along with London and Los Angeles. The air over Pittsburgh had become so foul that breathing in that city had become a matter of life and death. The cleanup in Pittsburgh has been so successful that the city no longer ranks among the 15 or 20 most air-polluted American cities.

Numerous rivers that were once so foul that they couldn't support aquatic life now have been sufficiently cleaned up that residents can use them for fishing, swimming, and other water-based sports and pastimes. In 1967 the St. Johns River at Jacksonville, Florida, was almost unbelievably polluted with raw sewage, pulp-mill effluents, and other contaminants. The city of Jacksonville itself was pumping 18 million

Bath may save a lucky loon's life after an oil spill fouled its feathers. Oregon's Willamette River receives a scrub at American Can Company lagoon, opposite, where rafts of air bubbles help detoxify pulp mill waste.

gallons of raw, untreated sewage into the river each day, and each teaspoon of river water was said to contain more than 100,000 bacteria, raising a serious threat of typhoid fever, dysentery, and other epidemic diseases. Now the bacteria count is down to 100 per teaspoon, and the tarpon and dolphin have returned to the river's mouth.

Whitehead, whose prescient warnings of the hazards of arrogant, unguided science went essentially ignored during his lifetime, said there were two "evils" to modern science: "the ignoration of the true relation of each organism to its environment; and the other, the habit of ignoring the intrinsic worth of the environment which must be allowed weight in any consideration of the final ends." We still don't fully understand the ecology of our complex environment, and we still haven't entirely broken the bad habits, but we have come a long way. Ecology has become a household word and a social platitude if not precisely a way of life, and with our new laws and the preparation of environmental impact statements we are at least heading in the right direction, giving the intrinsic worth of the environment its due weight in social and political decisions.

The question remains, though, whether we are changing fast enough, far enough. There are pessimists among us. In *The Human Prospect*, Robert L. Heilbroner gloomily concluded that "the outlook is for convulsive change—change forced upon us by external events rather than by conscious choice, by catastrophe rather than by calculation. As with Malthus's much derided but all too prescient forecasts," Heilbroner wrote, "nature will provide the checks, if foresight and 'morality' do not." But even so pessimistic an observer as Heilbroner conceded that "It is possible that . . . a new direction will be struck that will greatly ease the otherwise inescapable adjustments."

Having at long last realized that, environmentally at least, things are very wrong indeed, we can now set about righting the wrongs. It won't be easy, and it won't happen overnight; neither can we take the success of the cleanup for granted. Only time will tell. Perhaps, if we work hard enough at achieving and earning our progress, future historians will say that our age was one in which the idea of progress graduated from social mythology to social reality, that science and technology (and the society that guides and uses them) finally became motivated, as Einstein had said they must, by "concern for man and his fate," and that the Age of Environmentalism might also be called the Reenlightenment. In this I have not faith but hope, and only hoping and working can make it so.

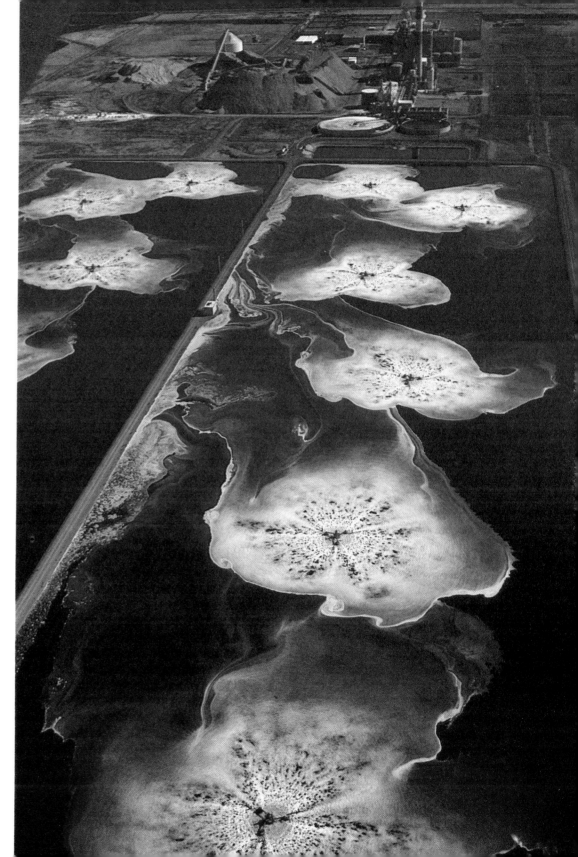

The Vital Estuary

By Arthur W. Sherwood

The Chesapeake Bay, the largest estuary in the United States, is a beautiful and productive environment to which millions of people have been attracted—all too often to the detriment of Bay resources. The full richness of the biology of the Chesapeake is a treasure rarely appreciated; it exists in a profusion of creatures and organisms great and small. The Bay, it can be fairly said, is one of the most productive ecosystems known to man. But its relatively short food chain is vulnerable because few plants and animals have learned to adapt to the rare combination of salt and fresh water that characterizes this shallow estuary. The price the Bay has paid for its popularity shows in overpopulated shores, overloaded sewage systems, underpopulated natural, renewable resources, and permits issued to thousands of point-source polluters. Yet many informed observers believe the worst is over; that an orderly management of resources is underway. There is evidence to substantiate their optimism.

Recent environmental laws and regulations have not brought instantaneous cleanliness and health to the Bay—its pollution began with the industrial revolution—but they have, as the following histories show, made the public's interest in the welfare of the Bay a dominant and enduring force.

In the lower Bay, the current hot issue is the proposed oil refinery at Portsmouth, Virginia. Reputedly a $600,000,000 investment, the project pits local and national conservationists, local watermen, the U.S. Fish and Wildlife Service, the Environmental Protection Agency, the National Marine Fisheries Service, and the Virginia Institute of Marine Science against the Hampton Roads Energy Co. (the proponent), the Mayor and City Council of Portsmouth, local trade associations and the U.S. Departments of Energy, Defense, and Labor. Fortunately for the opponents, the project requires dredging in navigable waters, for which a Corps of Engineers permit must be obtained. Pursuant to the National Environmental Policy Act of 1969, as amended, that means the Corps must consider the possible environmental impact of the proposed project.

The opponents' argument is rooted in a scientifically ultra-respectable special report prepared in 1974 for the Maryland Center for Environmental and Estuarine Studies by Dr. Curt D. Rose on the timely subject of Petroleum in the Estuary. Dr. Rose, at the time of the report head of the Shellfish Division at the Solomons Island Chesapeake Biological Laboratory, summed up oil-spill dangers to estuaries most succinctly: "Location [of oil refineries] in estuaries involves such exceptionally high and severe risks that it appears unacceptable from an environmental viewpoint."

On their side, the proponents came up with data so apparently compelling as to be almost totally irresistible. Citing benefits to the area should the plant be located in Portsmouth, Mayor Richard J. Davis listed a

potential local payroll of $50 million and an additional 2,200 permanent jobs (about 5 percent of the present work force). On the other hand, he warned, failure to build the plant would deprive the city of the facility's considerable real estate taxes. Added to those arguments was a letter from 32 U.S. Senators to Secretary of the Department of Energy James R. Schlesinger, calling for, among other things, more local (domestic) refineries, and the development of "respon-

sible siting policies consistent with Federal clean air and water standards."

Caught between these formidable forces, the Corps' district engineer was expected to reluctantly recommend issuance of the permit to build. Surprisingly, he did just the opposite, and recommended denial.

High glee and celebration among the opponents! But not for long. The permit's path had only just begun: from the local chief to the Corps' Chief of Engineers (per-

John Menke, arms folded, typifies Bay watermen, tied to the Chesapeake by family tradition, seasonal changes, and life cycles of the shellfish they seek. Spring brings soft crabs; summer, hardshells, moving toward the deeps that will be their winter home. As November's chill moves in, oyster boats move out to dredge. Maryland and Virginia supply 25 percent of U.S. oyster catch. Clams, opposite, processed on Eastern Shore, may show up at New England clambakes.

mit denial overruled); from the Corps Chief to Clifford Alexander, Jr., Secretary of the Army, where, as of now, the fate of the refinery rests. Whatever the outcome, no one can claim that the public's interest has been ignored. Before 1969, it might well have been.

At the northern end of the Bay, near the Port of Baltimore, the crisis of the moment centers on Hart and Miller Islands. The issue is whether to use the islands as dump sites for toxic spoil dredged from the shipping channels to Baltimore. What gives the case a special twist is its highly unlikely lineup of antagonists. On one side, in the opponents' corner, is a plucky group of nearby residents, most of whom live in Baltimore County and use the Hart-Miller area for boating, swimming, and fishing. Their avowed leader is their Congressman, Clarence D. Long. On the other side is a coalition of labor, commerce, conservation, state, and city interests—the institutional establishment of the area. Ten years ago, when Hart-Miller was proposed, the outcome seemed certain. Today no one is sure, and the institutional establishment is licking its wounds.

Those wounds run deep and red. No one denies that Baltimore's shipping channel must be kept open or that toxic spoil should not be dumped in the open Bay water, a common practice until recently. It's well known that the state of Maryland is fast running out of space to dispose of dredged spoil. And, of course, taxes, jobs, and transportation cost savings are thrown onto the scales. All this. Ten years of it. Permits secured from state and federal agencies. To date to no avail.

When the project finally got its Corps of Engineers permit, Congressman Long and his allies appealed to the Federal Court— and won. The latest chapter in this drama—the Court ruled the project did not have the needed Congressional approval!

The Hart-Miller Island case and the rumble over the proposed refinery at Portsmouth were commanding headlines long before the Clean Water Act of 1977 existed. Looking ahead, though, there's every reason to believe that this relatively unknown environmental blockbuster will be making history long after the current "big" cases are forgotten. It's a sleeper of immense potential—and a present disappointment.

The Act's central permit provision establishes a comprehensive regulatory scheme, the National Pollutant Discharge Elimination System (NPDES), the effect of which is to be nothing less than the elimination of the discharge of pollutants from "any discernible, confined, and discrete conveyance" (i.e., any point source) into navigable waters. Such scope, such an all-embracing gathering up of polluters into one bag, so to speak, makes the Clean Water Act a very dreamy piece of legislation. Very dreamy, that is, for everyone except those who are in the habit of dumping their waste into convenient waterways. The fact that the Act has, to date, been largely ignored, misused, and interpreted to death is understandable.

The population of the Bay region, now 8.2 million, more than doubled since 1940 and will double again during the next 50 years, if the Corps of Engineers' projections are regrettably right. That's enough statistical bad news to give the most intrepid planner/manager a headache. What are our problems? In a word—us.

Fortunately for the Bay, there are those among its friends who appear to have learned from past environmental disasters. Maryland Senator Charles McC. Mathias, Jr., is among them. He's been working for years to improve coordination among the various local, state, federal, public, and private agencies and organizations involved in Bay management. That means he's taken his licks—plenty of them. Senator Mathias has every reason, as the record discloses, to be discouraged. He isn't. "I am somewhat encouraged," he says, "about chances for devising an approach that will not impose

federal management on the Bay but will make federal resources available in a rational way to the Bay management process. I believe there is now a consensus that acknowledges if the Chesapeake Bay is to survive, it must be addressed as an entity, as a total system, without duplication and without omission. I hope that by the time this book is published that consensus will have produced tangible results."

There is reason for cautious optimism about the possibility of achieving more unified management of Bay resources. A joint Virginia/Maryland Bay Legislative Advisory Commission has been established (1978). That's an accomplishment that peace seekers throughout the world are no doubt studying carefully.

Intransigent traditionalists, unless they side with enlightened environmentalists, are the heavies of any piece like this. Identifying them can be difficult, for the rascals and villains are often the same guys we buy from and work for.

Russell R. Jones, general manager of Bethlehem Steel Company's Sparrows Point plant, for instance, makes no bones about how the Chesapeake fits into his plans. Says Jones: "The Sparrows Point plant's existence depends on our being able to recirculate large quantities of water in the production and finishing of steel. Since 1971 we have spent more than $62 million on water pollution control equipment at the Sparrows Point plant. In that time period, our discharges of suspended solids to tributary waters have been reduced by 85 percent. Total pollutant discharges have been reduced by 75 percent. However, the Clean Water Act requires that we now proceed to an even higher level of technology to further increase the cleanup efficiency. It is our belief that the additional expenditures of capital needed to achieve best-available technology, called for in the Clean Water Act, will far surpass the benefits derived."

Now that's laying it on the line. It's say-

Twin spans of Chesapeake Bay Bridge, above, speed sportsmen to marshlands rich with wildlife. Salt and fresh water mix constantly, creating an environment favorable to shellfish, rockfish, muskrat, otter, and flocks of wintering waterfowl. To navigate through the many shoals, watermen designed vessels unique to the region. Skipjack, top, saw many years of service in the oyster fleet. Opposite, recreational craft share Bay; sloops race as stiff October breeze fills spinnakers.

ing, as far as the Bay is concerned, that the Clean Water Act has done its job. But, in fact, the Clean Water Act has just begun to fight. Does that mean that Mr. Jones (Bay producers) and I (Bay environmentalists) have little in common? I think not. "We want to see the Bay flourish," Mr. Jones says, "from an industrial, recreational, environmental, and economic standpoint. And we will do our part to see that it does. However, we believe that this must be accomplished realistically using a balanced approach to Bay management that takes into account both socioeconomic and environmental factors." These are my sentiments exactly.

Kevin Sullivan, director of the Smithsonian Institution's Chesapeake Bay Center for Environmental Studies, cites the Wetlands Acts of the '70s, designed to protect the Bay's nutrient-rich marshes, as "one of the major environmental success stories . . . . Recent studies have indicated that these programs have resulted in a reduction of well over 80 percent of the amount of wetland acreage lost each year to development and that the health of the Chesapeake Bay system is not now being significantly threatened by modification of the Bay's shoreline."

So there are obviously many thoughtful people within the Bay community who haven't given up—and aren't about to. And they all have one thing in common—they know that they don't know enough.

While a new defense of the environment must be developed, it can't be done by opposing an oil refinery with an oyster. It can be done by putting in the balance man's yearning for the beautiful, by recognizing his dependence on an environment that sets his imagination free and cultivates his aesthetic sense.

Everyone who has read William W. Warner's Pulitzer Prize-winning book *Beautiful Swimmers* will remember how he sums up the Bay: "Delightsome, fruitful, pleasant. So it is, most would say, to this day."

"To me, nothing can be more thrilling than the whistling of wings, the sight of flocks against the sky, the knowledge that this ordered progression has begun again," writes Smithsonian Secretary S. Dillon Ripley. Migrating Canada geese, above, share Bay's ecosystem with mallard, left, and osprey, above left. Targets of gunners from Canada southward, mallards move to open water in autumn, may fly as far as Gulf Coast. Osprey finds channel marker ideal nesting place.

Environmentalists fear industrial damage to the largest and most productive estuary in the United States. "To paraphrase John Muir," writes author Arthur Sherwood, "any fool can destroy the Bay. Any fool can misuse its resources. The future of the Bay depends on whether we encourage or discourage such fools." Right, budding scientist at Smithsonian's Center for Environmental Studies, where scholars study the dynamic character of the Chesapeake and the richness of its biology.

By Joe Goodwin

Living in Harm's Way

Every silver lining has its cloud. And some are killers. Houses disintegrate at the touch of a tornado's furious funnel. Hurricanes churn up deadly tidal surges. Blizzards chunk millions of people back into the ice ages—or so it seems to those suddenly caught in nature's attack zone.

One stark fact emerges: Nobody is safe when disaster stalks the land.

Scientists who study the diverse species of disaster often discover curious similarities and family traits. For instance, blizzards have been called big white hurricanes. By the same token, hurricanes can be likened to big warm blizzards. Both probably serve the same function, helping to moderate Earth's extremes of temperature.

Some of the best places to observe both blizzards and tornadoes lie in the panhandle country of Oklahoma and north Texas. And the best place to run from both earthquakes and hurricanes is to high ground. Hurri-

canes kick up dangerous floods that sweep through coastal lowlands. Quakes engender tsunamis, the so-called tidal waves that devastate coasts.

Nature remains as cataclysmic as ever—but some of the sting is gone. With luck and plenty of sophisticated equipment, weather forecasters can predict some disasters aborning, and thus help us prepare our defenses in sufficient time to survive.

It was not always so. Take, for example, the hurricane that hit the Gulf Coast port of Galveston, Texas, in 1900. Signs of the storm were clear to anybody who looked up to the sky on that September 8th. But hardly anybody expected doomsday. It arrived in the form of a storm surge, a great moving dome of water, perhaps 50 miles across and a yard higher than the surrounding sea. The storm raised the already high tide an additional four feet. Water piled up, rushing past the wharf area into the business district and residential areas. Six thousand people drowned.

Survivors began construction of a seawall, fortunately completing it before 1915 when another hurricane arrived. This time only 275 people perished.

Mere mention of the name Camille and the year 1969 brings shudders to disaster professionals. This hurricane's path was correctly plotted, plenty of advance warning provided. Most citizens moved to high ground, especially from Pass Christian, Mississippi, the most likely place, weathermen calculated, for the storm to splash ashore. Evacuees took refuge in solidly built school buildings and other designated shelters.

A few people, though, elected to remain in town, gathering with friends to celebrate nature's rampage. Over cocktails at their hurricane parties, people reassured each other. Suddenly intensifying, Camille summoned up a storm surge. More than 140 people died in and near Pass Christian.

Another surprise punch landed during April 3–4, 1974. Tornadoes, nearly 150 of them, boiled out of a weather system that spread havoc across Alabama, Georgia, Tennessee, Kentucky, and Ohio. Dubbed the Super Outbreak by meteorologists, it claimed 315 lives. Without radio and television advisories, the death toll could have climbed higher.

Millions of people in the United States live in the country's two tornado alleys. One covers the lower half of the Great Plains. Researchers here, from the National Severe Storms Forecast Laboratory at Norman, Oklahoma, have gained fame through their tornado chases. Camera crews climb aboard vans; reports from radar watchers and from the pilot of a circling jet interceptor guide the cameramen to thunderstorms that may spawn twisters.

Photographic evidence and on-the-spot observation help scientists understand the life cycle of funnel-cloud episodes. The knowledge they gain also helps forecasters to react more quickly to tornado threats.

A second tornado alley runs across Dixie. More killer tornadoes are sighted in the county surrounding Birmingham, Alabama, than in any other county in the United States. Residents have long worked out survival plans and drills.

People often cling to each other when disaster moves in for the kill, but not so often in Birmingham. Husband and wife may separate. One runs to the front door to hold it open while the other runs to the back. In theory, the opening of doors helps equalize

Blizzard of 1978 stops New York City cold. Commuters struggle, opposite. Tornado transforms homes into a nightmarish lumberyard.

227

air pressure inside and outside the house, reducing the risk of collapse. Recent studies indicate, however, that the ploy doesn't work, and that simple construction techniques could strengthen houses so they might resist all but the strongest tornadoes, and thus reduce both damage and death.

Experts who study such events believe that many of our beloved twister curiosities—like wheat straws stuck clean through fence posts—may be myth or outright hoax. Experimenting along these lines, researchers fired a telephone pole out of a cannon directly into a brick wall. The pole disintegrated, much as a pencil does in an electric sharpener. But it certainly is no myth that severe tornadoes contain the fastest, hardest-hitting winds on earth, probably reaching 300 miles per hour.

Weather scientists are beginning to understand why some twisters are far more dangerous than others. In general, the more local the weather conditions that spawn a storm, the weaker the wind. Dust devils of the arid West may throw a little gravel, but a man can walk through many of those everyday whirlwinds without harm. They often occur in areas of clear air, drawing energy from heat convection and moderate winds aloft. But when combined with the vigorous drafts inside a thunderstorm, twisting wind becomes a good deal more dangerous. Such a local storm may lift a roof, but hardly ever shreds a house or barn, timber-from-beam.

Satellite imagery, a tool prized by weather scientists, reveals the truly massive parent storm systems that unleash outbreaks of dozens of super-tornadoes across several states. Though the disasters at first seem isolated, each tornado draws its power from the reservoir of energy held by the central weather formation.

Through a worldwide network of weather reporting, satellite eyes in the sky, and their own experience, forecasters can usually detect big trouble in the making. And while individual disasters happen with bewildering speed, dangerous cells within major storms can be tracked with radar and warnings quickly broadcast by radio and TV.

More than 300 automated stations of the

land endured its worst drought of the 20th century, a dry spell that lowered water in municipal reservoirs and brought summer water rationing. California and other western states experienced a drought in the mid-70s that brought scarcity to urban areas and real hardship to farmers.

In other parts of the land, so-called creeping disasters include: erosion of sand and soil, landsliding, subsiding land in settled areas near abandoned mines, water-level changes, contamination of standing water, and clay that swells and shrinks as its water content changes.

Perhaps due to the capriciousness of the phenomena which they study, disaster forecasters often reveal a streak of fatalism.

Survivors of San Francisco's 1906 quake, left, gather to stare in grim fascination as fire consumes the city. Aerial portrait, opposite, reveals sections of the city in ruins. Swollen Conemaugh River in 1889, engraving below, rolls through Johnstown, Pennsylvania, making the city's name a byword for flood tragedy.

National Oceanic and Atmospheric Administration (NOAA), form a network called National Weather Radio. Specially equipped receivers keep electronically alert for severe weather bulletins and signal their owners to turn up the set for warning of foul weather. In some of these radio sets the volume is automatically boosted. In addition, airline pilots, watermen, and law enforcement officers tune in to detailed early-morning weather briefings from NOAA, often aired on public service television channels.

One of nature's most protracted disasters, drought, is related more to climatology than to day-to-day weather forecast. For those caught in a drought, it's like living in a particularly long-term nightmare. Aside from the sheer discomfort of heat, lip-splitting dryness and grit, the crops and cattle suffer; farm income drops.

Up through the 1940s lack of wind brought a special kind of drought to places like the north Texas panhandle. Farmers here depended on windmills to pump water from deep wells. Children who grew up in such places remember going all summer without a tub bath, usually scrubbing hands and limbs daily in dry sand.

During the 1960s usually wet New Eng-

Take some maxims of the profession:

Anything can happen anywhere, and does. Nature simply can't be second-guessed. Nobody, for instance, expected the twister that splintered Worcester, Massachusetts, on June 9, 1953.

A disaster isn't a disaster unless people and their interests become involved. Otherwise it is an old-fashioned cataclysm, a good thing, in which nature operates to balance out the forces of destruction and creation which vie on our active planet.

A few places have a proved, serious disaster potential, and yet people not only persist but insist on living in harm's way. Towns too numerous to mention rise on floodplains, and eventually sink with the inevitable del-

uge. In Colorado's Big Thompson Canyon, a big flash flood killed 130 people in 1976. Some were vacationers who decided to break the camper's first commandment: Thou shalt not sleep near lowland watercourses in areas prone to flash floods.

In 1889, swollen waters of the Conemaugh River breached a dam and loosed a flood through built-up areas of Johnstown, Pennsylvania. Casualties included 2,000 deaths. Disastrous flood hit again in 1936. History also repeated itself in July 1977 with the loss of 70 lives.

Out West, considering the odds in favor of every variety of disaster, California probably shouldn't be lived in at all. Strains build up in the state's underpinnings. Only earth-

Fire storm sparked by fallen electrical cables travels on gale-force winds near Los Angeles. Reddened skies reveal forest aflame in the Napa Valley. Also in California, precarious Daly City not only clings to cliffs but straddles the earthquake-producing San Andreas Fault, here cutting the shoreline.

quakes can release the geological tension. Pacific hurricanes bring torrential rains that hardly ever arrive in time to quench brush and forest fires that repeatedly invade inhabited areas. The rains do trigger big mudslides. And when it doesn't rain, cattle, crops, and people thirst. The list goes on. . . .

Almost every hazard results from titanic forces at work in and under the state. The coastline nearly coincides with the juncture of two major crustal plates (see pages 68–75). Vigorous upthrust and subsidence of the landscape create a remarkable littoral transition from the High Sierras down to the cliff-bordered beaches. Here in canyons, valleys, deserts, mesaland, pockets, and plains, people find enchanting realms, both valuable and beautiful.

First and foremost, Californians share that great American folk belief that one day soon the whole of their beloved state will break off and set sail across the Pacific—but not today.

Nor, come to think of it, are residents of California unique in their disdain of disaster potential. One of the earliest great earthquakes recorded in the country's literature occurred not beside the Pacific, but on the Mississippi River, in 1811, with its focal point near New Madrid, Missouri. The town lies 150 miles from St. Louis. Other, lesser, shocks have been felt nearby in recent years.

The rival of far more famous shakes, New Madrid's biggest jolt probably reached an intensity of 7.2 on the Richter scale, compared to an estimated 8.3 for the San Francisco quake of 1906.

In a number of seismically active areas in New England, the Southern Appalachians of Georgia, Tennessee, and Alabama, and near Charleston, South Carolina, special danger of earthquakes exists, as well as in the Rockies and at scattered locations in the Middle West.

Volcanic eruptions are rare outside of Hawaii and Alaska, but Mount Lassen in California erupted in this century and

Washington state's Mount Baker threatened to blow in the mid-to-late 1970s.

Though seismic and volcanic prognostication is still in its infancy, experienced forecasters know that they can do a lot about the weather. Meteorologists blend hard fact and intuition in ways that to the outsider smack of magic. Or so it appeared to this visitor at the National Severe Storm Forecast Center in Kansas City.

I happened to remark that I planned to fly back home to Washington, D.C., late the next day. One forecaster glanced up from his charts and computer readouts.

"It's nothing that I can put my finger on yet," he volunteered, "but if you're scheduled to stop at the airport in St. Louis, you

may run into very heavy weather there about suppertime tomorrow."

Curious to test the meteorological hunch, or rather to profit from it, I changed my itinerary, choosing a flight that stopped in Indianapolis. As we came down for a landing, rain and moderate winds buffeted the plane. Then the airline captain announced that takeoff for Washington would be delayed a few minutes so that planes rerouted from St. Louis could land safely in Indianapolis. Sudden, intense storms had closed the St. Louis airport and snarled air traffic throughout the region. I quickly revised my personal estimation of much maligned weather forecasters. They may not always be right, but they're definitely getting better.

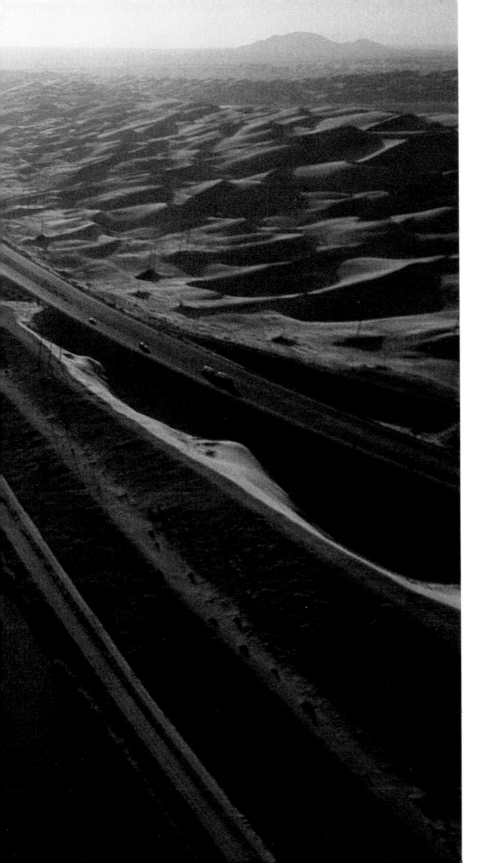

Resources

Slicing through golden dunes, tiny cars traveling its rim, the All American Canal sluices water from the Colorado River to California's thirsty Imperial Valley. Ditches and dams tame the once rambunctious Colorado, and from its lower reaches farmers draw water to irrigate their fields of lettuce and carrots.

Even while demand rises, the amount of available water grows smaller. And the Imperial Valley, a magnificent testimonial to the American dream, may one day experience shortages. Here, as in so many places, the popular vision of continued prosperity is based on the assumption that the mighty resource, the American land itself, will change but slowly, and in ways that can be anticipated and exploited.

For 350 years the land resource could keep pace with—even exceed—any American's dream. Beyond Connecticut's farmland was Ohio's, and beyond that, Oregon's. Beyond this river lay another; and anyway, irrigation could make the desert bloom. Beyond iron ore in the Mesabi, molybdenum in the Rockies. Beyond the coal of Appalachia, the Fort Union deposit of Montana. City, town, and transportation linkages followed the resources, and so did the immigrants. Enterprisers all, Americans availed themselves of the bounty.

Forest, water, and aesthetic resources were sacrificed to fuel the great industrial surge that followed the Civil War. Americans woke to the realization that the land

might not be limitless after all. The first national park was chartered in 1872, and in that same decade a precursor of the Forest Service emerged. By the early 1900s, three-fourths of today's 187-million-acre national forest had been established. Theodore Roosevelt and others had introduced the idea of resource conservation.

Policies of the day protected some resources, but by no means all, and America went on to lose 100 million acres of crop-land during the dustbowl '30s. President Franklin D. Roosevelt compared the Mid-west's plight to his own at Hyde Park, New York, saying, "I can lime it, cross-plough it, manure it, and treat it with every art known to science. But the land has just plain run out—and now I'm putting it into trees in the hope that my great-grandchildren will be able to try raising corn again."

Authors in this section of the book comment on the use and misuse of our basic resource. They suggest new ways to view the land, to help foster its restoration, and to conserve the remaining good soil and water for the future.

Generous land—the basic resource and great provider: Great Plains supply grain to much of Earth's population. Moist Southeast, traditional producer of cotton and citrus, turns to cattle and legumes in recent years; West Coast states ship a variety of vegetables and fruit, as does Hawaii, famed for pineapple and sugar; new petroleum sources in Alaska ease scarcity brought on by industrial development, paced by more than a century of mineral exploitation.

Confrontation in the West

By Alexis Doster III

When historian Frederick Jackson Turner presented his epochal essay on "The Significance of the Frontier in American History" in 1893, the last Oklahoma land rush, the end of the frontier, was still two months away. Today, the frontier and the open land it represented—the seemingly unlimited opportunities it offered to the strong, the quick, the doughty, the persevering—still exist as powerful images in the national memory. But the land itself, the water, the minerals, the grasses, the trees, the very soil are no longer open for the taking by the sturdy, land-hungry yeoman (except in Alaska). Instead these are the increasingly sought-after prizes of a great competition for control of the land and its fruits, a competition that pits special interest groups, states, and whole regions against the federal government in what may very well be the most serious confrontation over sovereignty since the Civil War.

Most of this eyeball-to-eyeballing over resources is taking place in and about the Mountain West—that nearly always dry stretch of the United States west of the 100th meridian, generally considered to encompass most of Washington, Oregon, California, Idaho, Utah, Nevada, Arizona, Montana, Wyoming, Colorado, and New Mexico. In these 11 states are found much of the nation's coal and other mineral resources, vast expanses of rangeland, breathtaking scenery, most of the wilderness left in the "lower 48," not much water, and a lot of frontier spirit.

I grew up in the southwestern part of the Mountain West. My family moved to Tucson, Arizona, in 1954, from a densely crowded corner of New Jersey just 20-odd miles from New York. The Southwest, as it did to so many others, beckoned irresistibly to my parents. It was warm, sunny, informal, a great place to raise your kids. More than that, it still had something of the frontier about it.

If the desert was not the Sahara I had imagined, it *was* dry. Water for all purposes, whether household, municipal, industrial, or agricultural, came almost exclusively from wells. Outside of the city, our community had its own well and storage. We didn't pay much for water, but those of us who came to love the desert and to marvel at the intricate adaptations of its wildlife could never quite shake a kind of subconscious awareness that water was a precious commodity. We manipulated our toilets to reduce water use, parsimoniously watered tiny lawns (incongruous in the desert, but the touch of green seemed necessary), and raised water-loving tomatoes over the septic tank.

All in all, though, the future of water resources was not a lively concern in the '50s. The three Cs were king: Cotton,

Copper, and Cattle. Long-staple Pima cotton, rivaled only by Egyptian in quality, and other crops greedily sucked up more than 80 percent of southern Arizona's pumped-up water, only to breathe most of it back into the dry, hot air. The copper mines used some, though they were not a major drain, and, of course, cattle needed a steady supply. Finally, there were the people, but the population of the Tucson area in 1954 was less than 90,000 people. Most of them, like us, were from the East or Midwest. And other than some University of Arizona scientists and precocious conservationists, few fretted about the source of tomorrow's water. Old-timers liked to tell the newcomers about the days back before the turn of the century when Tucson was a malarial swamp. "They used to die faster than they moved in," the old-timers would say of the early Anglo-American immigrants. Amazingly, they were telling the truth. The Tucson Basin had marshes complete with mosquitoes, beavers, and trout . . . until something dramatic happened in the 1880s. Within 10 years, once meandering streams had become deeply cut arroyos. Rainfall, once general over much of the year, became concentrated into two brief rainy seasons, one in late summer, one in winter. The reasons for this appallingly sudden shift—they range from overgrazing to a considerable change in the climate of the area—are still controversial, but few climatologists expect the trend to reverse.

Taking the climatic change and the heavy influx of humans together, it is now clear that those worriers of the 1950s had some basis for their concern, and they were not the first to voice their fears for the future.

The American West had been described throughout the early part of the 19th century as The Great American Desert. John Wesley Powell, geologist, ethnographer, explorer of the Colorado River, long associated with the Smithsonian Institution, said in a prophetic 1874 statement before Congress, "About two-fifths of the entire area of the United States has a climate so arid that agriculture cannot be pursued without irrigation. . . . Already the greater number of smaller streams such as can be controlled by individuals who wish to gain a livelihood by agriculture, are used for this purpose, the largest streams which will irrigate greater areas can only be managed by cooperative organization, great capitalists, or by the General or State Governments."

Much later, unexpectedly, came the great postwar rush to the Sun Belt, and the dry Southwest became the fastest growing section of the country. People began to compete in a serious way with the equally rapidly burgeoning agricultural industry's demand for irrigation water. The old three Cs had

Increasingly expensive water greens desert links in southern Arizona's Santa Cruz Valley, opposite, and grows crops in Idaho, below. Right, near Tucson, rainwater runs off quickly, leaving dry "washes."

to include a fourth: Communities. By the late 1970s, when the population of Tucson grew to half a million, Arizona agriculture was claiming over 90 percent of the state's water, while contributing 5 percent of its gross income.

Though the competing demands for the water resources of the Southwest would seem to demand a choice between water for people and water for other uses, the situation is by no means that simple. Farmers and ranchers produce a valuable product, and many would argue that agriculture is America's most important business. Furthermore, if irrigation water is available, the desert can be made to bloom dramatically. Others oppose the planting of such water-intensive and wasteful crops as cotton. Still others contend that the whole water issue is being approached in the wrong way. One of these is George F. Leaming, a southern Arizona mining engineer, economist, and resource management consultant. "Everybody knows that it doesn't rain here—so water is scarce," he says. "Except that water isn't scarce. Potable, usable water is probably more scarce in the Potomac Valley than it is in Tucson. Just because we have a slight rainfall per square foot, most of us don't project beyond our front yards to figure out how many square feet we have compared to the number of people we have.

Four Corners strip mine, below, scars the desert, yielding coal to fuel the West's bright lights, industries, and homes. Opposite, California's San Joaquin Valley Project brings water from distant rivers to fertile land.

"Take the Tucson Basin, for example—that watershed with its 11 inches of rain and 500,000 people is just as big as half of the state of New Jersey with its 40 to 45 inches of rain and four million people.

"We don't have a water shortage at all," he continues. "We have a shortage of capital, ingenuity, and willingness of people to utilize what nature has made available."

Dr. Leaming refers to what he calls the "grocery store" concept of resources. "Even people familiar with water and its economics tend to think that there's just so much water in the Basin—that it all comes like cans on a grocery store shelf. Everything's packaged in containers that are all the same size and price. You start taking them off the front of the shelf and when you get to the back, there's no more and that's it.

"It doesn't work that way. The cans of water are all different sizes, shapes, and prices. What you actually do is to take the cheapest ones first in whatever size you need. The farmers take big, cheap ones, the domestic users smaller, more expensive ones. You never get to the back of the shelf because by then the price has gone up so high that no one can afford it."

Backing up his argument, he points to already changing agricultural patterns. As the water table of the Santa Cruz Valley south of Tucson is lowered (from 200 feet to 300 feet

since World War II), pumping costs rise. Farmers there have recently shifted from cotton to more profitable pecans. Similar changes are being forced all over the Southwest. And interest is increasing in such naturally desert-dwelling plants as jojoba, whose seeds bear an oily substitute for sperm oil, and guayule, which yields a natural rubber.

Added to the economic woes of ever more expensive water are real fears expressed by some scientists that there is a threat of "desertification" in the arid parts of the West. Desertification is the slow encroachment of desert into formerly wetter zones that has brought tragedy to millions in the Sahel region south of the Sahara. Jack D. Johnson, director of Arid Lands Studies at the University of Arizona, speaking at a recent Smithsonian Associates lecture, estimated that up to a billion dollars in agricultural production in west Texas, New Mexico, and Arizona are being lost each year because of desertification.

Desertification can take place when arid lands with poor drainage are heavily irrigated. Minerals in the irrigation water are left behind when the water is evaporated by the sun, and salts build up in the soil until crops can no longer stand the salinity.

Overgrazing and mining also contribute to desertification

by reducing ground cover and accelerating runoff of rain water. Erosion increases, further reducing ground cover and promoting more runoff in a vicious cycle. Yet as much as 160 acres of grazing land are required to support one cow in many arid areas, and ranchers are hard pressed to maintain economical herds.

Indeed, as debates over exploitation and allocation of water and other western resources become more heated, decisions of the governing bodies which set resource-use policies become more critical. The much-talked-about Central Arizona Project (CAP) is a case in point. Conceived in the 1950s to bring water by canal to farmers in central and southern Arizona, the CAP will, by the time of its scheduled completion in 1985, be supplying much of its water to the urban areas of Phoenix and Tucson. This at the expense not only of Arizona farmers, but of Southern California farmers as well. California has been taking water from the Colorado River for Los Angeles and other cities and for agriculture since 1941. Harkening to their constituents' fears that water drawn off for the burgeoning population of Arizona will mean less for them, California legislators are understandably leery of letting any go without a fight. And just as with gasoline, rumors of impending scarcity send other parties with claims to Colorado River water—Nevada, Utah, Colorado—hurrying to the courts to see that they get their fair share. A number of Indian tribes, hitherto largely unheard in the melee for water rights, have added their claims to the Colorado and other rivers, including Arizona's Salt and Gila rivers.

Meanwhile, some federal agencies—the Bureau of Reclamation, for example—support projects to carry water from wetter to drier areas, while other agencies oppose them. Furthermore, many of these large-scale projects, much beloved by members of Congress for the benefits they may bring to constituents, are viewed by the Executive branch as economically wasteful, environmentally dangerous "pork barrels."

And yet, as we have seen, many of the water problems are genuine and are already causing hardship. Affecting even more states than the CAP is the Ogallala Aquifer, the great natural underground water system that supplies water to much of the Great Plains, from South Dakota to Texas. Many experts, within government and without, fear that it may soon be depleted to the point at which—both economically and in actuality—there will not be enough water to sustain that enormous agricultural area.

Some of the western water debates don't directly involve agricultural or municipal use, and yet have received national attention. Most of the great rivers of the area have been dammed over the years to provide reservoirs, hydroelectric power, or flood control. One sometimes has the feeling that, left unfettered, the agencies responsible for such projects would dam and channelize all of the Mountain West's rivers; only fierce opposition by conservation and environmental groups has kept dams from being built in such scenically irreplaceable areas as Marble Canyon, near the Grand Canyon. While some of the dams provide electricity, thereby reducing the need for other, even more distasteful sources, their critics point to practical as well as aesthetic problems. Huge Lake Mead, for example, impounded by Hoover Dam, is filling with silt dropped by the Colorado as it reaches the lake and suddenly slows down.

While water is at the heart of much of the Mountain West's resource conflicts, similar controversies rage over others. Of those old "Three C" cornerstones of Arizona's economic well-being, copper long bore the greatest part of the burden. Even recently, Arizona copper supplied about half of the nation's needs, and much of the rest came from the great mines in Montana. These are open pit mines, gigantic holes in the land, some as deep as 800 feet and a mile across. About 15 such mines are producing in Arizona today, and the state contains perhaps 15 other sites where ore bodies are known

The existence of an area of free land, its continuous recession, and the advance of American settlement westward, explain the American development.

–Frederick Jackson Turner

Beset by high costs and low prices, copper mining in Butte, Montana, below, and Globe, Arizona, right, may face an uncertain future. So may lush Montana grazing land, opposite, which could overlie a coal deposit.

to exist. But the copper industry is in a period of serious decline. Prices have plummeted since the high times during the Vietnam War, when millions of pounds were expended, mostly irretrievably, in the form of ammunition. Critics of the industry complain that it has been slow to keep up with the times, to develop new uses for its product. Aluminum has taken over some of copper's role as the wire used as an electrical conductor. And telephone conversations may soon be encoded in bursts of light traveling in strands of glass, leaving copper only the short-haul job of conducting the current from local telephone exchanges into the home.

Spokesmen for the copper industry point to rising costs of production. To be sure, all of the easy-to-get-at copper is gone. But, as George Leaming says of copper as well as water, there's no shortage. There is copper in the ground, and if economic conditions warrant, it will be extracted. Still, this is of small comfort to citizens of southern Arizona and Montana mining communities. While copper still contributes about 20 percent to the income of southern Arizona, the more uneconomical mines are closing one by one.

If the copper mines' unsightly and sterile tailing heaps and plumes of smelter smoke do not unduly offend their dependent communities, their economic woes are similarly local and

impinge little on the national consciousness. Not so for that other great western resource, coal.

It is estimated that nearly three *trillion* tons of coal underlie the mountain states, of which about 200 billion tons are minable. Although nationwide coal production has risen sharply in recent years, the still largely undeveloped western fields have contributed less than 20 percent of the total.

Coal, traditionally used in the 20th century for heating and production of electricity, is a dirty fuel; low oil prices, hopes of cheap nuclear energy, and strict clean-air standards have held down the development of coal resources in postwar years. Now, recurrent oil shortages and doubts regarding the economics and safety of nuclear power generation have put tremendous pressure on government and industry to relax environmental standards and stimulate the use of coal.

Western coal is attractive to miners for a number of reasons. The deposits are relatively thick and in many areas are located within a few feet of the surface, allowing easy removal by strip mining methods. Strip mining employs brobdingnagian machines called drag lines, some over 300 feet high and weighing 13,000 tons, to remove the soil over the coal, exposing it for removal. Western coal is also relatively low in sulphur, which during combustion creates the most noxious by-products of coal-fired energy production. The principal economic objection to western coal is that the fields are far from the great centers of population where power needs are greatest, and it must be transported by train or, mixed with water as a slurry, through pipelines.

Environmentally and socially, the price of western coal development may be very high. Not only will a large-scale return to coal for energy generation pollute the air with particulates, it will release vast quantities of carbon dioxide, which many scientists fear could cause a world-wide warming trend with possibly disastrous effects on climate. Locally, extensive strip mining removes vegetation and upsets drainage, accelerating erosion and in some cases damaging the quality of extensive underground water systems. The costs of returning the land to its present use, mostly grazing, are high, and in some areas nearly impossible at any price.

Furthermore, many small communities in these areas, traditionally the focal points of ranching life, have experienced great difficulty in absorbing the influx of coal miners and their families. Mining towns, particularly in Montana, Wyoming, and Colorado, have become the 20th-century counterparts of frontier boom towns, complete with rowdyism, shootings, and corruption.

Paradoxically, the great resource conflicts of the West present two entirely different problems. In the case of water, the rest of the nation has something the Mountain West needs. Coal, on the other hand, is abundant in the mountain states, but in great demand in other parts of the country. True to the spirit of their frontier forebears, many of the inhabitants of the arid lands say, "We can solve these problems, if only they'll leave us alone and let us do it," a sentiment that extends to bitter resentment of outside interference, particularly by the federal government. Yet it is to the federal government that farmers and city dwellers alike look for their water projects. Many wise decisions must be made by the people who live in the Mountain West, and by the people of the country as a whole, to see that all don't suffer in the long run. These decisions must be faced soon—before, in the words of essayist Joseph Wood Krutch, "the dreams of the boosters are realized as the nightmares such dreams have a way of turning into."

The problems of the Mountain West may seem at first glance to be regional. But as Frederick Jackson Turner so keenly perceived, in their power to affect us as a whole while inhabitants pursue their local interests, the various regions of the nation are both its weakness and its strength.

Field, Forest, and Mine

By Neil Sampson

S oil, sun, water, and plants are the basic elements of agriculture and forestry, as they have been for the 10,000 years that man has pursued those activities. But modern man, after spending centuries learning how to adapt to these elements, now concentrates on changing or controlling them. Instead of looking to the natural productivity of the land, today's harvester relies on technology, capital, and petroleum. He reaps not only the products of this year's sunshine, but those of the sun that shone hundreds of millions of years ago.

Today's farmer may start his day in the cab of a huge tractor. At the turn of a key, over 200 turbocharged horsepower roar to life. Monitoring dials arrayed in banks before him, he waits for proper oil temperatures and pressures to register. The radio is turned to the farm market reports and cab temperature is adjusted for comfort.

When all is ready, he moves at speeds up to 15 miles per hour to a field that may be some distance from his house, hooks onto an equally huge plow, and begins the day's work. A strip of black earth 15 feet wide unfolds at speeds faster than a man can walk, as 14 million pounds of soil turn over every hour. By sundown, he may have burned 100 gallons of diesel fuel and plowed 80 acres. Tomorrow, if the time is right, he will work the ground smooth and plant the crop. When ripe, the crop will be harvested by still other massive machines. The work of several days, even weeks, for

his father and grandfather is done in a matter of hours. It is a world of speed, power, and efficiency. It is a factory farm, where one farmer feeds himself and 59 others. It is the marvel of the world.

But this factory, with its petroleum-based, high-technology, capital-intensive, mass-production methods is not without its problems. The tractor costs over $50,000, and the machinery it pulls is expensive as well. Diesel fuel costs have risen dramatically, land prices have doubled in the last few years, and a center-pivot irrigation system will cost at least $50,000.

In the midst of these rising prices, the price of farm crops has stayed about where it was during the 1950s. As a result, farm profits are low. In 1977, the Congress's General Accounting Office estimated that farm prices were at their lowest ebb in 41 years, when compared to the rest of the economy. Agricultural policy, always troublesome, seemed to get more and more difficult for politicians, farmers, and citizens alike.

Beneath all this lies the American land. The United States Department of Agriculture estimates that the 400 million acres that grow commercial crops contain over 20,000 different kinds of soil, of which over half qualify as prime farmland. Wheat, the international food staple, is grown on some 10,000 different kinds of soil. This diversity helps to insulate the United States from nationwide crop failures. New fertilizers, crop varieties, pesticides, equipment, irriga-

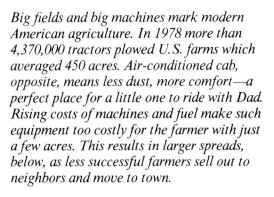

Big fields and big machines mark modern American agriculture. In 1978 more than 4,370,000 tractors plowed U.S. farms which averaged 450 acres. Air-conditioned cab, opposite, means less dust, more comfort—a perfect place for a little one to ride with Dad. Rising costs of machines and fuel make such equipment too costly for the farmer with just a few acres. This results in larger spreads, below, as less successful farmers sell out to neighbors and move to town.

Photographs by Kenneth Garrett

On a central Washington farm, above, a man and team cut hay much as his forebears did; hay baler, opposite right, works into the night in irrigated valley at foot of Cascade Range. Dams on Columbia River created farmlands from sagebrush desert. Hand labor still cuts asparagus, picks lettuce and beans, right and opposite top. Crop duster, far right, sprays large California cotton spread. But technology cannot prevent rain at harvest time, opposite, every farmer's nemesis.

tion, favorable weather, and the shift away from marginal soils to more productive areas have doubled yields since World War II. However, this rise in productivity has recently leveled off and, in some cases, even dropped slightly. Rising energy prices, it is thought, are largely responsible for this worrisome trend.

Despite its fantastic diversity and productivity, the American land does not always fare well under modern agriculture.

Increased power leads to the temptation to overwork the soil. This breaks down natural conditions, ruins soil structure, and allows wind and water to carry off precious topsoil. Recent surveys by the Soil Conservation Service indicate that annual soil losses from cropland range from two to four times the amount that can be replaced by natural processes. The inevitable loss of productivity that this will cause is another matter of growing concern.

A partial solution to these concerns may lie in the recent trend toward less cultivation. "No-till" farming is a fast-growing innovation that saves topsoil, reduces costs, and produces good yields.

Other American farmers don't use the high-technology methods, and some studies have shown that they do surprisingly well. These "organic" farmers use 60 percent less energy, lose 34 percent less soil to erosion, and keep their soil more fertile than their "conventional" counterparts. They must devote some land to hay, pasture, and other low-income crops, so they don't produce as much cash flow, but their operating costs are lower and annual net profits may be similar.

On America's timberlands, a similar harvest takes place, and there are comparable debates about appropriate methods and technologies. Here, as in farming, most of the product is generated by industrial methods. Cutting all the trees in large, checker-

Mechanical tomato picker, left, strips California acres in half the time of fieldhands. Plant breeders develop strains with tougher skin and flesh to stand up to rougher handling. While electronic sorters can distinguish red from green fruit, hand labor, below, separates stones and dirt from tomatoes. Portable irrigation pipes, above and opposite, transform western deserts into valleys of orchards and vegetables. One fifth of America's harvest comes from mechanically irrigated areas.

board-like blocks, called clear-cutting, is an efficient way to work with large machines. But soil erosion, water pollution, and problems with reforestation have created much controversy over this practice.

Growing and harvesting a tree crop that takes 60–100 years to mature is different from wheat farming, but the basics are the same. Both rely on sun, soil, water, and plants. Both must re-start a new crop as each crop is removed if they are to have a future, and both must protect the land in the process if the new crop is to thrive.

What of the future? To the miner who finds the mineral lode, there is little cause to mourn the fact that it will soon be used up. His minerals are inert and have no value unless extracted and used. There is always, he hopes, another lode to discover. But the farmer and forester need to develop a different outlook. If they protect the land while harvesting the crop, they can expect another

Industrial and family operations complement each other when it comes to harvesting timber. Weyerhaeuser loggers, opposite, clear-cut on 398,000-acre Vail-McDonald Tree Farm, Washington state, haul logs down miles of winding roads, opposite bottom. The Willard Lee family and their horses, right, salvage felled trees at edge of clear-cut area near Mount Hood National Forest. Horses do less damage to soil than mechanized equipment. Jodi Miller, below, thins out smaller trees.

harvest—and another—and another.

Man has, after all, harvested from portions of the Old World for millennia without ruining the land. But will the American industrialist-harvester find a way to achieve this? The answer, sadly, seems to be no, not on the path he is on, if at all.

There must, then, be another way. Perhaps today's giant machines must give way to less expensive, more labor-intensive, more technically sophisticated methods.

Perhaps there is a future for the family farmer—or logger—or miner. But that future must be found in the continued productivity of the American land.

Americans must turn their genius to the search for ways to work with nature, through science and the best technology: not to conquer or tame the land, but to understand it and use it wisely. With each bite of food, we must not consume a bite of the irreplaceable land that produced it.

Recalling the old days, prospector Jerry Borne regales a visitor with yarns of his search for gold. Self-sufficient in his cabin near Glacier, Washington, right, Borne generates electricity with waterwheel, foreground.

The Question of Alaska

By Jack Hope

"Hey, the stars up here are beautiful. They stretch across the horizon, and oh my God are they beautiful, cold and beautiful, probably the most beautiful things you've ever seen! But when you're up here walking across the tundra, and it's dark, and you're alone . . . then those stars are not the light you're looking for, are they? It's not the stars you want to see, because those stars can kill you. The cold can kill you. The tundra can kill you. That beautiful sky can kill you. So the light you want to see then, the finest light you can possibly see, is that first glimmer from a Coleman lantern, in somebody's cabin. . . ."

Spinning on his chair, barely pausing for breath, Wally Hickel talks on, giving his perceptions of the unique interaction of man and nature in Alaska.

". . . But the average American doesn't understand his Arctic, because he's down there in the lower 48, and Alaska is up here. The American thinks temperate. He thinks Alaska is Kansas. But the Arctic is cold and I think cold. The Alaskan thinks cold. It's tough up here! This country can kill you. That's why, when I hear some guy down there say he's worried about seeing an A&W Root Beer stand on the north slope, I know he doesn't have any idea what he's talking about!

". . . You cannot separate man and nature. So, the environmentalist's job is to make 'em compatible. And when I was Secretary, I considered myself a good strong environmentalist. But hey, these new guys are playing down man and building up the environment. They tell you how delicate the tundra is, but that tundra can kill you! They say, let's establish a wilderness, a formal, legal wilderness. But I say, why? . . . When God made this country, He zoned it Himself. If they wanted to leave it just as God made it, O.K. But they want to make it a wilderness, and that diminishes its value. It has value as wilderness. But it has value for minerals. It has value for hunting. It has value for oil. And there's not one American in a thousand who has the stamina or wherewithal to use it as wilderness. So I say, don't lock the people away from their land with this wilderness category. When you lock up the land, you lock up the human mind. You lock up the human spirit. And *that's* the only resource we might run short of in the future. Come on, trust the people on their land! Come on, trust the people!"

Everyone in Alaska today has an opinion on "land." And on that topic, the words of Walter Hickel—former Secretary of the Interior and Governor of Alaska, former boxer-dishwasher-carpenter, currently millionaire builder-developer—reflect the sentiments of a large proportion of the state's

Act in which the federal government agreed to transfer roughly 104 million acres to the new state, only about half of which transfer has been completed; to the Alaska Native Claims Settlement Act of 1971 which, many white Alaskans feel, gave native people far too much money and land ($962.5 million and 44 million acres); and, especially, to the imminent Alaska National Interest Lands Conservation Act (now in the form of bills HR 39 and S 222) which, when passed, will establish roughly 110 million acres of new, federally protected natural areas such as parks and park preserves, wild and scenic rivers, and wildlife refuges, thereby potentially limiting the scope of such conventional economic developments as mining, oil drilling, and lumbering.

But the strength of those sentiments is traceable not only to the land-use legislation itself, but to an Alaskan propensity that can be loosely defined as "frontier spirit." Notions that God zoned Alaska in such a way as to limit development, or

population. Large enough that, in the most recent gubernatorial election, with land and resource issues the primary plank in his platform but with his voters severely handicapped by the process of write-in ballot, Hickel nevertheless obtained 35 percent of the popular vote.

Another candidate in that election (for Lieutenant Governor), Joe Vogler, founder of the Alaskan Independence Party, speaks to the same issues with less metaphor: "I hate those bastards down in the lower 48 who think they own Alaska! They've sent these carpetbaggers up here—these environmentalists—and they're trying to tell us how to live our lives. Anybody who tells me this land was not put here to use is a socialist enemy of mine! Anybody who tells me trees shouldn't be cut, I'd use the axe on him! Anybody who says the ecology is fragile is an ignoramus or a goddamn liar! It's a struggle up here, all the way! Our climate protects the ecology. Our geography protects it. Sure, out of 220 million Americans you'll have a few who will come up here to build homes, to start businesses, whatever. But after a while, almost all of them will head back south with their tails between their legs. Our country has a way of weeding out the weak!"

Alaskan sentiments on land can be traced in part to a series of recent land-use legislation: to the 1958 Alaska Statehood

Under the fresh snow covering glacier near Seward, above left, rests some of Alaska's mineral wealth. Sea catch also brings in riches. Long hours of sun produce giant vegetables in Matanuska Valley, right.

that Alaska's rugged climate and terrain will protect its environment are lovely ideas, ideas that we all wish were true, but are in fact throwbacks to an era when the only human impacts upon the Alaskan landscape were the solitary diggings, scrapings, and choppings of individual homesteaders or placer miners. In Alaska, admittedly, that era was recent, probably as recent as the mid-1940s. Nevertheless, these notions do not hold today, and the evidence that they do not is painfully abundant. Beginning in 1974, for example, despite 60-below winters, dangerous working conditions, and the formidable task of crossing the rugged Brooks Range, the international oil consortium, Alyeska, almost instantly assembled 30,000 workers and, in a three-year period, sank oil wells and built an 800-mile pipeline from one end of Alaska to the other. Less dramatic but somehow more depressing evidence that Alaska's natural "toughness" no longer protects its ecology or limits its population by "weeding out the

Only true "city" in Alaska, with 198,000 residents, Anchorage serves as rail and air transportation center for virtually roadless state. Nearly 50 percent of Alaska's inhabitants enjoy Anchorage's ocean-moderated climate.

weak" is the fact that life in Alaska is fast becoming a carbon copy of life in the rest of America, complete with six-lane highways, McDonald's hamburgers, and the 9 to 5 commuter's lifestyle. Of the state's non-native population, only half a handful today live in a way that even vaguely resembles the rigorous frontiersman's lifestyle of hunting, fishing, trapping, or gold-panning for primary livelihood. The rest, the vast majority, live in urban or suburban situations identical to the ones they left, two years ago, in Cleveland or New York or San Diego in order to take a higher-paying job in Anchorage or Fairbanks. And the difference between living in a suburb of Anchorage and a suburb of Philadelphia is simply that it is black spruce instead of white pine that has been bulldozed aside to make room for Dairy Queen and Midas Mufflers and Waterbed World, Panoramic View Trailer Court, Ocean View North, and 18 Acres Zoned R-3.

But curiously, marvelously, evidence is not especially important in Alaska. There is the firm belief—held as strongly by newcomers as by long-term residents—that Alaskans and the Alaskan lifestyle are somehow "different," and that the Alaskan land will continue to accommodate this dream of difference by remaining always there and wild and undeveloped—a frontier. One of the reasons, then, for Alaska's lukewarm response to anything like land-use legislation, with its boundary lines and regulations, is that accepting it constitutes acknowledgment that the frontier is fading fast and that the Alaskan lifestyle is not that different after all.

It does not help either that this land-use legislation is being imposed upon Alaska by the foreign government of the United States of America. No self-respecting Alaskan considers himself a resident of the U.S. Rather, he is a citizen of the great northern nation of Alaska and feels that he has far more in common with his neighbors in the Canadian Yukon than with flatlanders from the lower 48.

Land is what Alaska has most of. With 376 million acres, the state is more than two and a half times the size of France, bigger than Texas, Florida, New York, Wisconsin, and California put together. The state's population is small—410,000. Yet it is up 35 percent from 1970 because of the pipeline— with most of the people concentrated in and àround the two largest cities of Anchorage (pop. 198,000) and Fairbanks (pop. 55,000). Another 25 or 30 percent live in small towns of from 2,000 to 14,000, like Juneau, Sitka, Bethel, Barrow, Nome, Ketchikan, all of which have jetports but most of which have no highway connection with the rest of the state. Ten to 15 percent, mostly Indians, Eskimos, and Aleuts, live in tiny bush settlements and practice a largely subsistence

In contrast to untouched acreage elsewhere, a camper park near Anchorage rents precious space to tourists, temporary workers. Pipeline construction brought thousands of drillers and welders averaging $1,200 a week.

lifestyle hunting moose and caribou, netting salmon, gathering berries, and trapping furbearers.

With a small and concentrated population, and with vast expanses of the state still roadless and undeveloped, there is considerable potential for any land-use regulations to interfere with conventional development. For the most part, then, this new and coming land legislation can be viewed in the context of the old "use versus preservation" controversy.

"Right here in Alaska," Robert Atwood says, "we have 32 of the 34 strategic materials the U.S. needs to wage war, and it seems a shame to leave those resources in the ground. Like oil. Right now, we're importing it. But that drains off dollars in foreign exchange and causes inflation. It weakens our currency and the position of the U.S. in the world."

What Bob Atwood thinks is important, not so much because of his private power and wealth (from oil, among other things), but because he owns and runs *The Anchorage Times,* the state's largest and most influential newspaper, with a circulation greater than the state's several other papers combined and with no real competition from out-of-state papers. With this monopolistic leverage over public opinion, Atwood has been described as "the most powerful man in Alaska," the man who is said to have initiated the Brasília-like move to construct a whole new state capital at the 50-person burg of Willow. His reputation, especially among environmentalists, is that of "Super Boomer," the voice of development.

"We know now," Atwood goes on, impatiently, "that Congress is not going to treat us any better than they have in the past, with this new legislation. They still think of Alaska as 'the red-haired stepchild' who has to be kept in the closet! So be it. But Alaskans do feel we should insist on three things. First, we want them to perform an intelligent inventory of our underground resources so we'll know just what we have. Why lock 'em up in a park somewhere? Why lock 'em up in a park that only the environmentalists with their planes can get to? Second!" (And he jabs me in the shoulder now, as he ticks off his points.) "We want them to leave us access to what little land we have left; don't surround state land with their parks and things so we can't get in there with a road or a railway to get a mineral out. Third!" (jab) "We want 'em to assure us that this is the last time the Feds are coming back for land! Alaskans want to know that this will be the last land grab!"

It is a moot point whether the federal government, with the Alaskan National Interest Lands Conservation Act, is about to "grab" land that rightfully belongs to Alaskans. Alaska never owned Alaska. The government of the United States bought it from Russia, in 1867, and thereafter owned it 100 percent, more or less, until 1959 statehood. So, the opposite point of view—that the federal government was indeed generous in granting Alaska 104 million free acres upon statehood, the largest grant of state land in U.S. history—is probably equally valid.

It is also questionable how well the image of the deprived "red-haired stepchild" holds up. While the U.S. has been painfully slow in transferring Alaska's 104 million acres, the state is nevertheless doing very well. Alaska has the highest per capita income in the United States. And that high income is in part due to the oil-rich lands of Prudhoe Bay, given by the U.S. to the state, in part due to the fact that the U.S. government is the largest employer of Alaskan residents.

The question of the extent to which land and resources will be "locked up" by the Alaska National Interest Lands Conservation Act is more complex. Speaking around the mounds of congressional reports, bumper stickers, and other debris in his Anchorage office, Assistant Sierra Club Representative for Alaska, David Levine, scoffs at the lock-up perception and offers another: "What we're saying is that we can almost have our cake and eat it too. We can have 110 million acres of protected land, and still have exceptional economic growth. I know that sounds unreal, but Alaska is a big place, don't

Wilderness is the raw material out of which man has hammered the artifact called civilization.

–Aldo Leopold

forget. And this legislation is no slipshod thing, hastily thrown together. It's compromise all the way. Most of the resource-rich areas have already been gerrymandered out of it. But people don't know that, here, because our media are so development-oriented. The thing people could use most, to make up their minds about this thing, is objective data, clear statements of fact. But they don't get that. What they do get, hammered into them day after day, is some generalization like the 'Feds' and the 'greenies' are turning the whole state into a national park."

Probably the most objective statements of the likely impact of current land-use legislation upon the Alaskan economy come from the Federal-State Land Use Planning Commission for Alaska. This group, with five federal and five state members, was set up to advise Congress on just such questions, and the Commission's general conclusion is that "... neither the State's fiscal base, nor, more generally, the State's broad economic well-being is dependent upon availability of resources on the [protected] lands." In other statements, analyzing the legislation's likely impact on jobs, balance of payments, and on individual industries (oil and gas, minerals, timber), the Commission again concludes that in all cases, the impact will be "not significant" . . . "negligible" . . . "not perceptible," either in Alaska or nationwide.

When passed into law, the Alaska National Interest Lands Conservation bill in combination with previous land-use legislation will define an Alaska in which approximately 132 million acres (a third of the state) will be protected by federal and state agencies, and 244 million acres (the remaining two thirds) under state or federal or private ownership will be subject to development. More or less as Levine contends, boundary compromises in the legislation—such as the removal of land from the proposed Gates of the Arctic National Park to make room for possible future mining in the Brooks Range's Ambler Mineral District—were worked out prior to the bill's presentation or in congressional committee. This means that roughly 65 percent of the state's known mineral-rich areas, 75 percent of the state's small supply of timber, and 95 percent of Alaska's probable oil and natural gas reserves are excluded from protection. Even on protected lands the legislation provides for an ongoing underground resource inventory by the U.S. Geological Survey, for access to these resources in the event of "national need," and grants "reasonable access" to existing mineral claims and private inholdings. The legal interpretation of "national need" seems to mean, simply, a demonstrated national shortage of a given resource. What "reasonable access" means will likely be in-

Massive flukes of humpback whale dwarf kayakers in Prince William Sound, near Anchorage. The humpback, seemingly unafraid of boats, performs its aerobatics in Alaska's coastal waters, then migrates as far as Hawaii.

terpreted on a case-by-case basis, but in most situations where private land or small placer claims fall within protected areas, such access already exists, by road, air, or water.

The possible impact of this legislation is diminished further by the facts of economics. While it is true that Alaska is a storehouse of still unexploited resources, the costs of gaining physical access to that storehouse and of getting the resources to market are astronomical. Alaska has few existing roads or railroads, and has the highest labor and energy costs in the United States. Its costs of producing minerals, for example, are at least two times greater than in the lower 48. This, combined with the fact that all these minerals are already available to U.S. industry from either domestic or foreign sources, dictates that Alaskan minerals cannot in the foreseeable future be developed at prices low enough to compete in world markets. The fact that little mining took place in Alaska even before land-use legislation tends to bear this out. With its vast supplies of coal, for example, the only producing coal mine in the state today is the small Usibelli mine near Fairbanks, whose output is used for local power generation.

Oil and natural gas development in Alaska, as we all know, *is* economical, at current prices. And one of the few specific use-versus-preservation conflicts that will be created by the

Is my share of Alaska worthless to me because I shall never go there? Do I need a road to show me the arctic prairies, the goose pastures of the Yukon, the Kodiak bear, the sheep meadows behind McKinley?

–Aldo Leopold

Alaska National Interest Lands Conservation Act will occur in the 18 million protected acres of the Arctic Wildlife Range, east of Prudhoe Bay. That region is the calving ground of the international Porcupine caribou herd, the continent's largest. Preliminary geological surveys indicate the likely existence there of a gas and oil deposit. But in this case, since 95 percent of Alaska's probable oil and gas reserves remain unprotected by the proposed legislation, and since 72 percent of the nation's oil and gas reserves are located outside Alaska, even the protection of this large area would potentially reduce U.S. output of oil and gas by less than 1 percent.

Development of Alaskan inland timber, in all likelihood, will never be economical. There isn't much of it, it is extremely slow-growing because of soil and climatic conditions, and, as with minerals, transport and development costs are very high. The Chugach and Tongass national forests, in the state's south-central and southeastern coastal areas, contain Alaska's only potentially commercial timber (about 5 percent of the United States' timber reserves), mostly in the form of virgin stands of Sitka spruce, western hemlock, and cedar.

Two firms now operate in Tongass National Forest, one American and one Japanese, cutting this timber for sale to Japan. But it is hard to say whether or not these operations are truly profitable. The Forest Service is subsidizing the two firms with about 9 million taxpayer dollars, annually. Multiply this by the 50-year term of each firm's contract, and you reach the correct conclusion that, once these logging operations are complete, Japan will have gained a half billion dollars worth of subsidized timber, and the United States will have gained a denuded landscape, a $450 million deficit, and no increased supply of timber for American industry.

Out of the 16 million-acre total of Tongass National Forest, roughly six million acres will be protected under the Alaska National Interest Lands Conservation Act. Predictably, environmentalists have seized upon the apparently uneconomic nature of timber harvest there to assert that even more wilderness could profitably be set aside—such as the magnificent but so far unprotected West Chichagof Island. Equally predictable, the two timber firms claim that the creation of any protected acreage within Tongass National Forest will mean reduction of their operations and a loss of jobs for mill employees.

In Alaska, apparently, there is much divided opinion not only among groups, but within individuals. One of the people of split opinion is Clark Engle, a professional hunting guide who sells trophy hunts to hunters from the lower 48 and Eu-

Conservationists fear development will hurt fragile ecology, note decline of caribou herds; natives and outfitters want land to stay open for hunting. Caribou, left, slows down bus; Guide Clark Engle, above, poses with kill.

Harsh climate, fragile tundra ecology, numerous earthquakes make difficult demands on Alaskan petroleum pumping and refining equipment. Opposite, famed cartoonist, Herblock, homes in on developers.

rope: "I sure don't want roads and mines and lumbering like the developers want," Clark says. "I'd fight it tooth and nail! If they want mining, let 'em restore the country. If they want lumbering, the hell with 'em, cause they're destroying wildlife, and they're just sending all that timber to Japan. And if they build roads, that'll destroy the state quicker than anything, because every cowboy and his brother'll be out there with his four by four or snow machine dropping beer cans and blasting away at the moose. But I have to oppose that bill, because they're going to take away two thirds of the hunting country in the state. If they pass it there's going to be bloodshed, I guarantee, and it's going to be on the President of the United States' hands. If the Feds come up here, they'd better bring bullet-proof vests and a priest!

"I said to Andrus, last year, 'Mr. Secretary, what are you going to do with people like me? I'm 47. I've got 20 more years in this business. I've got my whole life's blood in it, and

$200,000. What happens if I'm cut out?' He said, 'Mr. Engle, then there'll have to be some relief for you.' I said, 'Is that in the bill?' He said, 'No.' . . . I don't want to see this country ruined with development, but I sure don't want to lose this business I've spent 27 years building up."

Chances are Clark will not lose it. Because Alaska is Alaska, with a large number of subsistence and sport hunters and with about a thousand people who directly or indirectly earn their incomes from big game hunts for bear and moose. Ninety percent of the state will remain open to all hunting.

Nevertheless, for about 90 out of Alaska's 225 big game outfitters, there are cases when significant portions of their assigned hunting territories will be enclosed within the borders of new national parks.

Alaskans, many Alaskans, apparently also fear that their current access to the outdoors—by plane and motorboat and snowmobile—will be limited by land-use legislation. This is not the case. The Alaska National Interest Lands Conservation bill specifies that traditional routes and means of access to protected areas shall continue.

Alaskan state representative Michael Beirne feels that large-scale government ownership of land is tantamount to communism and suggests that government give away Alaska's land to anyone who has lived there at least three years.

This plan, the Beirne Homestead Initiative, which would transfer 30 million areas of Alaska state land, free, to residents, was passed 60-40 by Alaskan voters in November 1978. Since, the proposal has been struck down by the courts, but its opponents fear it will be repassed in some form, propelling millions of Americans slashing through the Alaskan landscape en route to that little cabin in the wilds.

It is not at all surprising that Alaskans passed the Initiative; it promises that people will get something for nothing. Alaskans, frustrated by high land prices and by the very slow rate at which state land is being made available for private purchase, are more than receptive to such promises. Equally appealing, the "Homestead" label conveys the soothing message that Alaska is still unique: Not only is the state still a frontier, it is a frontier vast enough to be given away.

"A few years ago, a native man in the Kuskokwim delta offered to share a fish camp with a white man. The white man was poor, and he needed the salmon, so the native man offered the camp in the spirit of generosity. Now, those fish camps are seasonal, and impermanent. Our society doesn't feel that any one person should 'own' them, and you certainly don't have the privilege of calling it 'yours.' But the white man immediately did two things when he came to the camp. First, he built a cabin, a permanent structure, for himself. Second, he applied to the state for title to the land."

Tony Vaska, a young Eskimo born in the Yukon-Kuskokwim delta country of the Bering coast, now serving as a staff employee of the delta's AVCP, Association of Village Council Presidents, comments on the apparently unbridgeable gaps between European and native perceptions of land and land ownership, and speaks on the persisting dominance of white culture over native in Alaska.

"When Columbus discovered America, he did it without any real perception of the fact that native people already lived there and maintained a viable subsistence lifestyle. That hasn't changed. In Alaska, when these 'outsiders' come here—the bureaucrats, the roadbuilders, the New Homesteaders, the miners, whoever—they see everything in traditionally capitalistic terms and, without even asking us, they assume that we see it the same. They want to get out in the Alaskan bush and do their thing—build a road, dig a mine, put up a cabin—and they think there's nothing out there. They are only vaguely aware that our people are already there, using that land for hunting and fishing and trapping, as we have for 15,000 years. But we haven't 'built' anything, we haven't dug anything up or surveyed anything. And to

CALL OF THE WILD
—copyright 1979 by Herblock in The Washington Post.

them, that doesn't count. Subsistence, they think, means that the land isn't being used. They think the native people and our lifestyle are part of the nothingness of the frontier that must be pushed aside to make room for them. . . . And that is what I call 'The Frontier Mentality.'"

In 1971, when the Alaska Native Claims Settlement Act (ANCSA) gave natives cash and land, it also decreed that that wealth should be managed collectively, corporately, by 13 regional and 225 village native corporations. Most of these corporations invested their cash in urban real estate, in canneries, banks, and in other conventional enterprises. A few natives, overnight, became high-paid managers of the new and unfamiliar corporate structure granted them or imposed upon them by Congress.

But for 60 to 70 percent of the native people, in the tiny and isolated villages, the subsistence lifestyle continued as always, except that they got periodic, small dividend checks. For these 40,000 people, who still obtain 90 or more percent of their food from hunting and fishing and who only minimally participate in the cash economy, the land—in its wilderness form—is the fragile stalk on which their lives and society depend. Ultimately, the land could be taxed away from them. Or they could sell it. Or, since much native land is adjacent to state or federal or (what will become) private land, the uses to which this adjacent land is put could easily diminish the fish and wildlife-producing capacities of subsistence land.

"I am very much in favor of preserving large tracts of land in the national interest," Tony Vaska continues, "for all its usual values—aesthetic, recreational, wildlife—and to those values or systems that the land supports, I would add, *people.* Our people. My concern is that these outsiders I mentioned will somehow get our land, or nearby land, and will want to change its uses from subsistence to traditional western uses, and that would destroy our way of life. . . . My worst fear, and this may be the ultimate in paranoia, is that some foreign government will buy into native land. Like Japan. Already, they're getting all of Alaska's timber. Already, they own 80 percent of Alaska's fisheries. What's to keep them from buying up 30 million acres of Alaskan land and developing or colonizing it? Nothing."

Chuck Hunt, also an AVCP employee and a Kuskokwim delta resident, describes a possible scenario of development and its impact, in and around the delta town of Bethel: "Our people are very opposed to mines. Our people are very opposed to oil. Our people are very, very opposed to roads. What would happen if they build a road out here from An-

259

chorage? We would be overwhelmed. Every weekend during hunting season 5,000 people would come out and shoot our moose and birds; they'd take our food away. Then, since they had a highway, somebody would start mineral exploration. They'd find mercury. They'd do their required impact studies on the wildlife and on the land, but they wouldn't do any impact studies on people. And they'd build their mine. But we're hunters and fishermen and trappers. The land is our supermarket. With a mine, with a lot of new people out here, with pollution, that would disappear overnight. And then what would happen to us? You're a writer, right? Suddenly, somebody tells you that you can't do the thing you've been doing for 20 or 30 or 40 years, the only thing you know how to do, writing or laying bricks or whatever. What happens? You lose your livelihood. You lose your self-respect, and the respect of your community. You lose your identity. You go on a long slide, take to firewater. . . . Same with us."

How long the subsistence lifestyle and subsistence land can withstand the pressures of development is impossible to predict. But the best some people seem to be hoping for is one generation, with a gradual exposure to the power and ways of industrial society, so that subsistence people will at least have some time for "adjustment."

All native leaders are aware of the inevitable conflict between rapid development and the subsistence lifestyle. But there seem to be considerable differences among them insofar as their sensitivity to the situation is concerned. A few of the native regional corporations, including Arctic Slope, Doyon, Nana, and Bristol Bay, are already actively involved in exploring for oil or minerals on their people's land. And two others, the Shee Atika village corporation of Sitka and the Goldbelt village corporation of Juneau, have already been involved in a use/preservation conflict with the Angoon village corporation on Admiralty Island: Shee Atika and Goldbelt wanted to log the island's timber around Angoon. But Angoon people—hunters and fishermen—opposed the logging because it would destroy wildlife and silt up the island's salmon-spawning streams.

Ironically, some of the state's white developers who 10 years ago hotly opposed native land settlement, claiming that the natives' 44 million acres would be "locked up," park-fashion, and who came very close to claiming that natives were not deserving of the land and money ANCSA gave them, are now courting and applauding the more development-oriented native leaders as "real Alaskans." Many observers feel that some of the state's first, large-scale resource development—after all current land-use legislation is in ef-

fect—will in fact occur on native regional corporation land.

Alaska's options for future development are open. Many of its industries and sources of income are already well-developed—oil, fisheries, retail trade, government, travel, construction, timber. In the near future, the most rapid expansion will likely occur in oil (with new finds), in fisheries (with the development of sophisticated "bottom-fishing" techniques), and in tourism, inspired at least in part by the formal designation of new parks and other scenic areas. Travel and tourism now is the state's fastest-growing industry and has just overtaken fisheries in dollar volume as its second largest.

In physical location, probably the first Alaskan resources to be developed will be those in coastal areas, along major inland water routes, and along existing highways and railways, where transport costs are lowest. In time, as prices rise and as shortages increase, there is no doubt that all the state's valuable resources will be developed, even those far inland, even the now uneconomical hardrock minerals, even the resources within now-protected areas.

The only real question and the only real difference in opinion between the staunchest environmentalist and the most hard-nosed developer is: How fast? It is conceivable that Alaska could embark upon a wholesale program of resource extraction tomorrow. It might not be economical, and might require taxpayer subsidies to build, for example, a 250-mile road from Fairbanks to the Brooks Range to extract copper. But it could be undertaken in a spirit of developmental exuberance, with the expectation that while this project alone would not break even, a subsequent network of additional highways, branching off the main road and penetrating other mineralized regions along the route, would enable extraction of zinc and iron ore and coal, and would ultimately reach a break-even point. This could be done. But if it were done now, chances are it would be a function of the push of the state's strong and impatient pro-development forces, and not of best economics.

Byron Malott, 35, Tlingit Chairman of the Board of the native Sealaska regional corporation, has thought about that: "Alaska possesses the development ethic, in spades! But why the hell should we be rushing pell-mell to develop our oil or timber or minerals? We're not now dependent on them. So long as we have access to other sources, elsewhere, I say we should use them before we rush to use up our own. In the meantime, we should be making honest assessments of what our supplies and demand for these resources are. We should be taking steps to cut our voracious consumer appetites for these resources. We should be developing cost/benefit ratios

On my land, I'm allowed.

–Song by Janette Carter

that include the real impact of resource development on our people and land. . . . If we find a mineral deposit whose development will benefit only a corporation and its stockholders, but will destroy a caribou herd or a people's subsistence lifestyle, I say that's not good enough! We should wait.

"The longer we wait, the more those resources will be worth. The longer we wait, the more likely that our resource development technology will improve, to become less environmentally disruptive. . . . The longer we wait, the more likely Alaskan society will learn the difference between real *need* and capricious *want*. . . . Otherwise, Alaska will become just like every other bloody place in America, and that doesn't have to happen."

Malott's view—with its emphasis on public costs, its attention to the future, and its focus upon trimming patterns of resource consumption rather than relying always upon escalation of resource extraction—offers a more flexible and human approach to development than our traditional one. The traditional approach, granted, is optimistic, in that it trusts the initiative of future generations to find solutions to resource problems we have created. But in the same breath, it is selfish, shortsighted, and not even good business sense, because it leaves the future with fewer options. In our enthusiasm over the private automobile, for example, we built a suburban commuting society in which the energy waste is inevitable, we permitted mass transit and urban centers to decay, and backed ourselves into the corner of having to depend upon foreign oil, having to build Alaska pipelines.

Perhaps the primary benefit of any land-use legislation would be to compel the kind of planning Malott speaks of. If that happens, if time is taken to think through the 49th state's future instead of pushing forward with hastily conceived development schemes, then Alaska will remain, if not exactly a frontier, a truly different kind of place.

Stark cliffs along the coast, left, provide nesting space for Alaska's horned puffin, above, kittiwakes, cormorants, and murres. Fears that oil spills may damage seashore ecology give environmentalists nightmares.

Text and Illustrations by Paul Hogarth

Cities of Hidden Delight

The Gritty Northeast

Initially I balked at the very idea of accepting assignments to portray various bits and pieces of Americana. The invitations had come thick and fast during the Bicentennial year; most of them I declined. But eventually—as I discovered that certain corners of some U.S. cities did in fact possess definite and even historical radiance—I succumbed to the general nostalgia for the epic quality of America.

As an English artist I found a perspective that involved me in the reclaiming of the American land. So, as successive years brought more opportunities to explore, I set forth with traveler's pack and artist's pad all the more eagerly. What made the adventure particularly illuminating was that I had the great advantage of having never learned any American history in school; I didn't feel tied down to any prescribed route or location. I simply drew those places that impressed me as humane or entertaining.

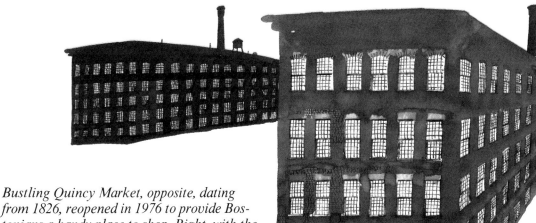

Bustling Quincy Market, opposite, dating from 1826, reopened in 1976 to provide Bostonians a handy place to shop. Right, with the textile industry's decline, Boot Mill, Lowell, Massachusetts, functions as a cultural center. Left, 1847 church graces Harrisonville, New Hampshire, a textile town saved by new industry. Below, James Lancaster Morgan residence (1869–70), New York City.

In the sooty, industrialized Northeast, for example, I was gratified that Boston's Brahmin-dwelling Beacon Hill had retained a certain elegance. Then, walking around old Faneuil Hall and its three-block-long annexes (Quincy, North, and South Markets), I marveled that this once grubby section had been restored to a new kind of life. Although no longer the bustling center of the Hub's tumultuous waterfront activity, Faneuil Hall now sustains a festive and congenial precinct with a variety of shops, serving the community differently but as vigorously as in its past heyday.

Even in that urgently immediate metropolis, New York City, I found a panorama of earlier eras. Urbanity, which I had regarded as a uniquely European virtue, was there manifesting itself: The city's elaborate Italianate brownstone row houses plus the Irish saloons of Third Avenue were emerging as a foreground subject, with the incomparable suspension bridges as the grand back-

drop linking Manhattan to the mainland.

The last stops on my northeastern exploration were the milltowns of New England (which I thought from previous travels would be no particular joy to revisit). Surprisingly, I discovered that many of the grim and satanic plants from Yankeeland's industrial revolution have been recycled for new uses. Lowell, for instance, once the "Spindle City on the Merrimac" and the principal manufacturing center in America, now flourishes as the Lowell National Urban Cultural Park, an historic site where more than 100 buildings have been placed on the National Register of Historic Places. Tourists marvel at the mills and machine shops that made Lowell world-famous. Such innovation serves as a refreshing reminder that as one journeys through a nation's past, more buildings than abandoned churches record the spirit of the region. Other stones can be built on, too, in the reconstruction of a threatened civilization.

An artist must take opportunities when and where he can. And in New Orleans' Jackson Square there was but a lunchtime hour of peaceful sketching before crowds would congregate and discover the fun of watching every stroke of my brush with garrulous enthusiasm. Absorbed in my studies of the romantic facades, I hadn't noticed that my hour was up. Suddenly a slim black youth started tap-dancing in front of my sketchpad. Then back into action swarmed the afternoon's onlookers: a joyous, uninhibited Vieux Carré jam session which included marching jazz bands, more dancers, and competition from a rival band of quick-sketching portrait artists.

"There's nothin' like this where I come

Romance in the South

from," drawled one blocky lady to the ice-cream vendor. Despite the interruption, I could only agree, and happily.

Other times throughout the South, I've been more relaxedly attuned to the unexpected and the exotic. Atlanta's fabulous Fox Theater, for example. Originally built in 1928 for the Shriners and covering almost one entire city block, it proved too expensive to complete. So the Shriners asked for financial help from motion picture tycoon William K. Fox. Enchanted by the auditorium (a dimly lit Moorish square with glowing barred windows and fortress-like turrets), domed minarets, blue and red tiles everywhere, and seats for 5,000 viewers, Fox thought it an ideal refuge from reality for

his Depression-troubled audiences.

In busy modern times, romantic attachment to the Atlanta Fox endures, despite threats to demolish it. But the theater was actually saved from the wrecker's ball by Atlanta Landmarks, an indefatigable non-profit volunteer group which raised $1.8 million to keep it going on downtown's restored Peachtree Street.

To many, the romance of the "real South" is in neither thriving Atlanta nor French-fashioned New Orleans but in Charleston, South Carolina, or Savannah, Georgia. And these observers have a point. Both of these beautiful and unforgettable cities were the southernmost tip of the English influence of the original Thirteen Colonies. Charleston,

especially, resembles 18th-century England while at the same time possessing an indefinable charm all its own. Many fine old houses have steep slate roofs and are built of stuccoed brick, showing the influence of English and Scottish architects from Wren to Adam. Wrought-iron gateways frame tempting glimpses of exquisite, shaded old gardens planted with azaleas, gardenias, and camellias. Paneled portals lead the visitor into long open piazzas on the side, facing south to catch the sea breeze in the long, humid summers.

A cultivated gentry grew up here, and the wealthy merchants' practice of sending sons to England to finish off their education brought a spirited social life. Charlestonians shared 18th-century London's passion for the theater; the finery and gaiety of dress and deportment gave the city a sophistication rare in America at that time. The essence and the form of that pre-Revolutionary spirit live on in the Dock Street Theater which I depicted with its fine cast-iron balcony and sandstone columns.

Savannah, an upstart compared to Charleston, was not founded until 1733. Here I delighted in the Georgian Colonial and Greek Revival buildings—many of them restored—that surround small parks planted with palms and tropical flowers.

Although romance withers and memorable halls continue to be torn down, there is always the compensating pleasure in hearing that some grand old objects, even loco-

motives, are being listed in the National Register of Historic Places. Once I found myself in Tennessee and was questioned by a state trooper. "I don't suppose," he asked, "that you've heard of the Chattanooga Choo Choo in England?" I replied that indeed I had. Then I added my own question, "Was it really a train or just a song?" The trooper told me gravely that not only had it always been a train but that it still exists. Now it sits in its original station-house right there in Chattanooga. Both a restaurant and hotel complex, the area can seat almost 1,500 visitors in the old baggage area, in the former waiting rooms, and even in the railroad cars themselves.

"A-W-L A-B-O-O-A-R-D!"

Opposite: Jackson Square, New Orleans, a mélange of French, Spanish, and British architecture and tradition. The turreted Fox Theater, top left, books family films and entertainment for Atlantans. Top right, Charleston's Dock Street Theater once served as a hotel for wealthy planters. The Chattanooga Choo Choo, right, made world-famous by Glen Miller's orchestra, became a restaurant-hotel in 1973.

Americans have an extraordinary facility for discovering a resource, exploiting and exhausting it, then obliterating it and moving on, only to repeat the process. But what memories, what tangible portraits in wood or masonry still exist of that original resource?

I have always wanted, for instance, to draw a typical Main Street. I know, however, that Main Street, U.S.A. has been in trouble for some time, bulldozed away by highways, urban renewal and, most of all, the pervasive shopping mall.

Yet in the reaches of the Midwest, Main Streets are making a comeback. Madison, Indiana (pop. 13,600), for instance, has one truly worthy of pride.

Laid out in 1808, Madison soon became a bustling Ohio River port. By 1830 the town had become the second largest pork-packing center west of the Alleghenies. There were iron foundries, too. Many of the ornate iron gates, fences, and balconies of New Orleans were made here and shipped down the Ohio and Mississippi by smoke-belching steamboat. Only the shift to railroad traffic later in the 19th century ended Madison's prosperity as an important river port. But the best of the past remains. Outlying farmers and tourists alike drive in to visit restored Federal and Greek revival houses along the riverside. They stroll and shop in the extraordinary variety of Victorian buildings that line Main Street, savoring over corner drugstore

sodas the unique social character of small-town America.

There's a degree of friendliness which you just don't get in a supermarket or mall. And even if you don't buy anything, the friendliness remains. "Come right in," said the lady proprietor of the dress shop I had chosen as a refuge and an artistic vantage point, "and make yourself at home." The shopkeeper agreed, as I painted Main Street swept by a rainstorm, that folks had been right to take down the lurid plastic sheets which for so long had covered up the ornate exteriors of their Renaissance, Gothic, or art deco stores.

There are not, on the other hand, many American cities where an artist can find the old and the new, the past and the present in

Welcome to the Midwest

one single effective image depicting change.

Chicago might be one exception to this rule. The immense Hancock Building looms over the Old Water Tower, built between 1867 and '69 in castellated pepperbox Gothic, advertising the speed of the Windy City's dizzy growth rate. All around it, Chicago's forest of thrusting skyscrapers—including the tallest in any land—expresses as nothing else does the vital, energetic, and competitive pulse of American life. Yet many older structures so necessary to sustain this visual drama of opposed moods have been demolished; the Stock Exchange by pioneering architects Dankmar Adler and Louis Sullivan is, for example, no longer on the scene. By contrast, St. Louis's

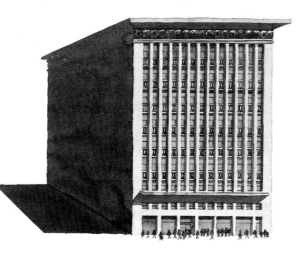

Opposite: Main Street, Madison, Indiana's restored business center, reflects the aspirations of westward expansion. St. Louis's Wainwright Building, left, and the Cleveland Arcade, below left, still serve original office/ shopping functions. The Chicago Water Tower, below, dwarfed by the John Hancock Building, is now the city's information center.

first and most ambitious office block, designed by Adler and Sullivan and built in 1891, was bought by the state of Missouri and still stands, restored as an office complex. And worshipers still gather at the Byzantine-style Cathedral of St. Louis, in the shadow of the soaring Gateway Arch.

Another triumph of preservation in the Midwest has been the celebrated Cleveland Arcade, a vast Victorian *galeria* reminiscent of an oriental bazaar. Hugely ornate iron staircases, bridges, and balconies join and link five floors around a vast central skylight. I was instantly transported back to the 1890s, the flamboyant years of its construction. In those days there were art stores, music publishers, dressmakers, jewelers, glove stores, shoe and umbrella stores. One was devoted entirely to "hair goods." There were several cigar stores, a very good barbershop, and a candy store and a florist. Last but not least, a brass band played on Saturday afternoons when people crowded the variety of stores.

Shops still ring the courtyard, increasingly so, attracting shoppers to a potpourri of items. Who knows, one day a band might play again as a new, respectful generation waltzes with ghosts of the old.

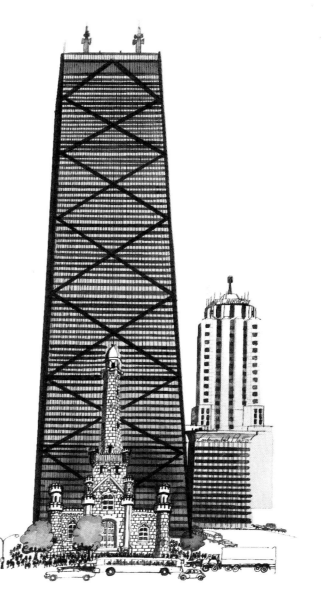

267

Georgetown Colorado Taos Street

High Style in the West

A lot of ghost towns aren't ghost towns any more. Some have been rejuvenated for summer tourists; Central City and Cripple Creek have long been emblazoned with ads and invitations to "enjoy" corny waxwork shows and bad food. Some, like Aspen, have become chic ski resorts in which only the very rich can afford to live. But others, notably Georgetown, Colorado, hold their heads high and resist temptation.

Once the "Silver Queen of the Rockies," Georgetown boasted two opera houses, the remarkable Hotel de Paris, and churches of five denominations. All but the opera houses still remain. This example of the past enduring with a modern flavor happened not because of an abstract effort by architectural aesthetes but because people wanted to live there—old-timers and young families alike.

In the Pacific Northwest similar efforts

have succeeded in preserving not only early mining camps but entire industrial neighborhoods. One of the more unusual examples is the refinery of the Seattle Gas Company, built in 1906 in Ballard, a turn-of-the-century milltown suburb of Seattle. Shut down following the widespread adoption of natural gas in the 1950s, this huge plant was acquired in 1963 by the city fathers as part of a rehabilitation project. Its monumental cooling towers and fantastic machinery prompted a landscape architect to propose that the former boiler house be filled with salvaged machinery, rendered suitably harmless, and painted in vivid colors to function as play sculpture for energetic children. It has been an unqualified success.

Near Taos, New Mexico, I found the exquisite adobe mission of St. Francis of Assisi, built by Spanish padres of the 1700s to win local Indians for cross and crown.

Even in California, the will to let it stand because you like it seems a secure philosophy. I give you Grauman's Chinese Theater in Hollywood, a remarkable confection which can only be described as Showbiz Eternal. But at the top of my California list is San Francisco, to quote Norman Mailer, "the Pearl of all American cities." From my

window I could see how the cable cars struggled over the dips in California Street. Looking up the famous street, you can see something of the influences which shaped this beautiful city: the banks and other financial institutions, the Kong Chow Temple on the fringe of America's second biggest Chinatown, and looking down on everyone, the prestigious Mark Hopkins Hotel. Perhaps an earthquake, but surely not people, will be responsible for San Francisco's eventual destruction.

And so I discovered and sketched landmarks that any proud nation could trumpet (many of them rescued just in the nick of time). For the rest, I covered thousands of miles across the land to find nothing but a gaudy display of gas stations, hamburger stands, and car lots cloned in 10,000 places.

Maybe I caught America just in time, before everything once beautiful or unique was washed out to sea. On the other hand, I found much to argue that there are Americans who respect their land sufficiently to be unembarrassed about admitting their love for particular places. They have turned their remarkable energies to recording them, understanding their potential, and using them for another day.

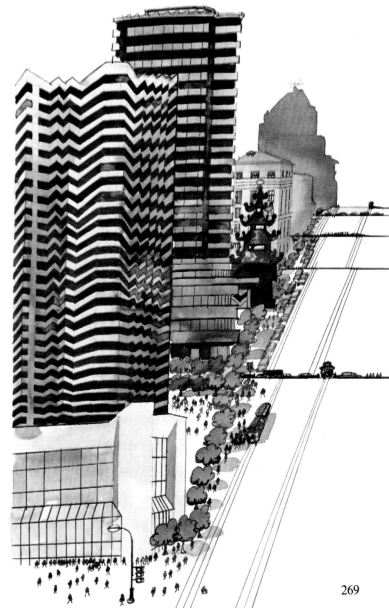

Georgetown, Colorado, opposite, lures vacationers with winter sports and fishing in clear lakes and streams. Top left: youngsters cavort on machinery from Seattle Gas Company; lower left, St. Francis Mission near Taos recalls the Southwest's Spanish heritage; below, California Street, San Francisco, distinguished by cable cars, pagoda, and the towering Bank of America.

269

The Land Between

By Charles E. Little

In the place of my bringing up—a small agricultural valley in what is now called the "Los Angeles Basin"—stately rows of table grapes (mostly, though there were some pinots, too), interspersed with orange groves here and there, have given way utterly to phalanxes of houses. The two-lane ribbon of a country road is 'now an expressway, one interchange of which covers the schoolyard where I got a bloody nose for wearing a Roosevelt button. I went home and commiserated with the chickens. I would guard them sometimes, single-shot .22 at the ready ($6.75, at the hardware store), from the marauding coyotes. The coyotes no longer howl from the mesa rim these days. The mesa is gone, literally removed for fill and "site improvement." The place is now called a "city." That's my story, and the important thing about it is how unremarkable it really is.

The late Aldo Leopold, America's premier conservation philosopher of the 20th century, and one whose name is often invoked in a wistful appeal to whatever authority can be mustered in defense of the land, put the problem pretty clearly at the end of his book, *Sand County Almanac* (1949). "We are remodeling the Alhambra with a steam shovel," he wrote, "and we are proud of our yardage. We shall hardly relinquish the shovel, which after all has many good points, but we are in need of gentler and more objective criteria for its successful use."

As a policy analyst for the American Land Forum, it is my job to evaluate the public criteria—gentle and otherwise—for dealing with land resources. This means that I should bring a certain scholarly detachment and evenhandedness to my analysis. But I must say, I am scarcely able to be anything but horrified at the casual destruction of mesas. This kind of ungentle use of steam shovels comes, I think, from viewing the American land simply as surface, rather than as resource. In terms of surface there are millions upon millions of acres. In terms of resource there is only one mesa, and the difference is a crucial one.

It is crucial because the mesa is representative of the *functional* American landscape—the living landscape, the working landscape, the productive landscape. This part of the American land comprises some 60 percent or so of the total

It is the "land between"—neither urbanized nor wilderness—that cries out for planning because that's where the people are going. The rigorous cowboy life and the simple joy of a rural upbringing may soon disappear.

land mass, a not inconsiderable fraction. It is the 1.4 billion acres of mostly privately owned land that are neither wilderness fastness nor the city and its immediate environs. It is, after all, "the land between" that gives the American land its real character—the everyday landscapes of dairy farms in Vermont, wheat fields in Kansas, and endless rows of corn in Iowa. It is the salt marsh behind the barrier beaches of the Carolinas, a giant sponge of biological diversity embroidering the southern coast. It is the New England woodlot; the rocky "cloves," as they call them, in the Catskills with ancient granite bearing the striations of glaciers come and gone. And it is rivers upon rivers; Great Lakes and lesser lakes and thousand lakes studding bog country. All in all this "land between" is the most astonishing aggregation of real estate one can imagine.

But is "real estate" quite the phrase for it? Aldo Leopold had some thoughts on this matter as well. "We abuse land," he said, "because we regard it as a commodity belonging to us. When we see land as a community to which we belong, we may begin to use it with love and respect." Real estate is in the realm of steam shovels altering a commodity. Land seen as a resource is in the gentle realm of "community" and of values held in common.

The fanciers of ungentle steam shovels argue that land *is* a commodity. Such is the whole idea of property rights, the market system, and the American way. We are not vassals to a landlord, they say, and especially not a philosophical-ethical principle standing in for a landlord. We can own the land ourselves. And we can sell it to people with steam shovels if we wish.

Of *course* land is a commodity. The real question Leopold is raising is to whom does it—with all its diverse "resource values"—belong? You see, I had assumed that the view of the mesa was deeded to me, and the rim to the coyotes for their evening use—an ownership necessary to my own aesthetic development and essential to the survival of coyotes. Such is the idea of community—to which I belonged, .22 and all.

And some other lad 40 years later might have been able to belong, too. But the choice was made for him, and made as well for some man and his wife who now own a house lot where the mesa used to be, and for whom a flash flood is a constant worry.

The economist says that land, like everything else, allocates its acres to the highest and best use in accordance with whatever society values. During my time, it has been house lots. But should society change its mind concerning the value of mesas and other ordinary marvels of the American

landscape, what then? It is doubtful that a boy not yet born could want to hear the coyotes again, and could somehow raise the money to rebuild the mesa. The decision, you see, really is permanent, and not everybody was properly asked. These are weighty and complicated matters and not often dealt with very well, although not for lack of trying.

In Santa Fe, New Mexico, Harry Moul, a city planner, told me once: "We have no vision here." And yet, like Sisyphus, Moul labors away to instill what vision he can in an historic and vividly beautiful resort area that is fast becoming a sprawling city. The scatteration of newcomers in this growing Sun Belt metropolis is worrisome, and Moul wants to find a better way for people to settle into the land, for the high desert is visually fragile—it depends on emptiness to have its full impact aesthetically.

This was why Moul applied for, and got, a grant to study the small Spanish-American agricultural communities that

A sprinkler driven by water-powered wheels creates a 130-acre circle in a 160-acre parcel of Washington land. Opposite, a highway near Palo Alto, California, where current state policy is to build no more.

abound in New Mexico. "In the tradition of Spanish-American land use," says Moul, "the only land you truly own is what you live on. The rest, the hills and valleys, are considered common land."

In another place, Oregon's Willamette Valley, the problems are similar, even if the land is different. One hundred miles long from the rise of the Willamette River south of Eugene to the bustling metropolis of Portland, the valley is as benign a swath of farmland as any in the Northwest, if not the whole United States. Flat and green and laced with gentle brooks, studded with sheep and cows a-pasture as well as planted to crops, the valley has a palpable "placeness" about it, a *genius loci* not lost on its residents. Rimmed by the coast range on the west and the Cascades to the east, the valley, as one civic leader told me, is finite. "You can understand its limits," he said. "When somebody sells off 160 acres for development, why it's a real loss."

The trouble is, the valley is bisected not only by a river, but by Interstate 5, which delivers people from California and elsewhere looking for a real "place" which ironically it could supply only by destroying itself. By the late 1960s it looked as though the saturation point had been reached, and former Governor Tom McCall fulminated against the "ravenous rampage of suburbia." But it fell to lean, lantern-jawed Hector Macpherson, a dairy farmer, to develop a way to retain the valley's "livability" as the Oregonians call it.

Said Macpherson, dour as his Highland forebears, righteous as John Knox: "We *must* plan. Visualize the alternative: a valley where neighbor encroaches on neighbor, a land unproductive agriculturally where hunger and want must surely follow, a land defiled and unsightly, a monument to man's greed."

So saying, Macpherson, a practical man, ran for and won a seat in the Oregon state legislature in order to save his beloved valley. From this platform he established, almost singlehandedly, a "land-use policy action group" which was to come up with legislative proposals to protect the valley and other landscapes of Oregon. In 1973 the legislature passed a series of measures which are by far the most forward-thinking in the United States. Under the aegis of Oregon's state-level Land Conservation and Development Commission, localities now draw "urban growth boundaries" outside of which, in agricultural areas, "exclusive farm-use zoning" is established. The effect of this procedure in the Willamette Valley is expected to protect upward of two million acres of agricultural land. Hector's land, you might say.

Of course, not all the living, working, producing land—the

land between the wilderness and the city—is cropland. In fact most of it isn't. Cropland totals 400 million acres; there's another billion in pasture, range, woods, and water.

Part of the woods—a fair-sized part in fact—is the six million-acre Adirondack region in the state of New York. This, too, has been regularly conceived of in terms of "community." As far back as 1857, a journalist by the name of S. H. Hammond, reacting to the excessive logging of the Adirondacks even then, complained: "Where shall we go to find the woods, the wild things, the old forests?" And then made this proposal: "Had I my way, I would make a circle of a hundred miles in diameter and throw around it the protective aegis of the constitution. I would make it a forest forever. It should be a misdemeanor to chop down a tree and a felony to clear an acre within its boundaries."

It took a while, but in 1892, the New York state legislature established a "blue line" describing six million acres, and three years later it dedicated some 700,000 acres within the line—a shade over 10 percent—as forever wild under Article XIV of the state constitution.

Today, some 38 percent of the land within the "blue line" is state-owned and constitutionally protected. But the remaining 62 percent is privately owned where it is not unconstitutional to chop down a tree or clear an acre—even thousands of acres, millions of trees.

Since Hammond, hundreds of journalists have championed the Adirondacks, most especially in the 1960s and 1970s when the future of this place was very much in doubt. The vulnerability of the Adirondacks was particularly troubling because of an interstate highway known as the Northway which put 55 million people within a day's drive, or less, of the region. The late Governor Nelson Rockefeller saw the chance for a rare accommodation among heretofore competing interest groups. He established a commission to study what could be done about keeping the Adirondacks whole by controlling the land uses on the troublesome 62 percent of land which, privately owned, intermingled checkerboard-fashion with the constitutionally protected public lands. The alternative was surely to watch the Adirondacks become degraded into alternating tracts of trees and ticky-tacky.

The result of the Commission's labor was as remarkable a social invention for the management of land resources as any yet seen on these shores. In 1971 the Adirondack Park Agency was established. Its job was not to buy land and equip it with picnic benches, as most park bodies do, but to *regulate* the private land within the blue line so that its use would not be inconsistent with the public lands.

If it is not against the law to clear a single acre of this land under the Adirondack Park Agency Act, it isn't all that easy either. On half the private land, owners may erect no more than one principal structure for every 43 acres. On another 37 percent of it, the limit is one structure per 8.5 acres. If this seems restrictive, it is. If it seems unconstitutional, in the sense of the Fifth Amendment stricture about not "taking" land without just compensation, the courts have so far sustained the Adirondack Park Agency Act in a score or more of lawsuits. Perhaps the point is that nobody's land is really "taken." It's just that owners must use it as if it were part of a community—that is, with love and respect.

The idea of the Adirondacks is catching. In 1978, the U.S. Congress passed legislation directing the Secretary of the Interior to help the state of New Jersey establish, Adirondack-style, protection of the Jersey Pine Barrens. The Pine Barrens constitutes about one-fifth the state of New Jersey; its giant aquifer contains 1.7 trillion gallons of water. Its pygmy forest is comprised of full-grown pines and oaks no higher than a grown man's shoulder.

There are a number of other places in the country interested in this approach, which I have called the "green-line concept." Borrowed in part from British national parks prac-

tice, green-lining America's outstanding landscapes, just as the British did the Lake District and nine other large areas, is one way to protect land that perhaps should not be publicly owned, really, but remain as living landscapes. These are places where, as William Wordsworth put it for his beloved lakes, "every man has a right and interest who has an eye to see and a heart to enjoy."

Turning to a different kind of landscape, the sea and its littoral, another Romantic, Lord Byron, wrote in *Childe Harold:* "There is rapture in the lonely shore,/There is society where none intrudes."

Byron was good at many things, but not economic forecasting. But then how could he know about the intrusions of oil companies, and the developers of Kiawah Island on the lonely shores of South Carolina? Or of the forays against the beaches and marshes of Florida? Or of the buzzing atoms of Calvert Cliffs, Maryland's nuclear plant? Some lonely shore!

And yet, of the total 36,010-mile coastline of the coterminous United States, only 16 percent of it is given over to nonrapturous uses. The remaining 84 percent still retains considerable recreational, aesthetic, and ecological quality. For this reason, the effort to manage coastal resources is neither too late nor quixotic.

In 1972, the Congress enacted the Coastal Zone Management Act to provide financial aid and technical assistance to states and localities wanting to guide development along the shore. All eligible states and territories signed up. Moreover, certain states have enacted coastal conservation and planning laws of their own. Maine, Delaware, and several other states have procedures that guide industry away from the coastal zone. Florida identifies and controls "critical areas" of wetland and beach, California has an elaborate citizen-led coastal planning program. Oregon and Texas have declared that the beach—to the line of vegetation rather than to the usual "mean high-water mark"—belongs to the people, by prescriptive right. Even more attention soon will be focused on coastal resources, as a powerful alliance of conservation organizations begins to plan a "year of the coast."

Clearly, as these cases show, the destruction of mesas has not abated since my childhood, but increased. Why this is so has surprised even the experts.

Calvin Beale is a soft-spoken demographer with an enviable national reputation who works out of a map-cluttered office at the Department of Agriculture. Recently he confessed his dismay to the Joint Economic Committee of the U.S. Congress. The population growth in rural and small town areas was "completely unpredicted in public discussion or in the literature of any of the social sciences ten years ago."

As it happens, rural land—seashore, farmland, woodland, mountain, and mesa—has been increasing in price at a rate two, and sometimes two and a half, times that of inflation. This fact is both a cause and an effect of what some demographers have called "reverse migration"—migration away from cities and suburbs into the pristine countryside. In fact, since 1970, rural counties that are themselves not adjacent to such metropolitan area counties are growing faster than cities or their suburbs, reversing a trend in place at least since the industrial revolution. The reversal of population flow in the United States (and Europe, too) has caught everybody but real estate agents with their statistics down.

These days, demographers, while not completely in agreement, generally believe that the rural growth trend will continue, and that it will affect every area of the country—rural and small town as well as areas closer to cities. The new resi-

dents will come to take (and create) new jobs not in the agricultural sector, but in offices and factories at the intersections of interstates deep in the country, at resort locations on their way to permanent year-round settlements, and in extractive industries related to minerals and energy resources.

What does this mean for the American land? There is both good news and bad news. The good news is that Americans will, in increasing numbers, begin to value and protect the vast American landscape. The bad news is that they may love it to death. Reverse migration is not really a reversal in anything but direction. Andy Hardy, in knickers and a bow tie idling on the tidy, white Main Street porch of the summer's day, is not to be recreated. Rather, he is hanging out, like teenagers everywhere, in a shopping mall. The dominant development pattern tends to be scattered in rural areas and along suburban patterns—brick ranchers strung out along the farm-to-market roads, subdivisions in the black dirt way

There are many charged with managing the land, some infrequently considered in this connection. Indians, like the salmon fishermen on the Klamath River, opposite, control much American land, as does the Department

of Defense. Below, the Blue Angels signal the Navy's sovereignty over a small portion of land in Maryland. Nearby, Baltimore's Fort McHenry is managed by that vast landholder, the National Park Service.

out beyond the edge of town, "industrial" and "office parks," and of course the ubiquitous shopping center.

It is of some importance, therefore, for aesthetic, economic, and social reasons that American citizens take an interest in the future of the living, working, productive landscape as a national rather than simply parochial issue. And this is, in fact, coming about—but painfully slowly.

The Coastal Zone Management program and the "green-line" parks attest to this. Moreover, now under deliberation by the Congress is legislation relating to the preservation of agricultural lands. Such legislation cannot come a moment too soon. Recent Department of Agriculture research has shown that the U.S. is converting rural land to urban uses at the rate of three million acres per year. And, they believe, the rate is increasing.

At the same time it is important for people like me not to succumb to the Potomac Fallacy—that the proper federal program will put everything to rights. There is in fact an opposite view, equally convincing, which is that nothing would have gone wrong in the first place if it hadn't been for federal programs.

I have observed over the years that the primary conservation impulse—the effort to make one's place livable, workable, and productive—is a kind of "back yard" impulse. That is, it relates to the land within one's own ken—not land in the abstract. What is happening now in America, given the aggregation of many, many local and state efforts such as those I have described, is that we may be beginning to have a larger view of our back yard, of the whole American land. Its values are beginning to transcend purely local, short-term economic considerations, and contain those larger values which have made the land itself the historical basis of our politics, our culture, and our enterprise.

If the mesas of our childhood have been destroyed, a million mesas remain—as pasture, woods, mountains, shores, and deserts. This is the community of the American land, and such is the enduring value of this most primary resource, that it can still determine our economic growth, social well-being, and environmental quality.

Does the thoughtful man suppose that . . . the present experiment in civilization is the last the world will see?

–George Santayana

In nation's capital, farmers help to repair damage to Mall caused by their winter 1978–79 protest rally against rising costs, falling profits. Picture symbolizes farmers' contributions, problems.

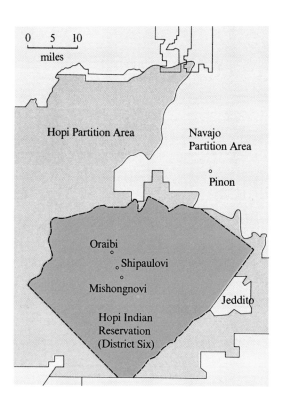

A View From the Mesas

By James K. Page, Jr.

Photographs by Susanne Anderson

Like most Americans, I don't live now where I grew up. We are restless, moving away, then searching for roots. Mine lay northeast of New York City.

But over the years I've spent some time trying to learn about an area where generation after generation of people have lived in the same spot for a millennium, where a sense of place is the central fact of life, dearly, sometimes desperately, to be preserved. It is the land of the Hopi Indians in the high desert of northeastern Arizona. I search there not for roots, obviously, but for a different perspective.

Arriving at Hopi, you are immediately impressed with the forbidding yellowish rock tumbling down the sides of the mesas in big geological junkheaps. And below stretch the flat endless miles of scrubby brown desert interrupted here and there by a distant, improbable butte jutting up like a tooth. Of course, in the spring and summer, you notice bright scarlet swatches of Indian paintbrush and yellow and

278

blue weedy-looking flowers along the road, but mainly it is a scene of arid desolation. Get a little closer and you are surprised to see, in the sandy, dry washes that descend from the mesas like so many ill-arranged sand traps, regular rows of corn, beans, squash, melon, even peach orchards. It is an unlikely place for human habitation.

Yet this is where the Hopi chose to be. They were not forced to move to their present locale; they were summoned to these parts over a thousand years ago by their prophecies.

Until modern times they lived in relative isolation, their culture intact. The Spanish soldiers, who were to scramble like so many eggs the cultures and populations of the pueblo peoples to the east in New Mexico, made only half-hearted attempts to conquer the remote Hopi. Missionaries were more persistent. In 1680, led by religious traditionalists, the Hopi rose and drove the missionaries out. Shortly thereafter, when the village of Awatovi invited them to return, other Hopi (the name means the peaceful people) swept down and exterminated the men of the village.

Utes, Apaches, Navajos, and other late-arriving tribes scourged the New Mexican pueblos, the Spanish settlements, and the Anglos who succeeded the Spanish, stealing horses, women, and other plunder. But their raids on Hopi were comparatively few and far between. Until the middle of the 19th century, with the exception of such interruptions, the Hopi lived in relative isolation on the mesas in compact villages, hunting, gathering wood, and visiting sacred shrines in the vast, empty surround. They were almost timeless, seeing things in the landscape that no one else could perceive, tending their gardens, making fanatically careful use of the water that magically arises here and there from improbable springs, and developing out of their perceptions of the land what one scholar has described with awe as the most profound works of art yet produced on the American continent: the Hopi ceremonies.

Among these, perhaps the best known is the snake dance that takes place in August. Black-painted snake priests issue forth from the kiva where they have spent the better part of a week. With antelope priests chanting, the snake priests in turn reach into an altar in the central plaza of the village and retrieve a snake—bull snakes and rattlers—and dance slowly around the plaza in pairs, one priest with the snake writhing in his mouth, the other with a feathered stick to distract the snake. After a circuit or two of the plaza, the snake is placed on the ground and heads off for the crowd, to be picked up at the last moment by a third priest. On and on it goes, groups of priests repeating the ritual. It *is* an

awesome, ominous piece of work. As Yale's Vincent Scully wrote, "it does seem to come right out of the ground." At the end, the snakes are released back in the desert, messengers to the spirits that the Hopi are doing their proper ceremonies as instructed and that the rains may now come. And the rains often do come, water writhing down the washes, like the snakes. Like so many Hopi ceremonies, each with its own special purposes, the snake dance is more than a prayer for rain. It is a prayer for the everlasting fruitfulness of the land and for the benefit of all creatures who live on the land and who are charged with its care.

By centuries of such rituals—bean dances, corn dances, all geared precisely to the seasonal rhythms of the land—the Hopi have dealt successfully with an inhospitable piece of real estate and the forces that govern it. One cannot lead a harmonious life, they believe, if one is out of harmony with the land. But modernity—the fruits of the Age of Reason, new procedures for dealing with land—was bound to come. And it came via the Navajo—late, but it came, beginning in the mid-19th century. The maraudings of the Navajo had become too much for the white settlers. Kit Carson was dispatched to round them up and kill their sheep. Ultimately in 1868 the tribe was sequestered by treaty on some

For a millennium, Hopi have lived in pueblos high on the mesas of northeastern Arizona. Mishongnovi, opposite, is in contrast to a lonely Navajo sheep camp of the kind that has more recently invaded ancient Hopi land.

three million acres lying across the New Mexico-Arizona border, along with new herds of sheep. Within 12 years, half the Navajo tribe lived outside the reservation—mostly westward, toward Hopi. To protect the Hopi's use of their lands, President Chester A. Arthur created the Hopi Indian Reservation in 1882, a rectangle of some 2,500,000 acres.

There is a great deal of legal and historical complexity in what happened next, but suffice it to say that the U.S. government, perhaps preoccupied, looked the other way as Navajo herdsmen moved into the Hopi's rectangle.

By the 1940s, the Hopi had found that all but a small portion of the rectangle—some 600,000 acres of what was now called Land Management District 6, surrounding the mesa villages—was inhabited by Navajo and had been seriously overgrazed by their sheep. Unlike the burgeoning Navajo, the Hopi population had meanwhile grown little—from 1,800 souls in 1882 to some 4,000.

By way of solution, about a decade later Congress authorized the U.S. District Court to settle title to the 1882 Hopi reservation lands. Eventually, in 1962, a court declared District 6 to be exclusively for the Hopi, but, the court added, since the government hadn't *discouraged* the Navajo from moving in, the rest of the rectangle, some 1.9 million acres, would be called the Joint Use Area—share and share alike. It was, you remember, the Age of Reason.

This sat ill with the Hopi, not surprisingly, the more so since they were for all practical purposes denied access to using rangeland in the Joint Use Area by the far more numerous and powerful Navajo settlers. Soon, their own sheepherding areas overgrazed to the point of uselessness, the Navajos began sending their sheep into the better-managed, relatively lush range of District 6 itself.

With the tribal governments unable to work it out, Congress passed the Navajo and Hopi Settlement Act of 1974, calling for the partition of the Joint Use Area, the eventual

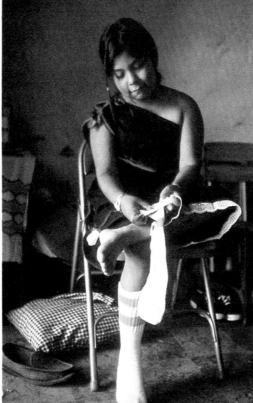

Tribal officials inspect a plundered ruin, an early Hopi settlement above Jeddito Wash. Shrines and ruins of long-abandoned dwellings, often marked by scattered shards, delineate a territory far greater in scope than the present reservation. These sacred areas, periodically revisited, are the lands from which the Hopi came and which they believe they have a duty to watch over and protect.

relocation of some 900 Navajo and 20 Hopi families that lived there, and a livestock reduction program. The partition line, by 1979, had been three-quarters fenced and 2,000 Navajo households had applied for the benefits of relocation (a new house and cash incentives).

All told, only 70 families had been relocated, with 400 scheduled to move by 1981. Those families were experiencing problems of employment and marital and family disputes, and the Navajo government was endeavoring to amend the original act and postpone the relocation effort. The Hopi were sympathetic toward the familial problems but firm in their resolve to reacquire the land. No one is particularly happy. As the Hopi Tribal Chairman Abbott Sekaquaptewa put it: "After all, suppose someone came and camped out in your back yard. Then a judge said the man could have half of your yard, even though he had no business there in the first place."

In the course of time the matter will settle down and the Hopi will take actual possession of their new/old land. I asked the Chairman just what the acquisition of this land meant to the tribe—what would be done with it.

"Our shrines," he said, "First, our shrines must be protected." Each year Hopi elders make a pilgrimage to the ancient shrines—sacred places and ruins—along the "traditional" Hopi border. The shrines mark the borders of what the Hopi consider to be their ancestral lands, lands they still feel responsible for. "The shrines are our standards," say the elders today, "just as the U.S. flag is the standard of the government." The treks go south of Flagstaff (100 miles west of Hopi), into the Grand Canyon, to the northeast to a mountain the maps call Navajo Mountain, and elsewhere—to the various places from which the Hopi clans gathered before history. (I stood with the Chairman one time in the rain inspecting some old Hopi ruins east of the mesa villages. Here and there the ground had been dug up

Kachinas, represented by this hand-carved doll, are the spirits who watch over the Hopi. Their home is San Francisco Peak, 100 miles away near Flagstaff, where Hopi leaders are battling developers who wish to enlarge a ski resort. Below, Hopi workers extend an old house in Mishongnovi on Second Mesa. Opposite, 600 feet above the frozen desert, Mishongnovi glows in the late afternoon sun.

by pothunters. Though against federal law, such offenses are hard to prohibit. "This is our history," the Chairman said then. "It should not be stolen.")

The new land will put several shrines, several ruins, within sole jurisdiction of the Hopi. It will also provide rangeland. "It would be best, once everyone is relocated, to restore the land before we use it," he said. There are several ways to do this. Various experiments are presently under way in cooperation with local universities and government agencies. "But that may be a little idealistic. If we don't start using the land right away, before it is restored, the Navajo will use that as an excuse not to move their people out.

"Later we'll use the land for new community development. There's no room here in District 6 for new communities. We will have public facilities there one day, too, a college maybe. A recreation area. Up north, near Black Mesa, I would like to see a wilderness area. My grandfather used to hunt antelope in the valleys up there. I'd like to bring them back. We're surveying the new land now for minerals, water . . . but you know there's not really all that much land out there. One million acres. That's not an awful lot when you realize there's no water on it.

"It's vital that we remember what is Hopi—the land. We must protect and cherish that land, not just for Hopis, but for all people."

All of this lies in the future. What of today? In what amounts to a long generation, the pickup truck has replaced the burro, most of the villages have electricity, some have running water. Many Hopi are employed by the tribal government or the Bureau of Indian Affairs, rather than traditional, subsistence agriculture.

A little while ago, a Hopi friend of mine, Alonzo Quavehema, stood on top of what is called Second Mesa where his village of Shipaulovi is located. He pointed to the flatlands intervening to the east between us and First Mesa.

"When I was a kid," said Alonzo, with the pleasing nasal lilt of a Hopi speaking English, "all that land was green with corn and peaches and melons. We did the ceremonies, all the dances, and things grew. Now a lot of men are too busy to work their fields. But that is what all our ceremonies are for, for the corn and all those things. Here in this village we do all the ceremonies still, but I don't know how long it will last, because without the corn the ceremonies aren't . . . what do you say, they don't have the same meaning."

Below us, the desert was brown except for a few cornfields. Alonzo worried that there might have been a climatic shift or that something was wrong with the Hopis and the way they were doing their ceremonies. Otherwise, he thought, the land would be green, the rains be more ample.

Who is to say? Will up-to-date land-use practices be a sufficient replacement for a thousand years of spiritual reverence for the land? Can the two modes coexist in one culture—science and magic, if you will? Again, who is to say? Nevertheless, I feel a particular confidence in the Hopi and their land. And a peculiar magnetism emanating from there. I am biased, of course. Now and then I imagine myself being invited to become a resident of Hopi one day, assigned to stand guard over the ancient ruins with a Winchester .30/30, discouraging the potsnatchers in the night.

But let's face it, I grew up alongside an ash tree in a suburb in the Northeast, not among mesas, dry washes, and Hopi corn. I believed mostly in baseball, not kachinas. Hopi land is for the Hopi. And since they've had a lot more experience living on their land than we've had on ours, I'd wager that they will survive us all one way or another, perched precariously on their mesas where they and they alone belong, reminders as long as we will listen that while there are many ways to perceive the land and to live on it, the only true way is to honor it. To look upon it and say: How awesome. How demanding. How generous.

Authors' Biographies

Edward S. Ayensu, director of the Office of Biological Conservation at the Smithsonian Institution, recently published a book on endangered and threatened plant species of the United States.

Sherwin Carlquist is Horton Professor of Botany jointly at Claremont Graduate School and Pomona College. Widely traveled, he is a leading researcher in the natural history of islands.

Robert C. Cowen is science editor of *The Christian Science Monitor* and a regular contributor to the Massachusetts Institute of Technology's *Technology Review.*

Vine Deloria, Jr., a member of the Standing Rock Sioux Tribe, is a widely known scholar and author in Indian Affairs. He is best known for his books, *Custer Died For Your Sins,* and *God is Red.*

William A. Douglass is an anthropologist and coordinator of Basque studies at the University of Nevada in Reno. He wrote *Beltran, Basque Sheepman of the American West,* among other Basque studies.

John Hay, president of the board of the Cape Cod Museum of Natural History, is widely known for his sensitive studies of nature which include *The Run, The Great Beach,* and *Spirit of Survival.*

Paul Hogarth, author and illustrator of *Drawing Architecture* and *Walking Tours of Old Philadelphia,* specializes in the drawing and painting of the urban landscape, here and abroad.

Jack Hope is a New York freelance writer specializing in environmental matters. He has traveled widely in the wild places of the continent, including the North, and is author of the book, *The Yukon.*

Nicholas Hotton III is research curator of the Smithsonian's Department of Paleontology. His research focuses on functional anatomy, especially of mammal-like reptiles, "but any old tetrapod will do."

Peirce Lewis, professor of geography at Pennsylvania State University, teaches and writes about human landscapes, arguing that we can "read" the character of nations from landscapes they have made.

Charles E. Little is president of the American Land Forum, a land-use policy research organization. He has written widely on land resource topics ranging from wilderness preservation to inner cities.

William G. Melson, a geologist and curator in the Department of Mineral Sciences at the Smithsonian's National Museum of Natural History, travels worldwide to observe land and sea volcanoes.

Alfred Meyer, executive editor of *Science 80,* is the former editor of *Natural History* and the author of several books including *The Armies of the Ant* and, most recently, a novel, *Cannibal.*

Roderick Nash, professor of history and environmental studies at the University of California at Santa Barbara, is also a wilderness explorer and white-water canoeist with experience on five continents.

Edwards Park's column "Around the Mall and Beyond" appears monthly in *Smithsonian* magazine. His book, *Nanette,* describes his love affair with an airplane in the days of World War II.

S. Dillon Ripley, Secretary of the Smithsonian Institution since 1964, is a noted ornithologist with a long-standing interest in the bird fauna of the Indian subcontinent, including the remote nation of Bhutan.

Alfred Runte is assistant director of the Institute of Environmental Studies at Baylor University. He was formerly with the Woodrow Wilson International Center for Scholars and wrote *National Parks: The American Experience.*

Neil Sampson, soil conservationist and land use specialist, is executive vice president of the National Association of Conservation Districts, representing 2,950 soil and water conservation districts.

Arthur W. Sherwood, author of *Understanding the Chesapeake,* is founder and director of the Chesapeake Bay Foundation, an organization devoted to the conservation and management of estuarine resources.

Bruce D. Smith is associate curator of North American Archeology in the Smithsonian's National Museum of Natural History. He has written widely on the Mississippi mound building cultures, and directed the excavation of the Gypsy Joint site.

Gary Soucie, a Connecticut-based freelance writer and senior editor of *Audubon* magazine, has served as an executive of numerous environmental organizations including the League of Conservation Voters.

Paul D. Spreiregen, a Washington, D.C., architect and town planner, is a lecturer and author and broadcasts a weekly commentary on urban planning on the National Public Radio network.

E. Ogden Tanner, a freelance writer and former editor of *Architectural Forum* and Time-Life Books, has lived in the same suburban Connecticut town for 20 years.

Joshua C. Taylor is director of the Smithsonian's National Collection of Fine Arts. Among his publications are *America as Art* and *Fine Arts in America.*

Wilcomb E. Washburn, formerly president of the Society for the History of Discoveries, is director of the Office of American Studies at the Smithsonian Institution.

Index

Picture Credits

Jacket: Shelly Grossman/Woodfin Camp & Associates. *Front Matter:* p. 1 J. Robert Stottlemyer/Lensman; 2–3 Ross Chapple; 4–5 Fred J. Maroon; 6–7 Joe Goodwin; 8-9 Glenn Van Nimwegen; 10-11 Fred J. Maroon; 12 George Hall.

Section I: p. 14–15 Jake Bair; 16–17 Celia L. Strain; 18 (top) T. Halter Cunningham; (bottom) Kent & Donna Dannen; 19 T. Halter Cunningham; 20 Kent & Donna Dannen; 21 Pamela Johnson Meyer; 22 (top) T. Halter Cunningham; (bottom) Dan Guravich/Photo Researchers, Inc.; (right) Kenneth Garrett; 23 Joe Goodwin; 24 Kenneth Garrett; 25–27 Pamela Johnson Meyer; 29 Huntington Library; 30 Shelly Grossman/Woodfin Camp & Associates; 31 Library of Congress; 32 Ross Chapple; 32–33 Dutton's Atlas, 1882; 34 Gary Ladd; 35 Library of Congress; 36–42 National Collection of Fine Arts/Smithsonian Institution; 43 Collection of Mr. & Mrs. Charles Gilman, Jr.; 44–45 Library of Congress; 47 Chapman & Hall, Ltd., London; 48–49 Library of Congress; 50 National Anthropological Archives/Smithsonian Institution; 51 Paul S. Conklin; 53–55 Susanne Anderson.

Section II: p. 56–57 Glenn Van Nimwegen; 58–59 Celia L. Strain; 60–61 Ross Chapple; 62 Bowring Cartographic; (right) Jake Bair; 63–65 Ross Chapple; 66 Schroeder/Eastwood; 67 David Alan Harvey/Woodfin Camp, Inc.; 68–75 Pierre Mion; 76 Bowring Cartographic; 77 Richard Cooper Kelsey; 78–79 Jan Adkins; 80–81 Richard Cooper Kelsey; 82 Beveridge & Associates; 83–84 Eleanor M. Kish; 85 (top) Chip Clark; (bottom) Beveridge & Associates; 86 (left) Beveridge & Associates; (right) Chip Clark; 87 Eleanor M. Kish; 88 (left) Beveridge & Associates; (right) Chip Clark; 89 Eleanor M. Kish; 91 Nicholas de Vore III/Bruce Coleman, Inc.; 92 (top) Paul Chesley; (bottom) Sherwin Carlquist; 94 Courtesy of Bishop Museum, Honolulu; 95 Bowring Cartographic; 96 DeWitt Jones/Woodfin Camp, Inc.; 97 Sherwin Carlquist; 99 Nicholas de Vore III/Bruce Coleman, Inc.

Section III: p. 100–101 Glenn Van Nimwegen; 102–103 Celia L. Strain; 105–107 Alan E. Cober; 108 Edward S. Ayensu; 109 George Hall; 111 Glenn Van Nimwegen; 112 Paul Chesley; 114 Shelly Grossman/Woodfin Camp & Associates; 115 James H. Carmichael, Jr./Bruce Coleman, Inc.; 116 Glenn Van Nimwegen; 117 Thomas Oberbauer; 118 Walter D. Osborne/Photo Researchers, Inc.; 119 Townsend P. Dickinson/Photo Researchers, Inc.; 120 (left) Glenn Van Nimwegen; (right) Shelly Grossman/Woodfin Camp & Associates; 121 Thase Daniel/Bruce Coleman, Inc.; 122 Smithsonian Institution Archives; 123 (left) Heidi Hughes; (right) Smithsonian Institution; 124 (top) Jen & Des Bartlett/Bruce Coleman, Inc.; (bottom). Una Flynn/Lensman; 125 Gary R. Zahm/ Bruce Coleman, Inc.; 126–135 William Albert Allard; 136 Linda Bartlett/Photo Researchers, Inc.; 137 Glenn Van Nimwegen; 138 Paul Chesley; 139 Glenn Van Nimwegen; 140 George Hall/Woodfin Camp & Associates; 141 Richard Frear/National Park Service photo; 142 (top) Charlie Ott/Photo Researchers, Inc.; (bottom) Bowring Cartographic; 143 Ralph Hunt Williams/Bruce Coleman, Inc.

Section IV: p. 144–145 Jay Bee/Lensman; 146–147 Celia L. Strain; 148 Charles H. Phillips; 149 John Douglass; 150–154 Charles H. Phillips; 155 John Douglass; 156 David Alan Harvey/Woodfin Camp, Inc.; 157 (top) Samuel Clemens Library; (bottom) Library of Congress; 158 State Historical Society of Wisconsin, SHSW Map Collections; 159 National Archives; 160 (top) Library of Congress; (bottom) National Ocean Survey (formerly Coast and Geodetic Survey); 161 George Hall; 162 Denver Public Library, Western History Department; 163 Harry S. Truman Library; 164 Charles H. Phillips, Courtesy of The Church of Jesus Christ of Latter-day Saints; 164–165 Bill Belknap/Photo Researchers, Inc.; 165 John S. Flannery/Bruce Coleman, Inc.; 166 (top) Harold B. Lee Library, Brigham Young University; (bottom) Kansas State Historical Society; 167 (left) Chicago Tribune; (right) Des Moines Register & Tribune; 168 George Hall; 169 (top) Harvey P. Smith, Restoration Architect; (bottom) Hank de Lespinasse/Photo Researchers, Inc; 170 (left) William Alan Garnett; (right) William Garnett; 171–175 William Garnett; 176 The Harry T. Peters "America on Stone" Lithography Collection, Smithsonian Institution; 177 Jonathan Blair/Woodfin Camp, Inc.; 178 George Hall/Woodfin Camp & Associates; 179 George Hall; 180 George Hall/Woodfin Camp & Associates; 181 (left) Schroeder/Eastwood; (right) Chip Clark; 182 George Hall; 183 Peirce F. Lewis; 184 Collection of Peirce F. Lewis; 185 Collection of Dr. Peter Ludwig; 186–187 George Hall; 188 (left) Peirce F. Lewis; (right) *Picturesque America,* American Heritage; 190 George Hall; 192 Joe Goodwin; 193 Paul S. Conklin/Lensman.

Section V: p. 194–195 James Sugar/Woodfin Camp, Inc.; 196–197 Celia L. Strain; 198–199 National Oceanic & Atmospheric Administration; 200 Wide World Photos, Inc.; 201 Boston Globe Photo; 203 Edward Rowe Snow; 204 DeWitt Jones/Woodfin Camp, Inc.; 205 (left) John M. Burnley/Bruce Coleman, Inc.; (right) William Garnett; 206 Gary Ladd; 209 Paul Chesley; 211 Harold M. Lambert Studios, Inc.; 212 Fred J. Maroon; 213 (top) John Dommers/Photo Researchers, Inc.; (bottom) David Hiser/EPA Documerica; 214 James Sugar/Woodfin Camp, Inc.; 215 Joern Gerdts/Photo Researchers, Inc.; 216 Kenneth Garrett; 217 Schroeder/Eastwood; 218 Tom Myers/Photo Researchers, Inc.; 219 Lowell J. Georgia/ Photo Researchers, Inc.; 220 (left) Bob Jones, Jr./ Woodfin Camp, Inc.; (right) Robert Madden/Lensman; 221 David Alan Harvey/Woodfin Camp, Inc.; 222 Bob Grieser/Lensman; 223 (top) Jim Ames/ Photo Researchers, Inc.; (bottom) Harold Flecknoe/ Lensman; 224 (top) William J. Jahodd/Photo Researchers, Inc.; (bottom) Bob Grieser/Lensman; 225 (left) Bob Grieser/Lensman; (right) Chesapeake Bay Center for Environmental Studies; 226 Ken Sherman; 227 George Hall; 228–229 Library of Congress; 230 (left) Ralph Starkweather/Life Magazine © 1978 Time Inc.; (right) Ron Larson/Lensman; 231 George Hall/Woodfin Camp & Associates.

Section VI: p. 232–233 Chuck O'Rear/Woodfin Camp, Inc.; 234–235 Celia L. Strain; 236 Gary Ladd; 237 (left) J.W. Mitchell/Bruce Coleman, Inc.; (right) Gary Ladd; 238 (left) Shelly Grossman/Woodfin Camp & Associates; (right) Norman Tomalin/Bruce Coleman, Inc.; 239 George Hall; 240 (left) Nicholas de Vore III/Bruce Coleman, Inc.; (right) Richard Weymouth Brooks/Photo Researchers, Inc.; 241 Joe Munroe/Photo Researchers, Inc.; 242–251 Kenneth Garrett; 252 Fred J. Maroon; 253 (left) Jack Hope; (right) Chuck O'Rear/Woodfin Camp, Inc.; 254 Fred J. Maroon; 255 Jack Hope; 256 Paul Chesley; 257 (left) J.D. Taylor/Bruce Coleman, Inc.; (right) Collection of Clark L. Engle; 258 (left) Jonathan T. Wright/Bruce Coleman, Inc.; (right) James H. Pickerell/Lensman; 259 © 1979 by Herblock in The Washington Post; 261 (left) Paul Chesley; (right) C. Gable Ray/Lensman; 262–269 Paul Hogarth; 270 Nicholas de Vore III/ Bruce Coleman, Inc.; 271 (left) Schroeder/Eastwood; (right) David Alan Harvey/Woodfin Camp, Inc.; 272 Kenneth Garrett; 273 George Hall/Woodfin Camp & Associates; 274 Robert Stottlemyer/Lensman; 275 (left) James Sugar/Woodfin Camp, Inc.; (right) George Hall; 276–277 Patricia Upchurch; 278 (left) Bowring Cartographic; (right) Susanne Anderson; 279–283 Susanne Anderson.